The Professional Caterer Series

(Volume 3)

The Professional Caterer Series

Volume 3

Croustades - Quenelles - Soufflés - Beignets
Individual Hot Dishes - Mixed Salads
Fish in Aspic - Lobsters - Poultry in Aspic

Denis Ruffel
assisted by
Roland Bilheux and Alain Escoffier
under the direction of
Pierre Michalet

Translated by Anne Sterling

A copublication of
CICEM (Compagnie Internationale
de Consultation *Education* et *Media*)
Paris

and

**Van Nostrand Reinhold
New York**

Table of Contents

Page

5

Presentation of the 9 Chapters

This branch of the cooking business is diverse and constantly changing. It encompasses specialty food shops and the informal restaurants that are often a part of the same establishment. Off premise catering includes functions from small sit-down dinners to large buffet receptions.

The nine chapters of this volume cover a variety of dishes. Croustades, individual savory pastries, filled crêpes and quenelles are dishes that can be prepared in advance and reheated just before serving. Soufflés and beignets demand last minute attention. Mixed salads are fresh and can be adapted to all methods of sale. For large buffets there are recipes for elaborate poultry and fish centerpieces in aspic and lobsters displayed on platters.

Chapter 1 - New Croustades

Very easy to prepare in large sizes or individual portions. Ideal for sale in specialty food shops, small restaurants.

Ingredients can rotate with the seasons and can be combined in original ways.

Chapter 2 - Quenelles

Quenelles are delicious when prepared properly with top quality ingredients.

They are not difficult to prepare and overall the food cost is not high. Cut in slices, they can be combined with other ingredients in savory fillings. Original sauces give thse quenelles a personal touch.

Chapter 3 - Soufflés

Light and delicious but fragile and therefore must be served at the last minute.

Soufflés can be made with many ingredients including fish, meat, cheese, and vegetables. They are always appreciated by customers.

Chapter 4 - Beignets

These original fritters are a wonderful addition to a selection of appetizers. Beignets are easy to eat and are appropriate served with cocktails before a dinner or at a reception.

They are often served with a sauce made with mayonnaise.

Volume 3 The Professional Caterer Series

Chapter 5 - Individual Hot Dishes

This chapter includes a variety of dishes that can be prepared in advance and reheated for serving.

This selection of savory items ranges from the most simple to very elaborate, from inexpensive to luxurious.

All of these dishes (except soufflé crêpes) can be sold in specialty food shops and reheated by the customer at home. They are also appropriate served as a first course at a sit-down dinner or as a selection on a buffet.

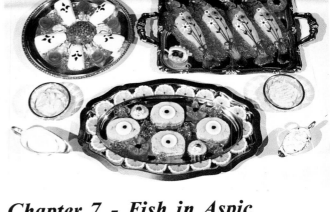

Chapter 6 - Mixed Salads

These colorful salads combine greens, vegetables, meats, seafood and other ingredients for a variety of textures and flavors. Salads are a versatile and popular part of the caterer's reperatoire.

Chapter 7 - Fish in Aspic

Individual portions can be made with small fish, filets, or slices. Large centerpieces using whole turbot, salmon and other large fish are a highlight on a buffet when elaborately decorated. These light dishes are delicious as well as beautiful.

Chapter 8 - Lobsters

These are prestigious dishes that feature the delicate and delicious meat of the lobster. The outstanding flavor stands on its own and is best when combined with a few simple ingredients. The color and shape of the lobster allow the caterer to create impressive presentations.

Chapter 9 - Poultry in Aspic

This chapter shows the variety of presentations that are possible using different poultry.

These classic dishes are personalized with special sauces and garnishes.

There is a recipe to suit every occasion.

Chapter 1
New Croustades

Innovative Taste Combinations

We begin Volume 3 with a variety of original " croustades ". In Volume 2 of this series, traditional and innovative quiches and croustades were presented. Here we complete the selection with 11 new combinations of flavors.

" Croustade " refers to the " crust " of basic pie pastry which is the base for all of these dishes.

The filling ingredients are chosen to reflect the seasons, and should always be of the highest quality.

The popularity of the classic quiche indicates that these savory, creamy croustades will become a successful addition to the caterer's repertoire.

General Advice for Making Croustades

Introduction

These new croustades marry delicious ingredients with a custard that has been seasoned to enhance these original combinations. Many of the creations feature seafood which is becoming very popular with clients who are " eating light ".

The wide variety of flavors and food cost permits the caterer to offer a continually changing selection of these savory pies. Customers appreciate new and interesting twists on old favorites.

Croustades can be made in individual portions or in large sizes that are cut in slices. They reheat easily and adapt to all methods of sale, making them a very important item for the caterer.

The Pastry Base

Beautiful and delicious croustades start with a pastry base that is made correctly.

The classic crust is basic pie pastry that should be made the day before and left to rest in the refrigerator, which makes it easier to work with and therefore more tender when baked.

The pastry is rolled out thinner for small individual croustades and thicker (about 3-4 mm (1/8in)) for larger ones. The molds which are about 3.5cm (1 1/2in) high are lightly buttered and the sheet of pastry is pressed into them with great care to ensure a crust that has neat edges and an attractive appearance. A border of pastry should be made around the top rim of the mold and crimped neatly with your fingers or a pastry crimper. This rim of pastry should not be too thin as the croustade bakes quite a long time; if the border is too thin it may brown too quickly and burn.

Once the pastry is pressed into the molds it should rest again in the refrigerator for 1-2 hours so that it does not shrink when it is baked. The pastry crust is then lined with a circle of parchment paper, filled with weights and blind baked.

The Filling Ingredients

The assortment of fillings should rotate with the seasons, using the very best and freshest that is available. The clients therefore have a new selection to choose from every few months.

Several combinations should be available at all times to offer a range of prices and flavors. To make this choice possible, the " mise en place " (advance preparation) for all of the croustades can be done at once--pie pastry made in sizeable batches, and custard

blended for several croustades at a time. The filling ingredients can often be prepared in advance in quantities large enough to make dozens of croustades.

The cost of the ingredients which is reflected in the price of the croustades should be selected with the method of sale in mind. Shelf life is also a factor when making croustades to be sold in a restaurant or specialty food shop.

The Custard

The custard sets around the filling ingredients and makes the

croustades moist and delicious. The classic recipe of cream and eggs is often enhanced with special seasonings that accent the flavor of the other ingredients.

The custard is easy to make; a simple blend of cream and eggs which should always be passed through a fine-meshed sieve to remove any egg shells or membrane from the egg and make the mixture homogeneous. Chopped herbs or other seasonings are then added to the smooth custard.

Preparation and Assembly

The preparation is done in three steps:

- Pressing the pastry into the mold and blind baking.

- Preparing the filling ingredients.

- Mixing the custard.

Great care should be taken with each of these steps to ensure a croustade that is attractive and delicious; pastry crust that is tender and crisp, custard that is well-seasoned and filling ingredients that are properly cooked and flavorful.

The ingredients should be arranged so that the presentation is balanced and eye appealing and each slice is the same.

Cooking

The cooking time and temperature varies slightly depending on the type of ingredients used. In all cases, attention must be paid to the three elements:

- The cooking of the filling ingredients.

- The custard should set but not overcook.

- The pastry crust must finish cooking but not become too brown.

When the custard has set, the pastry ring is removed and the croustade is glazed then returned to the oven for a few minutes so that the sides of the crust will brown and crisp.

It is recommended to cook croustades on heavy baking sheets which ensure even heating.

Pictured here are the croustades in this chapter.

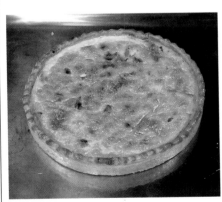

Salmon Croustade with Spinach and Sorrel

Introduction

This croustade can be made in all seasons. Salmon is usually available year round although the price may fluctuate. Spinach is easy to obtain, and the dish can be made without the sorrel if it is not available.

Choosing salmon that is perfectly fresh is important. The filets of salmon are cut on the bias in escalopes and marinated. The fresh spinach is sautéed in browned butter that gives it an agreeable nutty flavor. Sorrel is a delicious green with a lively acidic taste which marries extremely well with seafood.

The custard is accented with a fish based "Américaine" sauce that is reduced to concentrate the flavor. Finely chopped herbs and saffron add a zesty note to the classic custard.

Equipment

Cutting board, rolling pin, soft-bristled brush, thin-bladed flexible knife, serrated knife, 2-pronged fork, pastry brush, tablespoon, fork, ladle, whisk, fine-meshed conical strainer, mixing bowls, colander, hotel pan, sauté pan with cover, pastry ring (28cm (11in) x 3.5cm (1 1/2in)), round baking sheet, parchment paper, pie weights, plastic wrap

Ingredients

For a croustade 28cm (11in) in diameter and 3.5cm (1 1/2in) high, yielding 8 portions.

Spinach and Sorrel Filling
30g (1oz) clarified butter
750g (1 1/2lb) spinach
1 small bunch sorrel
30g (1oz) butter
Salt, pepper, nutmeg

Salmon Filling
500g (1lb) salmon filets
4 thin slices lemon
1 sprig fresh thyme
1/4 bay leaf
Few drops anise liqueur (Pastis or Ricard)
2cl (4 tsp) olive oil
Salt, pepper

Custard
3dl (1 1/4 cup) heavy cream
3 eggs
1 tablespoon finely chopped fresh herbs (chervil, tarragon, chives)
3cl (2 tbsp) reduced " Américaine " sauce
Salt, pepper, saffron

Procedure

The Pastry Base

It is best to make the basic pie pastry in advance and let it rest in the refrigerator. It will roll out more easily and be more tender when baked.

The rolled out sheet of dough is then pressed into pastry circles about 3.5cm (1 1/2in) high. Using these bottomless rings allows the pastry to brown and crisp on the bottom and the ring can be easily removed towards the end of cooking to brown the sides of the crust. It is important that the baking sheet be heavy to distribute heat evenly and avoid burning the pastry.

Once the pastry is pressed neatly into the bottom of the mold to ensure even baking and an attractive pastry crust, chill to rest the dough so that it does not shrink when it is baked.

Line the prepared mold with a circle of parchment paper and fill with weights (or dried beans or rice). Bake for about 15 minutes at 200C (375F), remove the paper and the weights, then bake for another 5-10 minutes to brown.

The Filling Ingredients

The Salmon

Slice the filets of salmon on the bias in escalopes about 1cm (3/8in) thick.

Place the pieces of salmon in a

flat dish and sprinkle with a little anise-flavored liqueur (Ricard or Pastis) and a few drops of olive oil. Place thin slices of lemon, the bay leaf and branches of thyme on top. Season with a little salt and pepper, cover with plastic wrap and mari-

nate in the refrigerator for at least one hour.

The salmon for many croustades can be marinated together and kept in the refrigerator for several days to make the croustades to order. Turn the escalopes over from time to time to distribute the marinade evenly.

The Spinach and Sorrel

Remove the stems from the leaves of spinach and sorrel and wash them thoroughly in a large basin of cold water, changing the water several times to remove all sand and dirt.

The spinach and sorrel are first cooked over high heat with a little clarified butter in a heavy pot with a tight-fitting lid which draws out the moisture in the leaves.

Drain the wilted leaves, then cook them in browned butter for a few minutes to evaporate the remaining liquid. Stir the greens as they cook with a two-pronged fork so that they will not stick to the pan and burn. Season the cooked spinach and sorrel with salt, pepper and nutmeg. Set aside to cool.

The Custard

Whisk together the cream and eggs and pass the mixture through a fine-meshed conical sieve.

Stir in the finely chopped herbs and the reduced and cooled " Américaine " sauce. Season the custard with salt, pepper and a pinch of saffron.

Assembly

Spread the spinach and sorrel mixture evenly over the bottom of the prebaked pastry crust. Ladle a little custard over the greens to cover. Arrange the marinated escalopes of salmon in an attractive pattern and pour in more custard to just below the rim.

Cooking

Bake the croustade at 200C (375F) for about 20-30 minutes. Be

Salmon, Spinach and Sorrel Croustade
Procedure Diagram

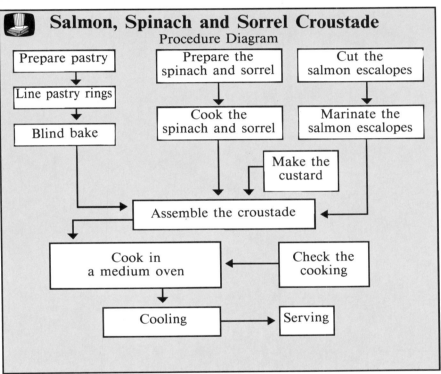

careful not to dry out the salmon which will cook quickly. When the custard has set, remove the pastry ring, brush a light coat of egg glaze on the rim and sides of the pastry to make it golden and help keep it fresh.

Return to the oven for a few minutes to brown the sides of the crust.

Carefully slide the cooked croustade onto a cooling rack so that the bottom of the crust does not become soggy.

Storage

This croustade will keep in the refrigerator for 2 days covered with plastic wrap.

Serving

Reheat the croustade in a medium oven and serve warm.

Croustade with Asparagus and Frogs' Legs

Introduction

This is a very light and refined croustade using an original and delicious combination of ingredients.

Fresh asparagus is plentiful during only a few months a year so this croustade should be offered in the spring when asparagus is available.

The delicate texture and flavor of the frogs' legs make this a very special dish.

The preparation of this croustade is quite simple, involving the preparation of two main ingredients combined with a classic custard seasoned only with salt, pepper and nutmeg.

Equipment

Cutting board, vegetable peeler, paring knife, chef's knife, pastry brush, tablespoon, fork, mixing bowls, colander, fine-meshed conical sieve, skimmer, ladle, whisk, sauté pan, pastry ring (28cm (11in) × 3.5cm (1 1/2in)), round baking sheet, parchment paper, pie weights, hotel pan, rolling pin, soft-bristled brush

Ingredients

For a croustade 28cm (11in) in diameter and 3.5cm (1 1/2in) high, yielding 8 portions.

Filling

a) 750g (1 1/2lb) green asparagus
   Salt

b) 500g (1lb) frogs' legs
   45g (1 1/2oz) clarified butter
   45g (1 1/2oz) shallots
   15g (1/2oz) garlic
   small bunch fresh coriander
   Salt, pepper

Custard

4dl (1 2/3 cup) heavy cream
5 eggs
8 sprigs chives, chopped
Salt, pepper, nutmeg

Procedure

The Pastry Base

Like all the croustades in this chapter, the basic pie pastry for the crust should be made in advance (1 day ahead) and left to rest in the refrigerator.

The rolled out sheet of dough is then pressed into pastry circles about 3.5cm (1 1/2in) high. Using these bottomless rings allows the pastry to brown and crisp on the bottom and the ring can be easily removed towards the end of cooking to brown the sides of the crust. It is important that the baking sheet be heavy to distribute heat evenly and avoid burning the pastry.

Once the pastry is pressed neatly into the bottom of the mold to ensure even baking and an attractive pastry crust, chill to rest the dough so that it does not shrink when it is baked.

Line the prepared mold with a circle of parchment paper and fill with weights (or dried beans or rice). Bake for about 15 minutes at 200C (375F), remove the paper and the weights, then bake for another 5-10 minutes to brown.

The Filling Ingredients

The Asparagus

Choose asparagus that are bright green and not too large. Rinse them thoroughly, trim the ends that tend to be tough and peel the stems to remove the fibrous skin.

Fill a large heavy pot with lightly salted water and bring it to rapid boil. Tie the asparagus in small bundles to protect them during cooking.

Plunge them into the boiling water and cook until tender but firm. Do not overcook at this point as the asparagus will cook again a little when the croustade is baked.

Verify the texture with the point of a small knife and remove the cooked asparagus to a basin of ice water to stop the cooking immediately. Drain the vegetables as soon as they are cool so that they do not become watery. Untie the bundles and dry them on a hand towel.

Cut the tips of the asparagus to about 4-5cm (2in) and set aside.

The tender stems are cut into small pieces, about 1cm (3/8in).

The Frogs' Legs

Choose fresh, meaty frogs' legs.

Cut the shallots into very fine dice, crush the garlic and chop it, and chop the coriander.

Heat a little clarified butter in a heavy-bottomed pan and sauté the

frogs' legs over high heat to brown them a little and cook them quickly

without drying them out, stirring them constantly.

Add the chopped shallots and garlic and cook without browning.

Assembly

Place the pre-baked crust on a heavy baking sheet. Fill the bottom of the crust with the pieces of asparagus and and boned meat from the frogs' legs. Ladle custard over these ingredients then arrange the asparagus tips in a neat spoke pattern on top.

Remove the frogs' legs from the heat, stir in the chopped coriander and cool a little.

While the frogs' legs are still warm, gently pull the meat off the bones. Discard the bones, reserving the chopped garlic, shallots and coriander, then add the pieces of meat and set aside to cool.

The Custard

Whisk together the cream and eggs and pass the mixture through a fine-meshed conical sieve to

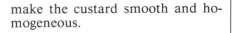

make the custard smooth and homogeneous.

Season the custard with salt, pepper, nutmeg and chopped chives. Set aside until ready to assemble the croustade.

Pour in more custard to just below the rim.

Cooking

Carefully place the croustade in the oven without spilling the custard. Cook at 200C (375F) for about 20-25 minutes.

Since the filling ingredients are already cooked it is only necessary to cook this croustade long enough to set the custard.

Insert the point of a paring knife in the center of the croustade to test the doneness of the custard. Do not overcook; the custard should be set but still soft and creamy.

When the custard has set, remove the ring, brush the sides of the pastry with egg glaze and return to the oven for a few minutes to brown the sides.

Carefully slide the cooked croustade onto a cooling rack so that the bottom of the crust does not become soggy.

Storage

This croustade will keep for two days in the refrigerator covered with plastic wrap.

Serving

Reheat the croustade in a medium oven and serve warm.

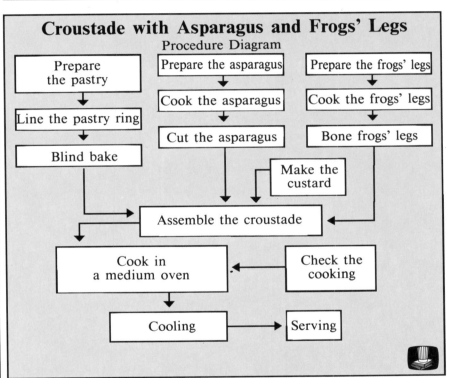

Croustade with Asparagus and Frogs' Legs
Procedure Diagram

```
Prepare                Prepare the asparagus      Prepare the frogs' legs
the pastry                      ↓                          ↓
    ↓                  Cook the asparagus          Cook the frogs' legs
Line the pastry ring            ↓                          ↓
    ↓                  Cut the asparagus            Bone frogs' legs
Blind bake
                                        Make the
                                        custard
                              Assemble the croustade

              Cook in                    Check the
            a medium oven                 cooking

              Cooling        →          Serving
```

Croustade with Artichokes, Zucchini and Frogs' Legs

Introduction

This croustade is a variation of the previous recipe which combined frogs' legs with asparagus. Here artichokes and zucchini marry equally well with the delicate meat of the frogs' legs. This is therefore a good alternative when asparagus is not in season.

The preparation of the artichokes requires skill to cut away the tough leaves, but otherwise the procedure for this croustade is not more difficult than the one we have just studied.

Equipment

Cutting board, paring knife, chef's knife, pastry brush, tablespoon, fork, mixing bowls, colanders, fine-meshed conical strainer, skimmer, ladle, whisk, frying pan, saucepans, sauté pan, hotel pan, pastry ring, round baking sheet, rolling pin, soft-bristled brush, parchment paper, pie weights

Ingredients

For a croustade 28cm (11in) in diameter and 3.5cm (1 1/2in) high, yielding 8 portions.

Filling

a) 3 large artichokes (750g (1 1/2lb))
Water, flour, olive oil, lemon, salt, pepper, coriander seed
3 zucchini (600g (1 1/4lb)
Olive oil, salt, pepper

b) 500g (1lb) frogs' legs
45g (1 1/2oz) clarified butter
45g (1 1/2oz) shallots
15g (1/2oz) garlic
6 sprigs fresh coriander
Salt, pepper

Custard

4dl (1 2/3 cup) heavy cream
5 eggs
8 sprigs chives, chopped
Salt, pepper, nutmeg

Procedure

The Pastry Base

The pastry base for this croustade is made exactly like the ones we have seen in the previous examples.

The Filling Ingredients

The Artichokes

Rinse the artichokes thoroughly and break off the stem. With a very sharp stainless-steel paring knife held against the side of the artichoke, cut off all the large bottom leaves, starting at the widest part of the artichoke and turning. Trim away all the leaves in this manner, then neatly trim the bottom so it is even and flat on the underside.

Rub the trimmed artichokes with lemon to keep them from darkening.

To keep them from darkening during cooking, it is recommended to use a " blanc ". This mixture consists of 25g (about 1oz) of flour stirred into 2L (2 qts) of water with a little olive oil and the juice of half of a lemon. Coriander can be added as well to season the water.

Add salt and pepper and bring the cooking liquid to a boil. Add the artichoke bottoms and cook until tender but still firm. Check the doneness with the point of a paring knife. Do not overcook as they will cook just a little more in the croustade.

Remove them from the liquid and let them cool a little before removing the fibrous choke.

Cut the prepared artichokes into dice about 1.5 cm (1/2in) on each side. Set aside until ready to assemble the croustade.

The Zucchini

Rinse the zucchini, dry them and cut off the ends. Cut them into slices about 1/2cm (about 1/4in) wide.

Heat some olive oil in a sauté pan, add the slices of zucchini and brown them on both sides. Season with thyme, salt and pepper. When they are cooked but still slightly firm, drain the slices in a colander and set aside.

The Frogs' Legs

The preparation of the frogs' legs is the same as in the previous recipe.

The Custard

The preparation of the custard is the same as in the previous recipe.

Assembly

Place an even layer of zucchini slices on the bottom of the pre-pared pastry crust. Top this layer with pieces of artichoke and frogs' legs as shown.

Pour the custard over these ingredients until it comes within 5mm (about 1/4in) of the rim.

Cooking

Carefully place the croustade in the oven without spilling the custard. Cook at 200C (375F) for about 20-25 minutes.

Since the filling ingredients are already cooked it is only necessary to cook this croustade long enough to set the custard.

Insert the point of a paring knife in the center of the croustade to test the doneness of the custard. Do not overcook; the custard should be set but still soft and creamy.

When the custard has set, remove the ring, brush the sides of the pastry with egg glaze and return to the oven for a few minutes to brown the sides.

Carefully slide the cooked croustade onto a cooling rack so that the bottom of the crust does not become soggy.

Storage

This croustade will keep for two days in the refrigerator covered with plastic wrap.

Serving

Reheat the croustade in a medium oven and serve warm.

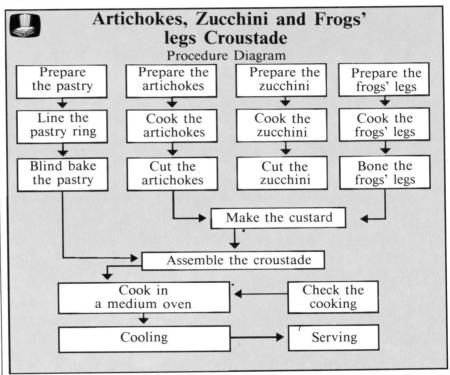

Artichokes, Zucchini and Frogs' legs Croustade
Procedure Diagram

```
Prepare          Prepare the      Prepare the      Prepare the
the pastry       artichokes       zucchini         frogs' legs
    ↓                ↓                ↓                ↓
Line the         Cook the         Cook the         Cook the
pastry ring      artichokes       zucchini         frogs' legs
    ↓                ↓                ↓                ↓
Blind bake       Cut the          Cut the          Bone the
the pastry       artichokes       zucchini         frogs' legs
                      ↓                               ↓
                     Make the custard
                          ↓
              Assemble the croustade
                   ↓
      Cook in                    Check the
      a medium oven       ←      cooking
           ↓
      Cooling          →          Serving
```

Seafood Croustade with Saffron

Introduction

This light and tasty croustade can be made with different assortments of seafood to take advantage of the freshest products available in each season. When one type of seafood becomes too expensive, it can be replaced with another.

A simple addition of sautéed mushrooms rounds out the filling ingredients in this croustade. Saffron and fresh herbs in the custard accent the delicious taste of the seafood.

Equipment

Cutting board, paring knife, chef's knife, thin-bladed flexible knife, tablespoon, fork, ladle, skimmer, whisk, sauté pans with lids, saucepans with lids, mixing bowls, colander, hotel pan, pastry brush, rolling pin, soft-bristled brush, pastry ring, round baking sheet, parchment paper, pie weights

Ingredients

For a croustade 28cm (11in) in diameter and 3.5cm (1 1/2in) high, yielding 8 portions.

Filling

Seafood Filling

Mussels " marinières ":
750g (1 1/2lb) mussels
1 shallot
1/2 small onion
20g (1/2oz) clarified butter
Small bouquet garni (parsley stems, thyme, bay leaf)
1dl (1/2 cup) dry white wine
Pepper
150g (5oz) shrimp
6 sea scallops with coral
200g (7oz) monkfish filets

Mushroom Filling

200g (7oz) mushrooms
5cl (1/4 cup) water
15g (1/2oz) butter
Few drops lemon juice
Salt, pepper

Custard

3dl (1 1/4 cup) heavy cream

1.5dl (2/3 cup) reserved mussel
cooking liquid
5cl (1/4 cup) reserved mushroom
cooking liquid
5 eggs
1 tablespoon chopped fresh herbs
(chervil, chives, dill)
Salt, pepper, saffron

Procedure

The Pastry Base

Like all the croustades in this chapter, the basic pie pastry for the crust should be made in advance (1 day ahead) and left to rest in the refrigerator.

The rolled out sheet of dough is then pressed into pastry circles about 3.5cm (1 1/2in) high. Using these bottomless rings allows the pastry to brown and crisp on the bottom and the ring can be easily removed towards the end of cooking to brown the sides of the crust. It is important that the baking sheet be heavy to distribute heat evenly and avoid burning the pastry.

Once the pastry is pressed neatly into the bottom of the mold to ensure even baking and an attractive pastry crust, chill to rest the dough so that it does not shrink when it is baked.

Line the prepared mold with a circle of parchment paper and fill with weights (or dried beans or rice). Bake for about 15 minutes at 200C (375F), remove the paper and the weights, then bake for another 5-10 minutes to brown.

The Filling Ingredients

The Mushrooms

Trim the sandy stems of the mushrooms. Wash the mushrooms in a large basin of cold water, changing the water several times until all of the sand has been rinsed away. Rub them with lemon to keep to keep them from darkening.

Bring the water, butter, lemon juice, salt and pepper to a boil. Add the mushrooms, cover the pot and

cook over high heat. When they are cooked but still slightly firm drain them in a colander.

Reserve the cooking liquid and reduce to about 5cl (1/4 cup). This mushroom essence will be added to the custard.

The Mussels

Choose fresh mussels and trim them of seaweed and barnacles. Rinse them in a large basin of cold water, changing the water several times.

To cook them " à la marinière ", first cook the chopped shallot and onion in clarified butter in a large pot without browning. Add the mussels, bouquet garni, white wine and pepper. (Salt is not added because the mussels are naturally salty.)

Cover the pot and steam the mussels over high heat until the shells open. Do not overcook, as they will cook a little more in the croustade.

Drain the mussels, reserving the liquid which is reduced to about 1.5dl (2/3 cup) and reserved to flavor the custard.

Remove the cooked mussels from the shells and pull off the dark " beard " around the edge of each mussel, which is chewy.

The Shrimp

Carefully remove the shells of the shrimp and cut them in pieces about the size of a mussel.

The Scallops

Remove the coral and set aside. Cut the scallops in slices about 1.5cm (1/2in) thick.

The Monkfish

Cut the monkfish into pieces about the same size as the other fish.

Note: The shrimp, the scallops and the monkfish are not pre-cooked at this time. The ingredients are added to the croustade raw and will cook during baking.

The Custard

Whisk together the cream, eggs, and the reduced cooking liquid from the mushrooms and the mussels. Pass this mixture through a fine-meshed conical sieve then add the finely chopped herbs.

Season the custard with a pinch of saffron which is delicious with seafood. Add pepper and a little salt.

Note: The reduced cooking liquids will be quite salty so very little salt if any will be needed for the custard.

Assembly

Arrange the ingredients evenly in the prepared crust so that each slice of croustade has an equal amount of each ingredient.

Pour the custard over the ingredients to within 5mm (about 1/4in) of the rim.

Cooking

Cook the croustade at 200C (375F) for 20-25 minutes.

The seafood will cook quickly. When the custard is set, the sea-

food will be cooked as well. The seafood should not overcook because it becomes dry and tough.

When the croustade is done, remove the ring, brush the sides of the pastry with egg glaze and return to the oven for just a moment to cook the glaze to a golden brown which will make the croustade attractive and will keep the croustade fresher.

Carefully slide the cooked croustade onto a cooling rack so that the bottom of the pastry does not become soggy.

Storage

This croustade will keep for two days in the refrigerator covered with plastic wrap.

Serving

Reheat the croustade in a medium oven and serve warm.

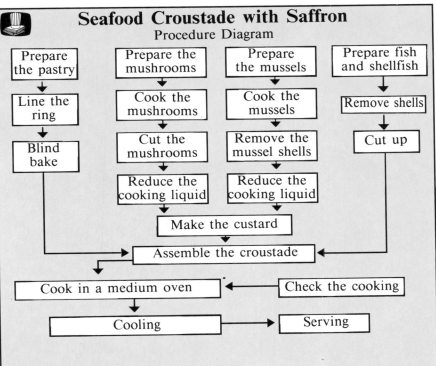

Seafood Croustade with Saffron
Procedure Diagram

Prepare the pastry	Prepare the mushrooms	Prepare the mussels	Prepare fish and shellfish
Line the ring	Cook the mushrooms	Cook the mussels	Remove shells
Blind bake	Cut the mushrooms	Remove the mussel shells	Cut up
	Reduce the cooking liquid	Reduce the cooking liquid	

Make the custard

Assemble the croustade

Cook in a medium oven ← Check the cooking

Cooling → Serving

Mussel Croustade with Pistou

Introduction

"Pistou" is a Mediterranean mixture of basil and garlic pounded in a "pestle" often with an addition of grilled, chopped tomatoes.

It is best to offer this croustade when fresh basil is plentiful and inexpensive. The food cost is quite low, allowing the caterer to offer this variation on the classic quiche at a reasonable price.

A touch of kirsch enhances the mussels and pistou giving this dish a distinctive flavor.

Equipment

Cutting board, paring knife, thin-bladed flexible knife, skimmer, ladle, spatula, tablespoon, fork, mixing bowls, colanders, fine-meshed conical sieve, large sauté pan with lid, rolling pin, soft-bristled brush, pastry brush, round baking sheet, pastry ring, parchment paper, pie weights, measuring cup, whisk

Ingredients

For a croustade 28cm (11in) in diameter and 3.5cm (1 1/2in) high, yielding 8 portions.

Filling

3.5cl (2 tbsp) olive oil
45g (1 1/2oz) shallots
15g (1/2oz) garlic
700g (1 1/2lb) tomatoes
2dl (3/4 cup) heavy cream
2kg (4 1/2lb) mussels
Salt, pepper, cayenne pepper, sugar
2 tablespoons chopped fresh parsley
1 bunch (about 20 leaves) basil
3cl (2 tbsp) kirsch

Custard

3dl (1 1/4 cup) heavy cream
5 eggs
Salt, pepper, saffron

Procedure

The Pastry Base

Like all the croustades in this chapter, the basic pie pastry for the crust should be made in advance (1 day ahead) and left to rest in the refrigerator.

The rolled out sheet of dough is then pressed into pastry circles about 3.5cm (1 1/2in) high. Using these bottomless rings allows the pastry to brown and crisp on the bottom and the ring can be easily removed towards the end of cooking to brown the sides of the crust. It is important that the baking sheet be heavy to distribute heat evenly and avoid burning the pastry.

Once the pastry is pressed neatly into the bottom of the mold to ensure even baking and an attractive pastry crust, chill to rest the dough so that it does not shrink when it is baked.

Line the prepared mold with a circle of parchment paper and fill with weights (or dried beans or rice). Bake for about 15 minutes at 200C (375F), remove the paper and the weights, then bake for another 5-10 minutes to brown.

The Mussels

Choose large, fresh mussels. Scrape the shells to remove seaweed and barnacles and rinse the mussels in a large basin of cold water, changing the water several times to rinse away sand.

Peel the shallots and cut into very fine dice. Peel the garlic, remove the the green sprout in the

center which tends to be bitter, crush the garlic then chop it finely. Pluck the leaves from the parsley, rinse, dry and chop finely. Pluck the leaves from the basil, rinse then cut into very thin strips. Trim the stem end of the tomatoes and

plunge them into boiling water for a few seconds to loosen the skin. Pull off the skin, cut in half and squeeze out the seeds. Cut the prepared tomatoes into large dice. Heat the oil in a large pan and add the diced tomatoes and the chopped shallots and garlic. Cover the pot and cook over medium-high heat a few minutes to draw the moisture out of the vegetables,

then remove the cover and continue to cook to dry out the mixture.

Add the cream, bring to a boil and add the cleaned mussels.

Season with a pinch of cayenne. The mussels are naturally salty so no salt is necessary. Add a pinch of sugar to counteract the acidity of the tomatoes.

Cover the pot and steam the mussels over high heat. They are done when the shells have opened. Remove the cooked mussels from the pot with a slotted spoon. Reduce the cooking liquid, now rich with mussel flavor, until it thickens slightly. Add the chopped parsley and basil and the kirsch. Taste and season if necessary.

Remove the mussels from the shells and pull off the dark "beard" around the edge of each mussel, which is chewy.

The Custard

Whisk together the cream and

eggs. Pass this mixture through a fine-meshed conical sieve to remove bits of egg shell and membrane. Season to taste with salt, pepper and a pinch of saffron.

Assembly

Place the pre-cooked pastry crust on a heavy baking sheet. Spread an even layer of the reduced " pistou " on the bottom of the crust. Place the mussels on top, then spoon the rest of the pistou on the mussels.

Ladle the custard over these ingredients to within 5mm (about 1/4in) of the rim.

Cooking

Place the croustade carefully into an oven preheated to 200C (375F).

It is cooked when the custard has set, about 20-25 minutes. Check the doneness of the custard with the point of a small knife inserted in the center.

When the custard has set, remove the ring and brush the sides of the pastry with egg glaze and return it to the oven for a few minutes. The glaze will be a golden brown and will keep the pastry fresh.

Carefully slide the cooked croustade onto a cooling rack so that the bottom of the crust does not become soggy.

Storage

This croustade will keep for two days in the refrigerator covered with plastic wrap.

Serving

Reheat the croustade in a medium oven and serve warm.

Mussel Croustade with Pistou
Procedure Diagram

```
Prepare          Prepare              Prepare
the pastry       the filling          the mussels
    |                |                     |
    v                v                     v
Line the         +-----------------------------+
pastry ring      |      Cook the mussels        |
    |            +-----------------------------+
    v                |                     |
 Blind           Reduce                Shell the
 bake            the liquid            mussels
    |                |
    |            Make the
    |            custard
    |                |
    +-----> Assemble the croustade <-----+
                     |
    +-----> Cook in a medium oven <----- Check the
    |                |                    cooking
    v                v
      Cooling  ------->  Serving
```

Five-Mushroom Croustade

Introduction

Lovers of mushrooms will appreciate this rustic croustade which features four wild mushrooms and white mushrooms. Truffle juice heightens the woodsy flavor of the croustade.

This is an ideal dish to offer in the fall when wild mushrooms are plentiful and less expensive.

Although dried mushrooms can be used, the flavor will be better if the croustade is made with fresh ones. If the types shown here are not available, similar wild mushrooms in season can be substituted.

Ingredients

For a croustade 28cm (11in) in diameter and 3.5cm (1 1/2in) high, yielding 8 portions.

Filling

45g (1 1/2oz) clarified butter
150g (5oz) chanterelles
150g (5oz) oyster mushrooms (pleurottes)
150g (5oz) morels
150g (5oz) mushrooms
150g (5oz) horn of plenty (trompettes de mort)
45g (1 1/2oz) shallots
15g (1/2oz) garlic
2 tablespoons chopped fresh chervil and parsley
2dl (3/4 cup) rich reduced veal stock
5cl (1/4 cup) truffle juice
Salt, pepper

Custard

3dl (1 1/4 cup) heavy cream
5 eggs
Salt, pepper, nutmeg

Equipment

Cutting board, paring knife, thin-bladed flexible knife, chef's knife, skimmer, ladle, spatula, tablespoon, fork, mixing bowls, colander, measuring cup, fine-meshed conical sieve, whisk, large sauté pan with lid, rolling pin, soft-bristled brush, round baking sheet, pastry ring, parchment paper, pie weights

Procedure

The Pastry Base

The preparation of the pastry base is the same as the other croustades in this chapter.

The Mushrooms

Sort through the wild mushrooms and remove leaves or straw that is often found with them. Trim the stems of all the mushrooms to remove the sand and dirt. Wash each type of mushroom separately in a large basin of cold water, changing the water several times until there is no sand or dirt left. Drain them and dry them thoroughly.

If the mushrooms are large, cut them into pieces so that they are all the same size.

The mushrooms do not cook at the same rate, so they must be kept separate at this point.

The Seasonings

Peel the shallot and cut it into very fine dice. Peel the garlic, remove the green sprout in the center, crush it and chop it finely.

Pluck the leaves from the parsley and chervil, then rinse and dry them. Chop them finely. Reserve the stems to make a bouquet garni.

33

Cooking the Mushrooms

Heat the clarified butter over medium-high heat and add the chanterelles and oyster mushrooms and cover the pot to draw some moisture out of the mushrooms. Add the morels and the white mushrooms, cover and cook for a few minutes. Finally add the horn of plenty and the chopped shallots and garlic.

Cover and cook a few minutes, then remove the cover and cook to evaporate the liquid. When the mixture is dry, stir in the chopped parsley and chervil.

Pour in the reduced stock and truffle juice, season with salt and pepper and cook until the liquid has reduced and is thick and syrupy. Set aside this mushroom mixture to cool until ready to assemble the croustade.

The Custard

Whisk together the cream and the eggs, and pass this mixture through a fine-meshed sieve to remove bits of egg shell and membrane.

Season the custard with salt, pepper and nutmeg.

Assembly

Place the pre-cooked pastry crust on a heavy baking sheet.

Spread an even layer of the mushroom mixture on the bottom of the crust.

Ladle the custard over the mushrooms to within 5mm (about 1/4in) of the rim.

Cooking

Place the croustade carefully into an oven preheated to 200C (375F).

It is cooked when the custard has set, about 20-25 minutes. Check the doneness of the custard with the point of a small knife inserted in the center.

When the custard has set, remove the ring and brush the sides of the pastry with egg glaze and remove it to the oven for a few minutes. The glaze will be golden brown and will keep the pastry fresh.

Carefully slide the cooked croustade onto a cooling rack so that the bottom of the crust does not become soggy.

Storage

This croustade will keep for two days in the refrigerator covered with plastic wrap.

Serving

Reheat the croustade in a medium oven and serve warm.

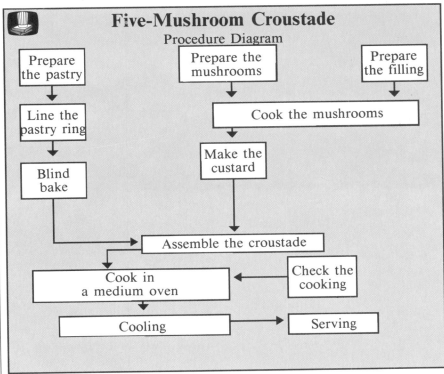

Five-Mushroom Croustade
Procedure Diagram

Prepare the pastry → Line the pastry ring → Blind bake

Prepare the mushrooms → Cook the mushrooms

Prepare the filling → Cook the mushrooms

Cook the mushrooms → Make the custard

Make the custard → Assemble the croustade

Blind bake → Assemble the croustade

Assemble the croustade → Cook in a medium oven

Check the cooking → Cook in a medium oven

Cook in a medium oven → Cooling

Cooling → Serving

Croustade with Eggs " Florentine "

Introduction

This croustade and the one that follows feature poached eggs. The custard used in the other croustades in this chapter is replaced by a flavorful mornay sauce.

All of the ingredients are cooked in advance, and since the sauce is cooked as well, these croustades are not baked in the oven but merely warmed through. Just before serving, grated swiss cheese is sprinkled on the top and browned under the broiler.

Close attention must be paid to the cooking of the eggs so that they remain soft. The eggs are held in place with a rich, thick mornay sauce.

These croustades are not expensive to make and are easy to prepare.

This croustade gets its name from the spinach used which was originally brought to France from Italy hence " Florentine ".

Equipment

Sauté pans with lids, large saucepan, whisk, skimmer, ladle, mixing bowls, colander, tablespoon, fork, 2-pronged fork, rolling pin, soft-bristled brush, pastry brush, round baking sheet, pastry ring, parchment paper, pie weights, scissors, spatula, measuring cup, fine-meshed conical sieve

Ingredients

For a croustade 28cm (11in) in diameter and 3.5cm (1 1/2in) high, yielding 8 portions.

Spinach Filling

750g (1 1/2lb) spinach
30g (1oz) clarified butter
45g (1 1/2oz) butter
1.5dl (2/3 cup) heavy cream
Salt, pepper, nutmeg

Poached Eggs

3L (3qts) water
8 eggs
1/4L (1 cup) white vinegar

To Finish

60g (2oz) grated swiss cheese

Mornay Sauce

45g (1 1/2oz) butter
45g (1 1/2oz) flour
3/4L (3 cups) milk
3 yolks
1dl (1/2 cup) heavy cream
Salt, pepper, nutmeg

Procedure

The Pastry Base

The preparation of the pastry crust is the same as the other croustades in this chapter. The rolled out sheet of dough is pressed into pastry circles about 3.5cm (1 1/2in) high. It is important that the baking sheet be heavy to distribute heat evenly and avoid burning the pastry.

Once the pastry is pressed neatly into the bottom of the mold to ensure even baking and an attractive pastry crust, chill to rest the dough so that it does not shrink when it is baked.

Line the prepared mold with a circle of parchment paper and fill with weights (or dried beans or rice). Bake for about 15 minutes at 200C (375F), remove the paper and the weights, then bake for another 5-10 minutes to brown.

When the pastry crust is lightly browned, brush the inside with egg glaze and return to the oven for a few more minutes, until the glaze is golden brown.

The Filling Ingredients

The Eggs

Bring the water and vinegar to a boil. White alcohol vinegar is recommended as it will not discolor the egg whites. The vinegar will coagulate the egg whites so that they will cling to the yolk and form more attractive poached eggs.

Break the eggs into a small bowl. Lower the heat so that the water is simmering, then slide the eggs into the water. It is recommended to poach only four eggs at a time. As soon as the white is set, carefully lift each egg out with a slotted spoon and stop the cooking by plunging it into ice water.

Drain the cooled eggs on a hand towel to dry completely.

The Spinach

Pull out the stem from the leaves of spinach and wash them thoroughly in a basin of cold water.

Melt the clarified butter in a large pot, add the spinach leaves, cover and cook over high heat to draw the moisture out of the spinach. Drain in a colander and heat more clarified butter, this time cooking it until it becomes golden brown and smells nutty.

Add the drained spinach to the browned butter and cook briefly to evaporate the remaining liquid, stirring constantly with a two-pronged fork to keep the spinach from sticking to the pot. Pour in the cream and cook until the mixture has thickened.

Season to taste with salt, pepper and nutmeg.

The Mornay Sauce

Make a classic béchamel sauce

by first melting the butter and whisking in the flour to make a roux. Whisk in the milk off the heat then return to medium-high heat and cook the sauce, stirring constantly.

When the sauce has thickened and no longer tastes of flour, re-

move the pot from the heat and whisk the cream and egg yolks into the hot sauce. Stir the sauce for a few moments over medium heat, being careful not to boil the sauce which would coagulate the egg yolks.

Season to taste with salt, pepper and nutmeg.

The cheese which transforms a be-chamel sauce into mornay is added on the top just before serving.

The sauce needs to be pourable when you assemble the croustade so that it coats the eggs easily. Since it is delicate to reheat due to the eggs, it is best to make the sauce shortly before assembling the croustade. If the sauce must be made ahead to facilitate the " mise en place ", after making the béchamel, cool it and incorporate the cream and egg yolks when the sauce is reheated for assembly.

Assembly

Place the pre-baked pastry crust on a heavy baking sheet. Remember that the crust for this croustade has been brushed with egg glaze on the inside to protect the pastry from the moisture in the filling.

In the bottom of the crust, spread an even layer of the spinach mixture. Place the eggs on top in a circle around the edge so that there is an egg for each slice of croustade.

Ladle the warm sauce over the top of these ingredients and sprinkle with grated swiss cheese.

Storage

The croustade can be made to this stage and kept refrigerated for 1 day.

Serving

Just before the croustade is to be served, warm it through in a medium oven.

When the croustade is warm, place it under the broiler for a few

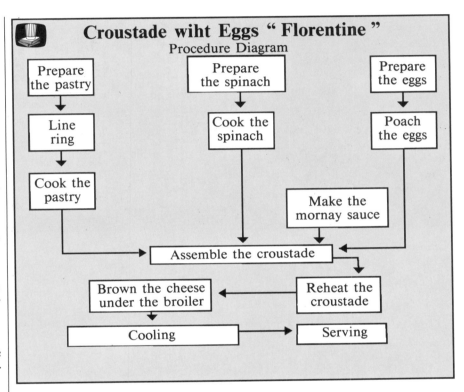

Croustade wiht Eggs " Florentine "
Procedure Diagram

```
Prepare            Prepare            Prepare
the pastry         the spinach        the eggs
   │                   │                  │
   ▼                   ▼                  ▼
 Line               Cook the           Poach
 ring               spinach            the eggs
   │                   │                  │
   ▼                   │                  │
Cook the               │          Make the
pastry                 │          mornay sauce
   │                   │                  │
   │                   ▼                  │
   └────────►  Assemble the croustade ◄───┘
                       │
                       ▼
Brown the cheese  ◄── Reheat the
under the broiler     croustade
   │
   ▼
  Cooling  ──────────►  Serving
```

moments to brown the cheese on the top.

It is very important that the croustade does not become hot enough to cook the eggs which should remain soft with a slightly runny yolk.

Serve the croustade immediately. Cut the portions between each egg so that the yolk remains intact.

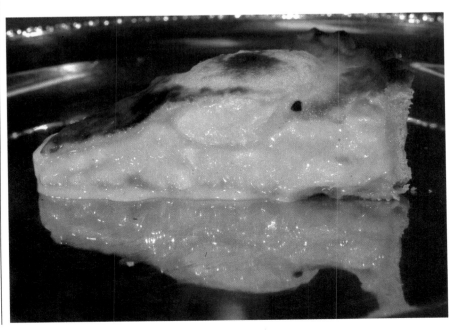

Croustade with Poached Eggs "Benedictine"

Introduction

This elegant and delicious croustade features poached eggs like the previous recipe. The procedure is similar but involves additional steps to prepare the "brandade" of salt cod and the sauce which is enriched with a sabayon.

Chopped truffles may be added to the sauce to intensify the taste. The cost of the truffles in this case must be reflected in the price.

Without the truffles, the food cost of this dish is relatively low.

The name for this croustade comes from the tradition of serving fish dishes on Fridays in Catholic countries, hence "Benedictine".

As with the previous croustade, the warming of this dish must be done very carefully so that the eggs do not overcook.

Equipment

Sauté pans, large saucepans, mortar and pestle or food processor, whisk, skimmer, ladle, mixing bowls, colander, tablespoon, fork, rolling pin, soft-bristled brush, pastry brush, round baking sheet, pastry ring, parchment paper, pie weights, scissors, spatula, measuring cup, fine-meshed conical sieve

Ingredients

For a croustade 28cm (11in) in diameter and 3.5cm (1 1/2in) high, yielding 8 portions.

"Brandade" Filling

500g (1lb) salt cod
1L (1qt) water
1L (1qt) milk
2dl (3/4 cup) oil
1.5dl (2/3 cup) milk
2 cloves garlic
Few drops lemon juice
Pepper

Poached Eggs

2L (2 qts) water
8 eggs
1/4L (1 cup) white vinegar

Sauce

4dl (1 2/3 cup) fish stock
4dl (1 2/3 cup) heavy cream
Roux, for thickening
5 egg yolks + 2 tablespoons water
  (for the sabayon)
Salt, pepper
30g (1oz) truffles (optional)

Procedure

The Pastry Base

The preparation of the pastry crust is the same as the other croustades in this chapter. The rolled out sheet of dough is pressed into pastry circles about 3.5cm (1 1/2in) high. It is important that the baking sheet be heavy to distribute heat evenly and avoid burning the pastry.

Once the pastry is pressed neatly into the bottom of the mold to ensure even baking and an attractive pastry crust, chill to rest the dough so that it does not shrink when it is baked.

Line the prepared mold with a circle of parchment paper and fill with weights (or dried beans or rice). Bake for about 15 minutes at 200C (375F), remove the paper and the weights, then bake for another 5-10 minutes to brown.

When the pastry crust is lightly browned, brush the inside with egg glaze and return to the oven for a few more minutes, until the glaze is golden brown.

The Filling Ingredients

The Brandade

Desalting and Poaching

The saltcod must be desalted before it is used in the recipe; this should be started one day ahead.

Cut the saltcod into large pieces and place them in a large mixing bowl. Place a grill on the top, to keep the pieces of saltcod from floating away, and let the cold water flow gently over the saltcod. Alternatively, soak the saltcod in cold water, changing the water very frequently. The saltcod must be desalted for at least 12 and up to 24 hours, otherwise the saltcod will be too salty.

The desalted saltcod is poached either in a mixture of half water and half milk or in water flavored with some aromatic vegetables and herbs.

Lay the pieces of saltcod in a shallow heat-proof dish containing the cold poaching liquid. Bring the

liquid just to a boil, then immediately reduce the heat and continue to poach over very low heat about 8-10 minutes. Skim off any foam that rises during poaching.

When the saltcod is poached, drain it, then with a fork, separate into flakes, removing any bones.

Flavoring and Blending the Brandade

Peel the garlic cloves, cut in half and remove the green sprout from the center.

Put the garlic in a small saucepan with some cold water and bring it to a boil, then drain them. This will soften them slightly.

The saltcod should be beaten with the other ingredients while it is still warm so that they are easier to incorporate. Heat the oil and milk as well.

The ingredients may be combined using a food processor or with a mortar and pestle. For the food processor, put the blanched garlic and the prepared, flaked saltcod in the workbowl and combine. Slowly add the warmed milk and oil until the mixture is well emulsified and light.

To combine by hand, work the blanched garlic and the prepared, flaked saltcod with the mortar and pestle until smooth, then gradually work in the warmed milk and oil until the mixture is well emulsified and light.

The brandade may be flavored with a few drops of lemon juice. Season with white pepper (the use of white pepper avoids the black spots that would be visible with black pepper).

Some versions of brandade call for the addition of a small amount of potatoes that have been cooked in their skins. If using the potatoes, add them at the beginning with the saltcod and garlic, before adding the liquid. Salt is not called for in the recipe because the saltcod will provide its own salty flavor, however additional salt may be added if necessary.

The Poached Eggs

Bring the water and vinegar to a boil. White alcohol vinegar is recommended as it will not discolor the egg whites. The vinegar will coagulate the egg whites so that they will cling to the yolk and form more attractive poached eggs.

Break the eggs into a small bowl. Lower the heat so that the water is simmering, then slide the eggs into the water. It is recommended to poach only four eggs at a time. As soon as the white is set, carefully lift each egg out with a slotted spoon and stop the cooking by plunging it into ice water.

Drain the cooled eggs on a hand towel to dry completely.

The Sauce

Reduce the 4dl (1 2/3 cup) of fish stock by half. Add the cream and reduce again until it thickens a little. If necessary, whisk in a little cooked roux to obtain a sauce that is velvety and will coat a spoon.

Make a sabayon with 5 egg yolks and two spoonfuls of water. Whisk this mixture over medium heat until it is thick and foamy. Fold the sabayon into the creamy fish sauce. Season to taste with salt and pepper.

Variation

The sauce can be further enhanced with the addition of 30g (1oz) of finely chopped truffle.

Assembly

All the components for this croustade may be prepared ahead of time, but the assembly and heating should be done only just when it is ready to serve.

Place the pre-baked pastry crust on a heavy baking sheet.

Spread an even layer of the brandade in the bottom of the crust.

Place the eggs on top in a circle around the edge so that there is an egg for each slice of croustade.

Ladle the warm sauce evenly over the top of the ingredients.

Just before the croustade is to be served, warm it through in a medium oven.

Croustade with Poached Eggs Benedictine
Procedure Diagram

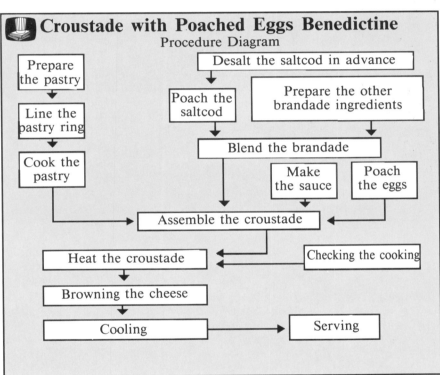

When the croustade is warm, place it under the broiler for a few moments to brown the sabayon sauce.

It is very important that the croustade does not become hot enough to cook the eggs which should remain soft with a slightly runny yolk.

Serve the croustade immediately. Cut the portions between each egg so that the yolk remains intact.

Cheese Croustade

Introduction

This is a very easy croustade to make and the food cost is not high.

The taste depends on choosing flavorful cheeses that have been aged correctly. The cheeses used in this recipe are Beaufort, Comté, and Cantal which could be replaced with other swiss type cheeses.

This makes an excellent light lunch when served with a refreshing green salad.

Equipment

Cutting board, chef's knife, mixing bowls, whisk, fine-meshed conical sieve, ladle, rolling pin, soft-bristled brush, pastry brush, round baking sheet, pastry ring, parchment paper, pie weights

Ingredients

For a croustade 28cm (11in) in diameter and 3.5cm (1 1/2in) high, yielding 8 portions.

Filling

350g (12oz) good quality cheeses

Custard

6dl (2 1/2 cups) heavy cream
5 eggs
Salt, pepper, nutmeg, paprika (optional)

Procedure

The Pastry Base

The preparation of the pastry crust is the same as the other croustades in this chapter.

The rolled out sheet of dough is pressed into pastry circles about 3.5cm (1 1/2in) high. It is important that the baking sheet be heavy to distribute heat evenly and avoid burning the pastry.

Once the pastry is pressed neatly into the bottom of the mold to ensure even baking and an attractive pastry crust, chill to rest the dough so that it does not shrink when it is baked.

Line the prepared mold with a circle of parchment paper and fill with weights (or dried beans or rice).

Bake for about 15 minutes at 200C (375F), remove the paper and the weights, then bake for another 5-10 minutes to brown.

When the pastry crust is lightly browned, brush the inside with egg glaze and return to the oven for a few more minutes, until the glaze is golden brown.

The cheese for several croustades can be cubed in advance and stored in plastic bags in the refrigerator to make the croustades to order.

The Custard

Whisk together the cream and the eggs and pass the mixture through a fine-meshed conical sieve to remove bits of eggshell and membrane from the egg.

Season the custard with salt, pepper, nutmeg and paprika.

The Cheese

Remove the crust from the cheeses. Cut them into large cubes about 1.5cm (1/2in) on each side.

45

Assembly

Place the pre-baked pastry crust on a heavy baking sheet.

Arrange the cubes of cheese on the crust as shown.

Ladle the custard over the cheese to just below the rim.

Cooking

Place the croustade in the oven, being careful not to spill the custard.

Cook at 200C (375F) for 20-30 minutes or until the custard is set. Remove the pastry ring and brush the sides with egg glaze and return to the oven for a few minutes to brown the sides.

Do not overcook; the pieces of cheese should be visible in the cooked croustade.

Storage

This croustade will keep for two days in the refrigerator covered with plastic wrap.

Serving

Reheat the croustade in a medium oven and serve warm.

Carefully slide the cooked croustade onto a cooling rack so that the bottom of the crust does not become soggy.

Storage

This croustade will keep for two days in the refrigerator covered with plastic wrap.

Serving

Reheat the croustade in a medium oven and serve warm.

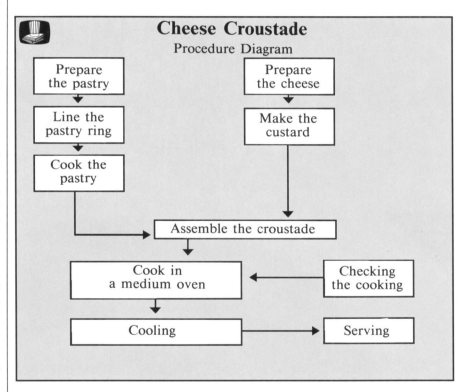

Cheese Croustade
Procedure Diagram

Prepare the pastry → Line the pastry ring → Cook the pastry → Assemble the croustade

Prepare the cheese → Make the custard → Assemble the croustade

Assemble the croustade → Cook in a medium oven ← Checking the cooking

Cook in a medium oven → Cooling → Serving

Chapter 2
Quenelles

A Gastronomic Tradition

Quenelles are part of the classic repertoire of French cooking. These delicate meat or seafood dumplings demand ingredients of the highest quality and attention to cook them properly.

An innovative touch in combining new flavors personalizes these quenelles and sets them apart from the ordinary.

The selection presented here spans the possibilities from the most simple to prepare and economical to the most luxurious.

General Advice for Making Quenelles

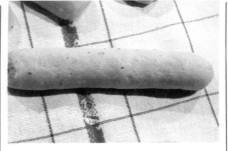

Introduction

Quenelles are elegant dumplings that can be made with meats and fish as well as semolina or potatoes.

The preparation of each quenelle is very similar so once you have mastered the basic procedure, the main ingredient can be altered to suit the occasion.

Each quenelle includes three elements:

- **Main ingredient**-the taste depends on a high proportion of the flavorful meat or fish etc. The price will reflect the cost of this ingredient.

- **Starchy base**-which is usually a " panade ".

- **Binding and enriching ingredients**-that include eggs, cream, butter or fat.

A flour-based " panade " is the classic starchy base for quenelles. The word is derived from " pain ", meaning bread in French, which was a medieval binder for meat purées.

To make delicious quenelles, the balance of ingredients is important. The right proportion of binding ingredients and meat or fish makes quenelles that are light and flavorful. Quenelles that are mass produced and pre-packaged are usually tasteless in comparison to these " homemade " quenelles.

Serving

Quenelles can be served in many ways. They are delicious with just melted butter and grated cheese and browned in the oven.

They are elegant when mixed with a delicate vegetable garnish and a sauce made to highlight the taste of the quenelles.

Quenelles can be combined with other meats to be included in the filling for " bouchées " or a " vol-au-vent ".

They can also be used to garnish an elaborate fish or meat dish.

The wide variety of shapes, flavors and presentation provides a quenelle for every budget and occasion.

Shaping and Poaching Quenelles

Quenelles can be made in different forms and sizes depending on the method of sale.

- With a pastry bag fitted with a large plain or notched tip.

- Scooped with one or two spoons to make the traditional oval shape.

They can be piped out onto a sheet of parchment paper and gently dropped into the poaching liquid or piped into a buttered hotel pan and covered with hot poaching liquid.

Quenelles are usually poached in lightly salted water. They can also be poached in veal, chicken or fish stock or milk, depending on the type of quenelle.

The poaching liquid should simmer gently (80-90C (175-195F)) and demands close attention to not let it boil, which would cause the quenelles to expand too quickly and break apart. The quenelles are done when they are firm and "springy" to the touch. Cooking time will vary depending on the size of the quenelle.

Remove the cooked quenelles from the poaching liquid with a slotted spoon and drain on a hand towel.

Sizeable quantities of quenelles can be made one or two days in advance and reheated in warm water or stock just before serving.

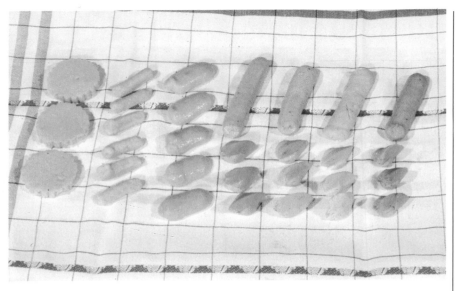

A Wide Variety of Quenelles

Quenelles are very versatile, adapting to a large variety of ingredients.

The selection presented here demonstrates some of the many combinations that can be used to make quenelles.

1) **Semolina Quenelles**

2) **Gnocchi " à la Romaine ", which are a variation on quenelles**

3) **Quenelles made with Choux Pastry**

4) **Potato Quenelles**

5) **Salmon Quenelles with Chive Cream**

6) **Pike Quenelles with Nantua Sauce**

7) **Turkey Quenelles with Suprême Sauce and a brunoise (tiny dice) of vegetables**

8) **Veal Quenelles with Perigueux Sauce**

Chive Cream Sauce

Equipment

Sauté pan, cutting board, knife, measuring cup, pastry scraper, whisk, fine-meshed conical sieve

Ingredients

20g (2/3oz) clarified butter
20g (2/3oz) shallots
30g (1oz) mushroom trimmings
10 chervil stems
8cl (1/3 cup) dry white wine
8cl (1/3 cup) dry vermouth
3dl (1 1/4 cup) fish stock
5dl (2 cups) heavy cream
Roux (optional)
45g (1 1/2oz) butter
Salt, pepper
10 sprigs chives, chopped

Procedure

Peel the shallots and cut them into fine dice. Chop the mushroom trimmings finely (trimmings are suggested simply to be economical- stems or whole mushrooms may be substituted). Chop finely the chervil stems.

Cut the chives in very small pieces starting from one end and set aside. Heat the clarified butter in a sauté pan. Add the shallots, mushrooms and chervil and cook until soft but not brown. Add the dry white wine and cook over gentle heat until reduced by half.

Add the vermouth and reduce by half again. Add the fish stock and cook over gentle heat until reduced by half. Be sure to skim off any impurities that accumulate during cooking.

Whisk in the cream and boil briefly to thicken the sauce. The sauce should be thick enough to coat the back of a spoon. If necessary, add a little of the cooked roux to achieve the right consistency. Pass the sauce through a fine- meshed conical sieve, pressing on the solids to extract all the flavorful liquid. Whisk in the butter and season to taste with salt and pepper. Add the chives only at the last moment, to keep their bright green color.

Suprême Sauce, with Brunoise of Vegetables

Equipment

Sauté pan, cutting board, knife, measuring cup, vegetable peeler, pastry scraper, whisk, fine-meshed conical sieve

Ingredients

8dl (3 1/3 cups) chicken stock
2.5dl (1 cup) heavy cream
Roux (optional)
30g (1oz) butter
Salt, pepper

Vegetable Brunoise
15g (1/2oz) clarified butter
100g (3 1/2oz) carrots
45g (1 1/2oz) onions
60g (2oz) leeks, white part only
Salt, pepper

Procedure

Gently simmer the chicken stock until reduced by half and very flavorful. Whisk in the cream and simmer a few minutes to thicken slightly. Be sure to skim off any impurities that accumulate during cooking. If necessary, thicken the sauce with a little cooked roux.

Pass the sauce through a fine-meshed conical sieve. Whisk in the butter. Season to taste with salt and pepper.

The Garnish

While the sauce is reducing, cut the brunoise.

Peel the carrots, onions and leeks. Wash the vegetables well, especially the leek which often is very sandy. Drain them well.

Cut the vegetables in tiny dice and combine them.

Cook the brunoise in clarified butter until soft but not brown. Season lightly with salt and pepper. Drain the vegetables well to remove any trace of butter, which would spoil the appearance of the sauce.

Nantua Sauce

Equipment

Sauté pan, cutting board, knife, measuring cup, pastry scraper, whisk, fine-meshed conical sieve

Ingredients

2dl (3/4 cup) "Américaine" sauce
4dl (1 2/3 cup) fish stock
Roux (optional)
1.5dl (2/3 cup) heavy cream
30g (1oz) crayfish butter
Salt, cayenne pepper
2cl (4 tsp) cognac
20 crayfish

Procedure

Gently simmer the "Américaine" sauce until reduced by half and very flavorful.

Add the fish stock and reduce by half again. Whisk in the cream and simmer a few minutes to reduce slightly. Be sure to skim off any impurities that accumulate during cooking. If necessary, thicken the sauce with a little cooked roux.

Pass the sauce through a fine-meshed conical sieve. Whisk in the crayfish butter. Season to taste with salt and cayenne pepper. To finish, add the cognac.

The Garnish

Add the crayfish tails and reserve the shells and claws to decorate the plate.

Perigueux Sauce

Equipment

Sauté pan, cutting board, knife, measuring cup, pastry scraper, whisk, fine-meshed conical sieve

Ingredients

4dl (1 2/3 cup) madeira
5dl (2 cups) reduced veal stock
15g (1/2oz) roux
5cl (1/4 cup) truffle juice
20g (2/3oz) butter
Salt, pepper
30g (1oz) truffles

Procedure

Gently simmer the madeira until reduced by half and very flavorful. Add the veal stock and reduce again by half. Be sure to skim off any impurities that accumulate during cooking.

Thicken the sauce with the roux, then add the truffle juice. Pass the sauce through a fine-meshed conical sieve and whisk in the butter. Season to taste with salt and pepper.

The Garnish

Garnish with chopped or julienned truffles.

Semolina Quenelles

Introduction

These quenelles are inspired by Italian gnocchi.

In this recipe, the semolina is not cooked in advance and therefore the assembled quenelles must poach for quite a long time--20-30 minutes, as opposed to the usual 5-10 minutes required for most quenelles.

Equipment

Mixing bowl, spatula, whisk, pastry scraper, pastry bag, plain tip, skimmer, plates, sauté pan, sheet pan, hotel pan

Ingredients

75g (2 1/2oz) butter
1 egg
60g (2oz) semolina (fine ground)
30g (1oz) flour
Salt, pepper, nutmeg

Procedure

Making the Quenelle Mixture

In a large bowl, cream the butter until smooth. Beat the egg, then

whisk it gradually into the creamed butter. Gradually add the semolina to the mixture, letting it pour in a fine stream to avoid lumps, then add the sifted flour.

Combine with a spatula and mix until the dough is firm and smooth.

Season with salt, pepper and nutmeg.

Shaping the Quenelles

The quenelles are piped out with a pastry bag fitted with a plain tip. They may be shaped large or small.

Pipe the quenelles onto a piece of lightly buttered parchment paper that has been cut to the same size as the poaching pan.

Poaching the Quenelles

Heat the poaching liquid (lightly salted water or stock) until just simmering.

Place the piece of parchment paper upside down in the pan, so the quenelles are in the liquid. Peel off the paper, leaving the quenelles in the pan; the steam and moisture will make the paper come off easily.

Cooking

These quenelles must be cooked

for a long time (20-30 minutes) because of the uncooked semolina. To test them, cut open and taste.

Remove the quenelles from the poaching liquid with a slotted

spoon and lay them on hand towels to drain.

Serving

Arrange the quenelles on heatproof plates. Baste them with melted butter and sprinkle with grated cheese. Just before serving, brown them in a hot oven.

Semolina Quenelles
Procedure Diagram

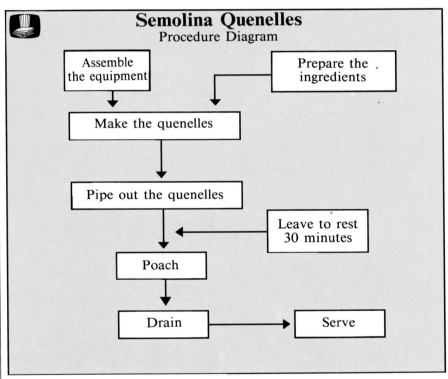

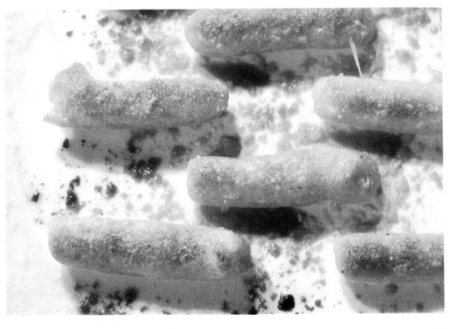

Gnocchi " à la Romaine "

Introduction

These Italian-style quenelles are not featured in French cuisine as often as the lighter, moister French quenelles " à la Parisienne ". They are, however, delicious in their own right.

Made with semolina cooked in milk and bound with egg yolks, the mixture is then cooled in a flat sheet and shaped with a pastry cutter. This method enables the caterer to make gnocchi in different sizes and shapes to suit the occasion.

In addition, this delicious quenelle is easy to make and the food cost is quite low, making it an excellent addition to the caterer's repertoire.

Equipment

Mixing bowls, ramequins, measuring cup, plates, saucepan, pastry scraper, sheet pan, palette knife, chef's knife, pastry cutter, spatula, whisk

Ingredients

8dl (3 1/3 cups) milk
250g (1/2lb) semolina (fine ground)
Salt, pepper
5 eggs yolks
To finish:
45g (1 1/2oz) butter
30g (1oz) grated parmesan

Procedure

The Quenelle Mixture

In a heavy pot, bring the milk to a boil. Incorporate the semolina in a fine steady stream, pouring from a sheet of parchment paper as shown, whisking constantly to avoid lumps.

Continue to stir as the mixture thickens. Remove from the heat and season to taste with salt and pepper.

Stir in the egg yolks one at a time. Stir the mixture until it is smooth and creamy.

Spread out the mixture on a sheet pan that is lightly buttered or covered with a piece of plastic

wrap. Smooth the surface with a wet palette knife.

To prevent the formation of a dry skin, coat the surface of the semolina with butter or cover with a piece of plastic wrap.

Refrigerate until firm and completely cool.

Shaping

Cut out the desired shapes using a pastry cutter, or cut out shapes with a knife.

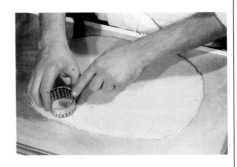

Lay the shapes carefully on a hand towel or on the platter or plate to be used for presentation.

Serving

Just before serving, pour a little melted butter on the gnocchi and sprinkle them with grated swiss or parmesan cheese. Heat the gnocchi in the oven or under the broiler until golden brown.

Gnocchi " à la Romaine "
Procedure Diagram

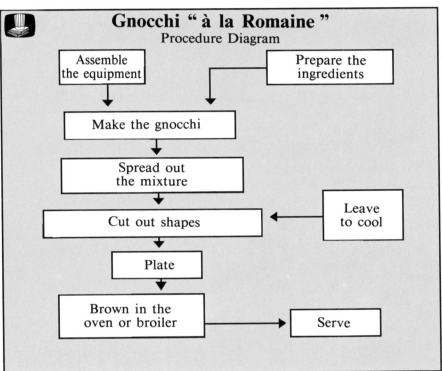

Assemble the equipment → Make the gnocchi

Prepare the ingredients → Make the gnocchi

Make the gnocchi → Spread out the mixture → Cut out shapes ← Leave to cool

Cut out shapes → Plate → Brown in the oven or broiler → Serve

Cream Puff Quenelles

Introduction

This is one of the simplest quenelles to make. Variations of cream puff pastry (" pâte à choux ") are often used as the " panade " or binding for meat or fish quenelles. Here, the cream puff dough is poached " plain " to make delicious quenelles that are traditionally served in a creamy bechamel sauce, " à la Parisienne ".

It is important to season these quenelles adequately with salt, pepper and nutmeg so they are not bland.

Equipment

Saucepan, measuring cup, spatula, mixing bowls, sifter, parchment paper, pastry scraper, pastry bag and plain tip, sauté pan, metal skewer, plates

Ingredients

1/4L (1 cup) milk
100g (3 1/2oz) butter
150g (5oz) flour
4 eggs
Salt, pepper, nutmeg

Procedure

The Cream Puff Dough

Bring the milk to a boil in a large heavy saucepan with the butter and seasonings. Remove the pan from the heat and add all the flour at once. Stir until the milk absorbs all

the flour and forms a ball. Return the mixture to the heat and dry it out a little, stirring constantly.

Transfer the mixture to a large bowl. Add the eggs one at a time, stirring until it is smooth before adding the next egg. Do not over mix.

Poaching the Quenelles

Bring the lightly salted water to a simmer. Depending on the size of the quenelles to be made, fit the pastry bag with a tip measuring between 7-10mm (1/4-3/8in).

Hold the bag over simmering water and cut off the pieces of the mixture as it is extruded through the tip, as shown. A metal skewer works well to cut of the mixture from the top and should be dipped into the hot water from time to time to keep it from sticking.

The quenelles can be made longer or shorter at this stage, but each " batch " should be the same size so they cook evenly.

Poach the quenelles for about 3-5 minutes depending on their size, stirring from time to time to cook them evenly.

When they are done, plunge them into ice water to stop the cooking. Drain thoroughly and set aside until ready to serve.

Storage

These quenelles will keep for one day in the refrigerator covered with plastic wrap.

They are so easy to prepare that it is recommended to make them fresh to order.

Potato Quenelles

Introduction

This quenelle is not well know, but is a delicious alternative to plain potatoes.

In fact, in taste and texture they are similar to " pommes duchesse " which is a purée of potatoes with the addition of butter and eggs. The potato quenelle, however, is slightly more sturdy due to the flour in the mixture.

As a result, they can be shaped more easily to make individual shapes with a piping bag or can be cut out like the " gnocchi à la romaine " and baked in the oven.

The quenelle will only be as good as the potato chosen to make them, so start with flavorful, waxy potatoes. Season them carefully, not forgetting the pinch of nutmeg that accents the flavor.

Equipment

Hotel pan, sheet pan, plates, ramequins, serving platter, mixing bowl, large saucepans with lid, colander, drum sieve, skimmer, pastry scraper, spatula, pastry brush, pastry bag and plain tip, ladle, pastry scraper, chef's knife, vegetable peeler

Ingredients

1kg (2lb) waxy potatoes
60g (2oz) butter
3 eggs
150g (5oz) flour
Salt, pepper, nutmeg
To finish:
75g (2 1/2oz) butter
100g (3 1/2oz) grated swiss cheese

Procedure

Preparing the Potatoes

Peel the potatoes and rinse them. Cut them into large dice so that they will cook quickly and evenly.

Put them in a pot with cold, lightly salted water to cover, bring it to a simmer and cook them until tender but not falling apart.

Drain the cooked potatoes in a colander. Spread them on a baking sheet and dry them out a little in a low oven.

Purée the hot pieces of potato by passing them through a drum sieve or food mill.

The potatoes should always be hot when they are puréed because they become very gluey if puréed when they are cold.

Scrape off the purée that adheres to the mesh of the sieve and put all the purée in a large saucepan.

Stir the butter into the warm purée, mixing until it is completely incorporated and smooth.

Dry the purée out a little on the stove, proceeding as with the cream puff dough, stirring constantly.

Transfer the purée to a large bowl. (The eggs will cook too quickly if they come in contact with the hot pot.) Beat in the eggs one at a time, stirring well between each one.

Sift the flour and add it in a slow steady stream with the help of a sheet of parchment paper as shown. Blend until smooth.

Season to taste with salt and pepper and a pinch of nutmeg, which enhances the flavor of the potatoes.

Shaping the Quenelles

Pipe the quenelle mixture onto buttered sheets of parchment paper to be transferred to a pot of simmering water, or pipe them into a buttered hotel pan and ladle boiling water over them.

These quenelles can be served in different ways:

• Brushed with melted butter, sprinkled with grated swiss cheese or parmesan and browned.

• Covered with a cream-based sauce, sprinkled with grated swiss cheese or parmesan.

• Served as an accompaniment to a meat dish.

Baking the quenelles in the oven melts the cheese and browns the surface, for a delicious taste and lovely presentation.

Cooking

Poach them in simmering water for 5-10 minutes, depending on their size. Do not let the water boil, which would cause the quenelles to

expand too quickly.

Remove the quenelles with a slotted spoon and place them on a hand towel to dry completely.

Serving

Arrange the quenelles on plates or platters.

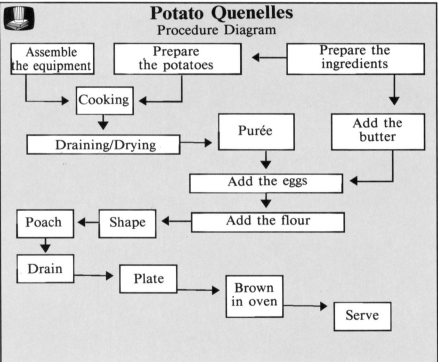

Potato Quenelles
Procedure Diagram

Assemble the equipment → Prepare the potatoes ← Prepare the ingredients

Cooking → Draining/Drying → Purée

Add the butter

Add the eggs

Add the flour → Shape → Poach → Drain → Plate → Brown in oven → Serve

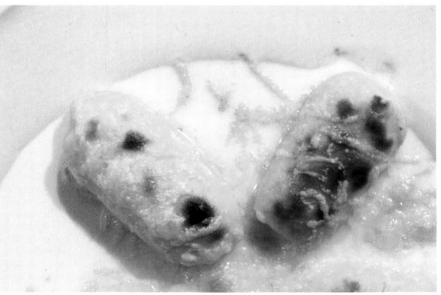

Salmon Quenelles with Chive Cream

Introduction

This is a very refined quenelle and is more expensive than the others in this chapter, due to the high price of salmon.

It is important to choose a fresh, top quality rosy salmon which will ensure that these quenelles are lovely as well as delicious.

A " panade " is used to bind the mixture, which is made of water, butter and flour. It is made just like cream puff dough but without the eggs which are added raw later in the preparation.

The salmon is puréed and blended with the panade, passed through a sieve, then bound with eggs and enriched with butter.

They can be shaped with a pastry bag, as shown, or with two spoons.

In this recipe, the salmon quenelles are served with a cream reduction accented with chives.

These quenelles can be cut in pieces and combined with other seafood and served with a creamy sauce.

Equipment

Cutting board, large saucepan, sauté pan, paring knife, thin-bladed flexible knife, pastry scraper, spatula, pastry brush, measuring cup, hotel pan, mixing bowl, 2 plates, small bowls, food processor, drum sieve, pastry bag and tip

Ingredients

300g (10oz) panade (made with 2dl (3/4 cup) water, 45g (1 1/2oz)

butter, salt, pepper, 100g (3 1/2oz) flour
500g (1lb) salmon filets
Salt, pepper, nutmeg
200g (7oz) butter
2 eggs
4 yolks

Procedure

The Salmon

Remove the filets and pull out any small bones that remain. Rinse off any scales. Keep the salmon chilled.

The Panade

This panade is essentially a cream puff dough without eggs.

Bring the water, butter, salt and pepper to a boil in a large saucepan.

Off the heat, add the flour all at once and stir until the mixture comes together in a ball.

Return to the heat to dry out the mixture slightly, stirring constantly. Transfer it to a stainless steel hotel pan, flatten it out so it cools quickly, and coat the surface

with butter to prevent formation of a dry skin.

Cut the filet of salmon in pieces, then purée in the food processor. Add the panade and blend until smooth.

Break the eggs in a bowl and add them in a steady stream to the salmon mixture.

Soften the butter and blend it into the salmon.

Pass the mixture through a fine-meshed drum sieve set over a hotel pan. Notice that the sieve and hotel pan are stainless steel, which avoids discoloring the purée. Use a plastic scraper as shown to push the salmon mixture through the sieve and also to remove the mixture that adheres to the sieve.

Transfer to a stainless steel bowl, stir until smooth.

Poach a spoonful of mixture, taste and adjust seasoning if necessary.

Shaping the Quenelles

• Pipe out the quenelles about the size and shape of an eclair, using a pastry bag and large plain tip onto a sheet of buttered parchment paper.

• Other forms can be piped out using a special notched pastry tip as shown.
• Two spoons can be used to achieve the classic ovals as well. Dip the spoons in cold water to keep the mixture from sticking.

Poaching the Quenelles

The quenelles can be poached in simmering salted water, fish stock or court bouillon. The poaching

liquid should be maintained at 85-90C (185-195F) and should not boil.

Remove the quenelles with a slotted spoon and drain them on a hand towel.

Serving

Reheat in warm stock or in the oven. Arrange on plates and serve with the chive cream.

Salmon Quenelles with Chive Cream
Procedure Diagram

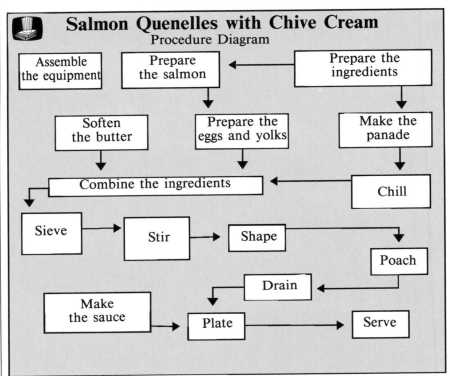

Assemble the equipment → Prepare the salmon ← Prepare the ingredients

Soften the butter → Prepare the eggs and yolks → Make the panade

Combine the ingredients ← Chill

Sieve → Stir → Shape → Poach

Make the sauce → Plate → Serve

Drain

Pike Quenelles with Nantua Sauce

Introduction

Pike is often used for quenelles because the flesh is very flavorful so it blends well with other ingredients.

Pike is also a very bony fish that is rarely served in filets. By puréeing and passing the flesh through a sieve, the small bones are eliminated.

This river fish marries naturally with the assertive taste of the crayfish-based Nantua sauce and the conbination has become a classic in French cooking.

This recipe differs from the salmon quenelles. A panade made with egg yolks is used and the mixture is bound with egg whites and enriched with a purée of the fat found around beef kidneys, also known as suet.

Equipment

Cutting board, large saucepan, sauté pan, paring knife, thin-bladed flexible knife, pastry scraper, spatula, pastry brush, measuring cup, hotel pan, mixing bowls, plates, small bowls, food processor, drum sieve, pastry bag and tip, meat grinder and fine disk

Ingredients

300g (10oz) panade (with 75g (2 1/2oz) flour, 3 egg yolks, 30g (1oz) melted butter, 1.7dl (approx. 2/3 cup) milk, salt, pepper, nutmeg)
300g (10oz) pike filet
250g (1/2lb) beef suet
3 egg whites
Salt, pepper, nutmeg

Procedure

The Pike

Bone and skin the pike and chill the filets until ready to use.

The Panade

Stir the egg yolks into the flour. Stir in the melted butter. Bring the

milk to a boil, and pour it into the egg, flour and butter mixture. Stir until smooth. Dry the mixture slightly by stirring over the heat, as for the cream puff pastry.

Transfer the panade to a stainless steel hotel pan, spread it out to cool quickly and coat the top with butter to prevent the surface from drying out. Chill until ready to use.

The Suet

To prepare fresh suet, peel away

the thin skin that envelops the fat. Trim the nerves and tendons. Cut the fat into pieces.

Pass the fat through a meat grinder fitted with a fine disk.

Making the Quenelle Mixture

Cut the filets of pike into pieces

and purée them in the food processor. Add the ground fat and blend. Add the egg whites in a steady stream and mix until smooth.

Finally, incorporate the cooled panade and blend until smooth. Season with salt and pepper.

Pass the mixture through a stainless steel drum sieve set over a

stainless steel hotel pan.

Transfer the sieved mixture to a bowl set over ice and stir until perfectly smooth.

Shaping the Quenelles

Pipe out the quenelle mixture in the desired shape and size on

sheets of lightly buttered parchment paper. The classic shapes are the " éclair " and three-sided ovals, or " little flames ".

Alternatively, shape the mixture with two spoons, dipped in cold water.

Poaching

Poach the quenelles in salted water, fish stock or court bouillon. Bring the poaching liquid to a simmer (85-90C (185-195F). Cook the quenelles a few at a time for 5-10 minutes, depending on the size. Do not let the liquid boil.

Remove the cooked quenelles with a slotted spoon and drain on a hand towel.

Serving

Warm the quenelles in hot water or stock, arrange them on plates with the Nantua sauce and a garnish of crayfish.

Pike Quenelles with Nantua Sauce
Procedure Diagram

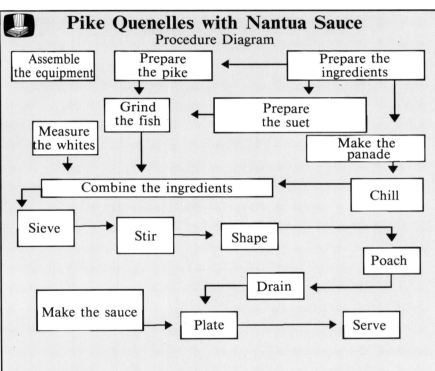

Turkey Quenelles Suprême Sauce

Introduction

Turkey or chicken breast can be used to make these delicate quenelles. Turkey is often less expensive and gives very good results.

The turkey breast is puréed in the food processor like the meat in the other quenelles in this chapter, bound with a panade and egg yolks, and enriched with cream.

The shaping and poaching is identical to the other quenelles in this chapter.

The suprême sauce, velouté enriched with cream, is further enhanced with a colorful garnish of brunoise (tiny dice) of vegetables.

Ingredients

150g (5oz) panade (made with 1dl (1/2 cup) water, 20g (2/3oz) butter, 45g (1 1/2oz) flour, salt, pepper, nutmeg)
400g (14oz) turkey filets
75g (2 1/2oz) butter
3 yolks
45g (1 1/2oz) heavy cream
Salt, pepper, nutmeg

Equipment

Cutting board, large saucepan, sauté pan, paring knife, thin-bladed flexible knife, pastry scraper, spatula, pastry brush, measuring cup, hotel pan, mixing bowls, plates, small bowls, food processor, drum sieve, pastry bag and tip, meat grinder with fine disk

Procedure

Preparing the Turkey

Trim the turkey breast of skin and tendons and cut it into pieces. Chill until ready to use.

Making the Panade

Proceed as for cream puff pastry dough. Bring the water and butter to a boil.

Off the heat, add the flour all at once and beat until smooth and the mixture forms a ball.

Season with salt, pepper and a pinch of nutmeg. Return to the heat and dry out the mixture a little, stirring constantly.

Transfer to a stainless steel hotel pan, spread the panade out so that it cools quickly and coat the surface with butter to prevent a dry skin from forming.

Chill until ready to use.

Making the Quenelle Mixture

Pass the pieces of turkey through a meat grinder fitted with a fine disk. Put the ground meat in the food processor. Add the chilled panade and blend until smooth.

Add the egg yolks and cream to the mixture and blend until smooth.

Pass the quenelle mixture through a stainless steel drum sieve, using a pastry scraper as shown. The sieve should be placed over a stainless steel pan.

Scrape the sieve to remove the mixture that adheres to it. Place all the mixture in a stainless steel bowl and stir over ice to make it smooth, light and homogeneous.

Shaping the Quenelles

Pipe out the quenelles as shown on a sheet of lightly buttered parchment paper. They can be different sizes and shapes.

Poaching the Quenelles

Poach the quenelles in salted water or chicken or veal stock. Bring the liquid to a simmer (85-90C (185-195F)) and poach for 5-10 minutes.

Remove the quenelles with a slotted spoon and drain on a hand towel.

Serving

Arrange the quenelles on plates, and serve with suprême sauce and a colorful brunoise of cooked vegetables.

Turkey Quenelles with Suprême Sauce
Procedure Diagram

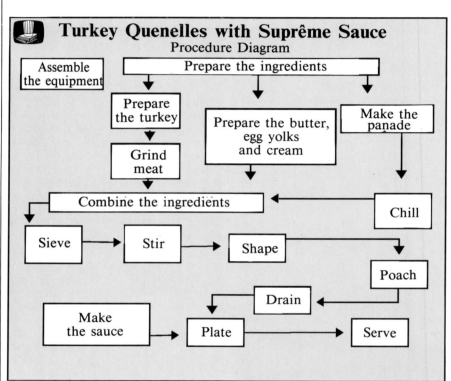

Assemble the equipment

Prepare the ingredients

Prepare the turkey → Grind meat

Prepare the butter, egg yolks and cream

Make the panade → Chill

Combine the ingredients

Sieve → Stir → Shape → Poach → Drain

Make the sauce → Plate → Serve

Veal Quenelles with Perigueux Sauce

Introduction

This quenelle is made with ground veal bound with the egg yolk panade enriched with suet outlined in the recipe for pike quenelles.

They are shaped and poached like the other quenelles in this chapter.

These delicate quenelles adapt well to many sauces. Here, they are served with a meaty Perigueux sauce, which is accented with the intense flavor of truffles from the Perigord region in southwest France.

Equipment

Cutting board, large saucepan, sauté pan, paring knife, thin-bladed flexible knife, pastry scraper, spatula, pastry brush, measuring cup, hotel pan, mixing bowls, plates, small bowls, food processor, drum sieve, pastry bag and top, meat grinder and fine disk

Ingredients

260g (1/2lb) panade (made with 60g (2oz) flour, 45g (1 1/2oz) egg yolks, 30g (1oz) butter, 130g (1/2 cup) milk, salt, pepper, nutmeg)
450 (1lb) sirloin tip of veal
150g (5oz) suet
Salt, pepper, nutmeg

Procedure

Preparing the Veal

Trim the veal of silverskin and tendons, cut into pieces. Chill until ready to use.

Preparing the Panade

Stir the egg yolks into the flour. Stir in the melted butter. Bring the milk to a boil and pour it into the mixture, blending until smooth.

Season with salt, pepper and nut-meg. Dry the mixture out a little over medium heat, stirring constantly. Transfer to a stainless steel hotel pan, coat with a little butter and chill.

Preparing the Fat

If using fresh suet, peel the thin

Put the ground veal and fat in the food processor along with the cooled panade. Blend until smooth.

Poach a spoonful of the mixture, taste and adjust seasoning if necessary.

Pass the mixture through a fine-meshed sieve using a plastic scraper as shown.

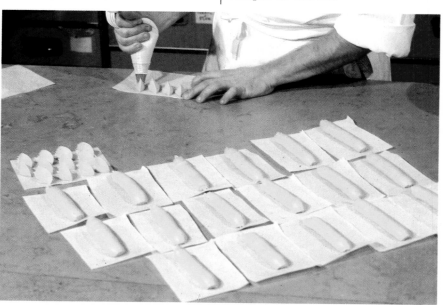

skin that envelops the fat. Trim the nerves and tendons. Cut the fat into pieces.

Making the Quenelle Mixture

Pass the veal and the fat separately through a meat grinder fitted with a fine disk.

Put the quenelle mixture into a bowl.

Set over ice and stir to make it smooth and light.

Shaping the Quenelles

Pipe out the quenelles on sheets of lightly buttered parchment paper. They can vary in size and shape to suit the occasion.

Poaching the Quenelles

Poach the quenelles in salted water or veal stock. Bring the liquid to a simmer (85-90C (185-195F)) and poach about 5-10 minutes.

Remove the quenelles with a slotted spoon and drain on a hand towel.

Serving

Arrange the quenelles on a plate and serve with the Perigueux sauce.

These quenelles are also an ingredient in classic " vol au vent " dishes--elegant combinations of different meats in a rich sauce served in a puff pastry shell.

Veal Quenelles with Perigueux Sauce
Procedure Diagram

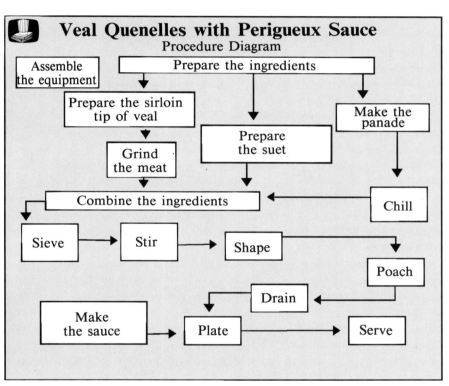

Assemble the equipment

Prepare the ingredients

Prepare the sirloin tip of veal

Prepare the suet

Make the panade

Grind the meat

Combine the ingredients

Chill

Sieve → Stir → Shape

Poach

Make the sauce

Drain

Plate

Poach

Serve

Chapter 3
Soufflés

Light and Delicate First Courses

Soufflés are delicate dishes made airy and light with beaten egg whites.

They are a popular dessert, made with fruits or chocolate, and are delicious when made with savory ingredients.

In this chapter, we present five savory soufflés ideal to serve as a first course. This selection only scratches the surface of the possibilities; soufflés can be made with shellfish and fish, meat and poultry and vegetables of all kinds.

They are not difficult to prepare, but must be served directly from the oven while they are hot and puffed.

Therefore many chefs nowadays shy away from this fragile dish.

Soufflés are more popular than ever and are a valuable part of the caterer's repertoire.

General Advice for Making Soufflés

" Mise en Place "

Even though soufflés cannot be made in advance, the separate ingredients can be prepared in sizeable quantities so that soufflés can be made to order.

The molds are generously buttered before the mixture is added so that the soufflés can " slide up " the sides easily for maximum height and lightness.

Cooking the Soufflés

To puff the soufflés and cook them through without drying them out, they are cooked in two stages.

They are first placed on a heavy baking sheet then put into an oven preheated to 215C (420F). This high heat immediately expands the air that is trapped in the tiny bubbles formed by beating the egg whites.

The heat is then lowered to 190C (about 370F) and the soufflés continue to cook until firm but still soft and creamy in the middle.

Small soufflés (6-8cm (2 1/2-3 1/2in) in diameter) will require about 25 minutes, larger ones (12-16cm (5-6 1/2in) should cook for about 35-40 minutes.

Serving

Once cooked, the soufflés must be served immediately.

They are most often served in a restaurant or at a catered event where the chef is present and can oversee the process personally.

The egg whites are beaten and folded in at the last minute.

Two flavors can be combined in one soufflé if the texture of the two mixtures is similar.

The cooking must be timed precisely to insure that the soufflés are served directly from the oven.

The Molds

The best molds to use are made of earthenware or porcelain, which conduct heat evenly.

The Selection of Soufflés in this chapter

A vast assortment of ingredients can be used to make soufflés.

1 - Salmon Soufflé

2 - Soufflé with Chicken Livers

3 - Spinach Soufflé

4 - " Harlequin " Soufflé

5 - Cheese Soufflé

Salmon Soufflé

Introduction

Salmon is one of the most popular seafood soufflés, due to its flavorful "meaty" flesh. The rosy color makes this soufflé attractive as well.

It is important to choose fresh, top quality salmon. Since salmon is often very expensive, it is best to offer this soufflé when salmon is most plentiful and therefore less expensive.

Equipment

1 large soufflé mold (4 servings) and 5 individual molds, cutting board, mixing bowls, small bowls, plates, paring knife, thin-bladed flexible knife, fork, spoon, pastry brush, pastry scraper, frying pan, saucepan, large saucepan, whisk, spatula, measuring cup, food processor, drum sieve, copper bowl for egg whites and balloon whisk, round or rectangular baking sheets

Ingredients

250g (8oz) salmon filets
30g (1oz) clarified butter

Basic Sauce
30g (1oz) butter + 30g (1oz) flour (roux)
1dl (1/2 cup) fish stock
5cl (1/4 cup) reduced " Américaine " sauce
3 egg yolks
4 egg whites
Salt, pepper

Procedure

The Salmon

If using a whole fresh salmon, begin by rinsing the fish and scrap-

ing off the scales. Trim the fins, clean it and rinse out the inside of the salmon. Remove the two filets and skin them.

If using frozen salmon, defrost it slowly in the refrigerator.

Cut the salmon into large pieces and sear them in clarified butter.

Purée the seared pieces of salmon in the food processor. This step can be done in advance.

Set the purée aside on a plate.

The Sauce Base

Most savory soufflés are based on a thickened sauce that holds the

beaten egg whites in suspension. For this recipe a flavorful fish velouté is used.

Heat the butter and add the flour to make a roux. Cook this mixture a little without letting it get brown. Pour in the fish stock, whisking constantly. Whisk in the reduced " Américaine " sauce which adds a distinctive seafood flavor. Simmer the thick sauce over medium heat for about five minutes.

Separate the eggs. Incorporate the yolks into the warm velouté and stir until smooth. Mix the puréed salmon into the sauce and stir until smooth.

Beat the egg whites until stiff peaks are formed. Fold the beaten egg whites into the salmon mixture, taking care to not deflate the egg whites too much.

Filling the Molds

Use a plastic scraper to transfer the light soufflé mixture into the molds. Fill them to within 1cm (3/8in) of the rim.

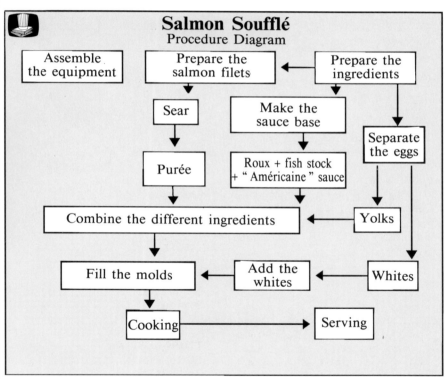

Salmon Soufflé
Procedure Diagram

Assemble the equipment → Prepare the salmon filets ← Prepare the ingredients

Prepare the salmon filets → Sear → Purée → Combine the different ingredients

Prepare the ingredients → Make the sauce base → Roux + fish stock + " Américaine " sauce → Combine the different ingredients

Prepare the ingredients → Separate the eggs → Yolks → Combine the different ingredients

Separate the eggs → Whites → Add the whites → Fill the molds

Combine the different ingredients → Fill the molds → Cooking → Serving

Cooking and Serving

Place the soufflés in a hot oven preheated to 215C (420F). When the soufflés are puffed, lower to 190C (about 370F) and finish cooking.

Place the soufflés on a plate or platter and serve immediately, directly from the molds.

Soufflé with Chicken Livers

Introduction

This is a very delicious way to serve chicken livers. Livers from ducks or other poultry as well as calf liver can be substituted.

The food cost is not high, which enables the caterer to offer a wonderful dish at a reasonable price.

In French cuisine, the livers are often served alongside the meat. The soufflé, made in small individual molds would make a light and tasty accompaniment to a hearty chicken dish.

Equipment

1 large soufflé mold (4 servings) and 5 individual molds, cutting board, mixing bowls, small bowls, plates, paring knife, thin-bladed flexible knife, fork, spoon, pastry brush, pastry scraper, frying pan, skimmer, saucepan, large saucepan, whisk, spatula, measuring cup, food processor, drum sieve, copper bowl for egg whites and balloon whisk, round or rectangular baking sheets

Ingredients

250g (8oz) chicken livers
30g (1oz) clarified butter
1cl (2tsp) oil
Salt, pepper

Béchamel Sauce

45g (1 1/2oz) butter + 45g (1 1/2oz) flour
1/4L (1 cup) milk
Salt, pepper, nutmeg
2 eggs, separated

Procedure

The Chicken Livers

Degorge the livers in a basin of cold water to draw out blood and impurities. Dry them thoroughly on a hand towel.

Trim each liver of any ducts or tendons and any portion that is stained green or yellow from the bile sack.

Sear the livers in a blend of oil and clarified butter. Brown them on all sides in the hot fat without cooking them too much.

Season with salt and pepper and drain on a paper towel.

Purée the livers in the food processor until very smooth. Pass the purée through a fine-meshed sieve if necessary.

The Sauce Base

This soufflé uses a classic béchamel. Melt the butter, whisk in the flour and cook the roux a little without browning.

Pour in the milk, whisking constantly and simmer the thick sauce for a few minutes. Season with salt,

pepper and nutmeg.

Separate the eggs and incorporate the yolks into the warm sauce and stir until smooth.

Incorporate the purée of chicken livers and stir until smooth.

Beat the egg whites until stiff peaks are formed and gently fold them into the chicken liver mixture.

Filling the Molds

Use a plastic scraper to transfer the light soufflé mixture into the

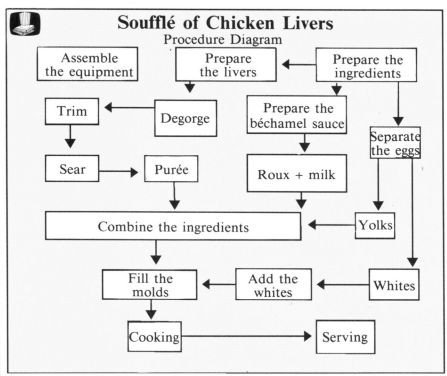

Soufflé of Chicken Livers
Procedure Diagram

```
Assemble            Prepare            Prepare the
the equipment       the livers    ←    ingredients

                         ↓                    ↓
       Trim  ←  Degorge        Prepare the      Separate
                              béchamel sauce     the eggs
        ↓                          ↓                ↓
       Sear  →  Purée          Roux + milk
                    ↓               ↓             Yolks
         Combine the ingredients        ←          ↑
                    ↓
        Fill the    ←   Add the    ←   Whites
         molds          whites
            ↓
         Cooking   →   Serving
```

molds. Fill them to within 1cm (3/8in) of the rim.

Cooking

Place the soufflés in a hot oven preheated to 215C (420F). When the soufflés have puffed, lower the heat to 190C (about 370F) and finish cooking.

Serving

Place the soufflés on a plate or platter and serve immediately, directly from the molds.

Spinach Soufflé

Introduction

In French cuisine, dishes that feature spinach are often called "Florentine" because spinach was brought to France from Italy.

This colorful soufflé is enhanced with parmesan which adds a zesty flavor as well as extra moistness to this delicious soufflé.

Nutmeg is an indispensable seasoning which accents the combination of creamy sauce and spinach.

Equipment

1 large soufflé mold (4 servings) and 5 individual molds, cutting board, mixing bowls, small bowls, plates, paring knife, chef's knife, fork, spoon, pastry brush, skimmer, spatula, whisk, saucepan, large saucepan, copper bowl for egg whites and balloon whisk, heavy casserole with lid, colander, pastry scraper, hand towels

Ingredients

500g (1lb) spinach (250g (1/2lb) after cooking and draining)
30g (1oz) clarified butter
Salt, pepper, nutmeg

Bechamel Sauce

20g (2/3oz) butter + 20g (2/3 oz) flour
125g (1/2 cup) milk
Salt, pepper, nutmeg
45g (1 1/2oz) grated parmesan
2 eggs, separated

Procedure

The Spinach

Pull the stems from the leaves of spinach and wash the leaves in a large basin of cold water, changing the water several times to remove all sand and dirt. Drain the clean leaves in a colander.

Put a little clarified butter in a large pot, add the spinach, cover the pot and cook over high heat for

a few minutes, stirring occasionally to prevent the spinach from sticking to the bottom.

The spinach will render quite a lot of liquid. Drain the spinach, then squeeze it dry in a hand towel.

Chop the dried spinach with a chef's knife and set aside in a bowl.

The Sauce Base

A classic béchamel is used in this soufflé. Melt the butter, stir in the flour and cook the roux for a few minutes without browning.

Pour in the milk, stirring constantly and simmer the thick sauce for a few minutes.

Add the spinach and stir until smooth. Season the sauce with salt, pepper and nutmeg.

Beat the egg whites until firm peaks are formed, then gently fold the beaten egg whites into the spinach mixture without deflating them too much.

Filling the Molds

Use a plastic scraper to transfer the delicate soufflé mixture to the molds. Fill them to within 1cm (3/8in) of the rim.

Cooking

Place the soufflés in a hot oven preheated to 215C (420F). When the soufflés are puffed, lower the heat to 190C (about 370F) and finish cooking.

Serving

Place the soufflés on a plate or platter and serve immediately, directly from the molds.

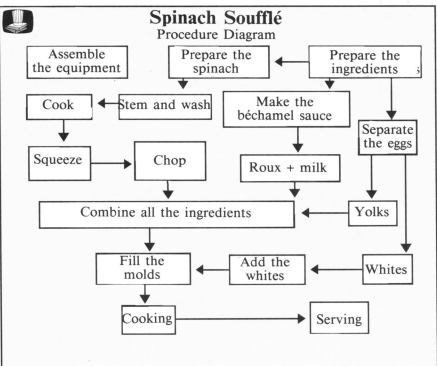

Spinach Soufflé
Procedure Diagram

Assemble the equipment → Prepare the spinach ← Prepare the ingredients

Cook ← Stem and wash | Make the béchamel sauce | Separate the eggs

Squeeze → Chop | Roux + milk

Combine all the ingredients ← Yolks

Fill the molds ← Add the whites ← Whites

Cooking → Serving

"Harlequin" Soufflé

Introduction

This dish combines two flavorful vegetables in one soufflé to make an attractive "harlequin" design.

Carrot and celeriac marry well to give this inexpensive soufflé special appeal.

It is inexpensive to make and is a versatile first course or accompaniment for any menu.

Equipment

1 large soufflé mold (4 servings) and 5 individual molds, cutting board, mixing bowls, small bowls, plates, large saucepans, colanders, sauté pans, casserole, skimmer, paring knife, chef's knife, pastry brush, pastry scraper, spatula, spoon, fork, drum sieve, cardboard, copper bowl for egg whites and balloon whisk, food processor (optional), round or rectangular baking sheets

Ingredients

Carrot purée - Celeriac purée 500g (1lb) raw carrots (250g (1/2lb) when trimmed and cooked) 500g (1lb) raw celeriac (250g (1/2lb) when trimmed and cooked)

Béchamel Sauce

(Prepare once, for both purées)
30g (1oz) butter
+ 45g (1 1/2oz) flour
2dl (3/4 cup) milk
Salt, pepper, nutmeg
2 eggs, separated

Procedure

The Carrots

Peel the carrots and rinse them. Cut them into slices and cook them until vey tender in lightly salted water.

Drain the slices thoroughly in a colander then spread them on a baking sheet and dry them a little in a low oven.

Pass the cooked carrots through a fine-meshed sieve using a plastic scraper as shown. Scrape the car-

rots that adhere to the underside of the sieve and set aside.

The Celeriac

Cut the tough peel off the celeriac with a sharp, stiff-bladed stainless steel knife and rub it with lemon to keep it from darkening. Cut the peeled celeriac into cubes and cook in lightly salted water until very tender. Dry the pieces and purée them like the carrots.

The Sauce Base

A classic béchamel is the base for this soufflé. Melt the butter, stir in the flour and cook the roux for a few minutes without browning.

Pour in the milk, stirring constantly, then cook the thick sauce

for a few minutes. Season with salt, pepper and nutmeg.

Separate the eggs and incorporate the yolks into the warm sauce; stir until smooth. Divide the sauce into two parts and add the carrot purée to one and the celeriac purée to the other.

Beat the egg whites until stiff peaks are formed, then gently fold half of them into the carrot mixture and the rest into the celeriac mixture.

Filling the Molds

Small individual molds are filled with carrot soufflé on one side and celeriac on the other.

To fill the large molds with alternating portions of the two soufflés,

make a form from stiff cardboard that will divide the mold in four parts. Spoon in alternating portions of purée, then lift the cardboard straight up to remove it.

Cooking

Place the soufflés in a hot oven

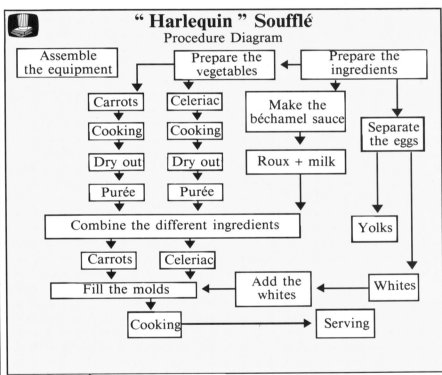

" Harlequin " Soufflé
Procedure Diagram

Assemble the equipment → Prepare the vegetables ← Prepare the ingredients

- Carrots → Cooking → Dry out → Purée
- Celeriac → Cooking → Dry out → Purée
- Make the béchamel sauce → Roux + milk
- Separate the eggs → Yolks / Whites

Combine the different ingredients

Carrots / Celeriac

Fill the molds ← Add the whites ← Whites

Cooking → Serving

preheated to 215C (420F). When the soufflés are puffed, lower the temperature to 190C (about 370F) and finish cooking.

Serving

Place the soufflés on a plate or platter and serve immediately, directly from the molds.

Cheese Soufflé

Introduction

This is the most popular of the savory soufflés. Different cheeses can be used with the recipe outlined here.

If you have never made a soufflé before, this easy recipe is a good one to acquaint yourself with the basic techniques used to make soufflés.

It is important to use a lot of cheese to make a soufflé that is flavorful and not too fragile.

Once again a béchamel is used, seasoned with a hint of nutmeg which accents the taste of the cheese.

This is an inexpensive soufflé to make which is sure to please.

Equipment

1 large soufflé mold (4 servings) and 5 individual molds, cutting board, cheese grater, mixing bowls, small bowls, plates, chef's knife, spatula, whisk, pastry brush, pastry scraper, large saucepan, measuring cup, copper bowl for egg whites and balloon whisk, round or rectangular baking sheet

Ingredients

Béchamel Sauce

45g (1 1/2oz) butter
60g (2oz) flour
3dl (1 1/4 cup) milk
Salt, pepper, nutmeg
90g (3oz) grated swiss cheese
4 eggs, separated

Procedure

The Cheese

Choose a swiss type cheese that has a lot of flavor. The best ones include Gruyère, Comté, and Emmenthaler.

Cut the waxy coating from the cheese and grate it.

The Sauce Base

Classic béchamel is used as the base for this soufflé. Melt butter and stir in flour and cook the roux for a few minutes.

Pour in the milk, stirring constantly and cook the thick sauce for a few minutes.

Season with salt, pepper and a pinch of nutmeg.

Separate the eggs and incorporate the yolks into the warm sauce and stir until smooth. Stir the grated cheese into the sauce.

Beat the egg whites until firm peaks are formed. Gently fold the

beaten egg whites into the sauce without deflating the egg whites too much.

Filling the Molds

Use a plastic scraper to transfer the delicate soufflé mixture into the molds. Fill to within 1cm (3/8in) of the rim.

Cooking

Place the soufflés in a hot oven preheated to 215C (420F). When the soufflés are puffed, lower the temperature to 190C (about 370F) and finish cooking.

Serving

Place the soufflés on a plate or platter with a doily and serve immediately.

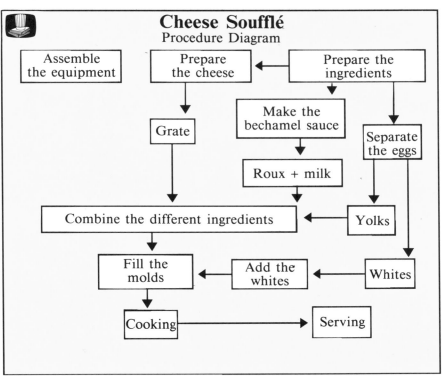

Cheese Soufflé
Procedure Diagram

Assemble the equipment

Prepare the cheese

Prepare the ingredients

Grate

Make the bechamel sauce

Separate the eggs

Roux + milk

Combine the different ingredients

Yolks

Fill the molds

Add the whites

Whites

Cooking → Serving

Chapter 4
Beignets

Delicious and Crispy Hors d'Œuvres

"Beignets" get their name from the "bath" ("bain" in French) of hot oil that these tasty fritters are deep fried in.

They are first dipped in a batter, deep fried and served hot. This chapter also includes beignets that are breaded and pan-fried.

Sweet beignets made with fruits or jam are more common than savory ones. These crispy bite-size hors d'œuvres are a welcome alternative to the usual appetizer.

The possibilities are endless as many ingredients are suitable for making beignets. The choice includes beignets made with:

- *Beef, lamb, veal, pork, poultry*
- *Fish and shellfish*
- *Vegetables*

General Advice for Making Beignets

Introduction

There are two basic ways to prepare beignets:
- Beignets dipped in batter
- Beignets that are breaded

Both methods are explained in this chapter. Among the 13 varieties, 9 of the beignets are dipped in batter and 4 are breaded.

The food cost will depend on the price of the main ingredient so the caterer can choose a variety that offers different tastes, textures and price.

The selection presented here provides a wide variety to show the range of possibilities.

The ingredients should always be cut into bite-size pieces and precooked if necessary so that they are easy to eat as " fingerfood ".

A sauce can be served alongside for dipping.

These are usually served at functions where the chef is present to oversee their preparation personally.

The Deep-Frying Batter

Many recipes exist for deep-frying batter but they are all based on similar ingredients.

The major ingredient is flour which is blended with eggs and a liquid. Depending on the recipe you will use whole eggs, egg yolks or beaten egg whites in varying combinations to create different textures. If beaten egg whites are used, add them just before frying the beignets as the batter will deflate quickly.

The liquid as well varies to give different results. Water, milk or beer are the most common choices.

A little oil is sometimes added to tenderize the batter by relaxing the gluten a little. Salt has a similar effect and flavors the batter as well.

Allowing the batter to rest before frying the beignets allows the gluten in the flour to rest which results in beignets that are more tender and crispy.

Recipe for Deep-frying Batter

500g (1lb) flour
10g (2tsp) salt
4 eggs
1/2L (2 cups) beer
1dl (1/2 cup) oil
5 beaten egg whites

Breading " à l'Anglaise "

This method of breading food that is to be fried keeps the ingredients moist but not greasy and creates a crust that is crisp and delicious.

The eggs are beaten and passed through a fine-meshed conical sieve then seasoned with salt and pepper. A little oil is added for flavor and lightness.

The prepared ingredients are then coated with the beaten egg and drained briefly to remove excess egg. They are then rolled in dried breadcrumbs. Excess breadcrumbs are removed by tapping each beignet gently.

The beaten egg will keep for about one day in the refrigerator. The breadcrumbs can be kept in a closed container and passed through a sieve after each use and dried if necessary.

Recipe for Breading

6 eggs
Salt, pepper
5cl (1/4 cup) oil
400g (14oz) dry breadcrumbs for coating

Cooking

Two methods of cooking are used depending on the type of beignet.

Beignets dipped in batter

Deep fry these beignets in a large pan of oil so that they will " swim " in the oil and can be turned easily.

Use a top quality oil that is neutral in taste and can withstand high temperatures. Peanut oil is a good choice.

Preheat the oil to 160C (325F) and maintain a constant temperature throughout cooking. Heating the oil above 160C ruins the taste and will give a disagreable flavor to the beignets.

The oil used to fry savory preparations should be kept separate from oil used to make sweet items.

When you are ready to cook the beignets, assemble the prepared ingredients, the deep-frying batter then heat the oil.

Dip each item to be fried in the batter using a fork or your fingers for those foods that have a stem. Coat completely with batter and place in the hot oil. Cook only a few at a time so that you can regulate the cooking and turn them easily.

The finished beignets should be golden brown on all sides. To achieve this, turn each one with a fork or slotted spoon as it cooks to brown on all sides. The cooking time will vary according to the size and characteristics of the ingredients.

Remove the cooked beignets from the oil with a fork or slotted spoon and drain them on a cooling rack covered with paper towel. Drain them well to remove excess oil which would make them greasy and unappetizing.

Breaded Beignets

The breaded beignets are pan-fried rather than deep fried.

Use a deep heavy skillet and add oil to fill about one third. A light tasting oil such as peanut oil would also be appropriate for these beignets. Heat the oil to 135C (275F). The temperature is lower than for the deep fried beignets so that they do not brown too quickly.

Assemble the prepared ingredients and the beaten egg and the dried breadcrumbs. Heat the oil, bread each item then place it in the oil. Half way through the cooking, turn the beignet over to brown the other side. Do not cook too many at a time so that you can regulate the cooking and turn them easily.

Remove the cooked beignets with a fork or slotted spoon and drain them on a cooling rack covered with paper towel to remove excess oil.

These beignets are best if served immediately, however to serve large quantities they can be made in advance and gently reheated in a low oven.

Choice of Ingredients

The possibilities are endless as many foods are delicious when made into beignets. In all cases, choose ingredients that are fresh and flavorful.

The Selection of Beignets in this chapter

Nº	Name	Category	Cost	Advance preparation	Coating	Cooking	Serving
1	Peppers stuffed with cheese	Vegetables/cheese	Average	Stuff with herbs and fresh cheese	Frying batter	Deep fat 150C (300F) 8 min	Lemon
2	Zucchini	Vegetables	Inexpensive	Cut into slices	Frying batter	Deep fat 160C (325F) 7 min	Lemon
3	Eggplant	Vegetables	Inexpensive	Peel and cut into slices	Frying batter	Deep fat 160C (325F) 7 min	Lemon
4	Baby corn	Vegetables	Inexpensive	Drain, cut in half	Frying batter	Deep fat 150C (300F) 8 min	Lemon
5	Chicken	Meat	Average	Cut into strips	Frying batter	Deep fat 150C (300F) 9 min	Sauce
6	Brains	Variety meat	Average	Cut and peel	Frying batter	Deep fat 150C (300F) 9 min	Sauce
7	Crayfish	Shellfish	Costly	Shell and rinse	Frying batter	Deep fat 150C (300F) 7 min	Lemon sauce
8	Squid	Fish	Average	Shell, rinse and cut	Frying batter	Deep fat 150C (300F) 8 min	Lemon sauce
9	Mussels	Shellfish	Average	Scrub and wash	Frying batter	Deep fat 150C (300F) 6 min	Lemon
10	Ground meat	Meat	Inexpensive	Season, shape	Breading	Shallow fat 130C (265F) 5 min	Lemon
11	Oysters	Shellfish	Costly	Open, empty and drain	Breading	Shallow fat 135C (275F) 3 min	Lemon
12	Red mullet	Fish	Costly	Dress and filet	Breading	Shallow fat 135C (275F) 3 min	Lemon
13	Salmon/green beans	Fish	Costly	Cut, fill and roll	Breading	Shallow fat 130C (265F) 5 min	Lemon

1. Pepper Beignets Stuffed with Cheese

Pipe some cheese into each pepper with a pastry bag and small tip. Chill the peppers to set the cheese before frying.

Holding the stem, dip each pepper into the deep-frying batter, then into the preheated oil. Cook until golden brown on all sides. Drain and serve immediately.

Choose small mild peppers (do not confuse them with hot peppers). Slit each pepper, leaving the stem intact, remove the seeds and rinse them. Dry them inside and out with paper towel.

Season " fromage frais " (or cottage cheese passed through a sieve) with salt, pepper and chopped chives.

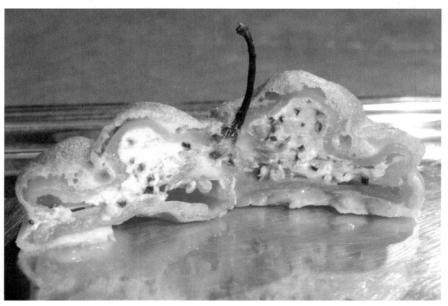

2. Zucchini Beignets

Turn the beignets over as they cook to brown them evenly on all sides. These beignets will cook very quickly.

Remove them from the oil with a fork or slotted spoon and drain on paper towels.

Choose medium-sized zucchini that are firm and bright green.

Rinse and dry them. Do not peel the zucchini. Cut them in slices about 1cm (3/8in) thick. The zucchini needs no further preparation.

Dip each slice into deep-frying batter with a fork, then put them, a few at a time, into the hot oil.

3. Eggplant Beignets

Degorge the slices for about 10 minutes on one side, wipe off moisture and excess salt with a paper towel, turn the slices over and repeat the process.

Dry the slices well before dipping each one in the deep-frying batter. Cook and drain as previously explained.

Choose small, firm eggplant. They should feel heavy for their size which indicates a less " seedy " interior.

Rinse and peel them. Cut into slices about 1cm (3/8in) thick and place them on a hand towel. Sprinkle the slices with salt which draws moisture out of the eggplant which tends to taste bitter otherwise. Some of the salt is absorbed, flavoring the eggplant.

4. Miniature Corn Beignets

Dip each piece in the deep-frying batter with a fork and cook in the hot oil until they are golden brown on all sides.

Since the corn is already thoroughly cooked, it is only necessary to cook the batter.

These attractive miniature ears of corn are available ready to eat in jars.

Drain the corn on a hand towel to dry them completely.

If they are large, cut them in half so that all the pieces are about 4cm (1 3/4in) long.

5. Chicken Beignets

Dip each piece of chicken into the deep-frying batter with a fork and cook in the hot oil until the beignets are golden brown on all sides.

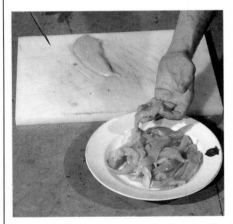

These beignets should be made with pieces cut from the tender breast of chicken. If a whole chicken is being used, reserve the legs for another recipe. The breast of other poultry (duck or turkey) can be substituted.

Trim the breast of skin and sinews and cut into strips about 4-5cm (about 2in) long and about 1cm (3/8in) wide.

6. Beignets Made with Brains

Trim the brains with a sharp paring knife to remove the membranes that are attached as well as any bits of blood that remain.

Dry them thoroughly on a hand towel, then cut them into small pieces.

Dip the pieces in the deep-frying batter with a fork and cook the beignets in the hot oil.

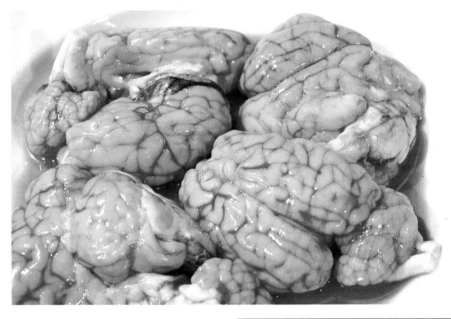

Veal or lamb brains may be used and they must be perfectly fresh.

Degorge the brains under cold running water to remove blood and impurities.

7. Gambas Beignets

Twist the head to remove it. Pull the shell off the tail without damaging the meat.

Leave the tail fins attached which will make the beignets more attractive and serve as a " handle " for dipping into the batter as well as for eating.

Slit along the back of the tail and pull off the dark vein. Rinse them to remove any portion of this vein that remains.

Dry the gambas thoroughly on a hand towel.

Dip each one in the deep-frying batter and cook in the hot oil until brown on all sides.

Gambas are large meaty shrimp which are often an ingredient in Spanish paella. Other large shrimp or salt water crayfish can be substituted.

8. Squid Beignets

Choose small tender squid. They are usually sold with the tentacles and the clear central cartilage.

Pull out the head and tentacles which come out of the body in one piece. Pull the central cartilage out of the body and discard. Remove the flaps on either side and pull off the black skin.

Rinse each squid under cold running water.

Cut the cleaned squid into slices crosswise, which will produce small rings of meat and dry thoroughly on a hand towel.

Dip each piece of squid in the deep-frying batter with a fork and cook the beignets in the hot oil until golden brown.

9. Mussel Beignets

Using a stiff thin-bladed knife, open the shells and carefully remove the mussel. Reserve the best looking shells for the presentation.

Pull off the dark rim or " beard " of each mussel and thoroughly dry them on a hand towel.

Dip each mussel in the deep-frying batter with a fork and cook in the hot oil until golden brown.

The mussel beignets can be served arranged in their shells.

Choose fresh large mussels.

Scrape the shells to remove seaweed and barnacles, then wash the mussels in a large basin of cold water, changing the water several times until there is no sand left.

10. Ground Meat Beignets

Ingredients

500g (1lb) pork, 500g (1lb) beef, 1 egg, 2 shallots, 1 clove garlic, parsley, salt, pepper

Pass the meats through the medium disk of the meat grinder. Peel and chop the shallots and garlic. Rinse, dry and chop the parsley.

Stir an egg into these ingredients, blending until completely incorporated. Season with salt and pepper. Poach or pan-fry a spoonful of the meat, cool, taste and adjust the seasoning if necessary.

Roll the meat into small balls. Chill the meatballs a little to make them firm. Roll the meatballs in the beaten egg then cover completely with dried breadcrumbs. Tap to remove excess.

Pan-fry in hot oil as explained at the beginning of this chapter.

These beignets can be made with different combinations of ground meat. It is important to select meats that have a little fat so that the beignets will be moist. Fresh herbs give these hors d'œuvres a delicious flavor.

The mixture is rolled into regular balls. The size can vary but if they are too large it will be difficult to cook them through without browning the breading too much.

11. Oyster Beignets

Reserve the best looking shells for the presentation.

Drain them, then dry thoroughly on paper towels.

Dip the oysters in the beaten egg, then cover completely with dried breadcrumbs. Gently fry them in the hot oil, turning them carefully to brown them on both sides.

After the excess oil has been drained, serve them immediately in their shells.

This is a delicious way to serve oysters. They are easy to make but the food cost is slightly higher than the other beignets in this chapter.

Choose large fresh oysters. Open the shells and remove the oyster, making sure that there are no bits of shell attached.

12. Red Mullet Beignets

Cut the filets into small pieces, place them in a shallow dish to marinate. Sprinkle them with salt, pepper and olive oil.

Place lemon slices and thyme and bay leaf on top. Cover and marinate in the refrigerator for about 30 minutes.

Dip each piece of fish in the beaten egg, then cover completely with dried breadcrumbs.

Fry the fish in the hot oil as described at the beginning of this chapter.

These beignets can be made with many other types of white fish as well, such as sole, cod or snapper.

Choose small fresh red mullets and remove the filets. Rinse them and pull out any bones that may remain, by feeling with your fingers.

13. Salmon Beignets with Green Beans

Cut very thin escalopes on the bias from a fresh filet of salmon, (about 15g (1/2oz)) each.

Choose very thin green beans, remove the ends and the strings and rinse them. Plunge them into rapidly boiling salted water and cook until tender but still firm. Drain, dry on a hand towel and cut them the same length as the escalopes of salmon.

Make little bundles of green beans tied together with a sprig of chive or a thin piece of blanched leek green. Wrap the bundles in the salmon and chill.

Roll each one in beaten egg then cover completely with dried bread crumbs. The cooking is the same as the other breaded beignets.

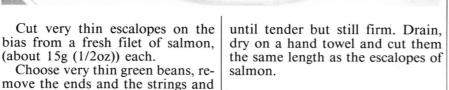

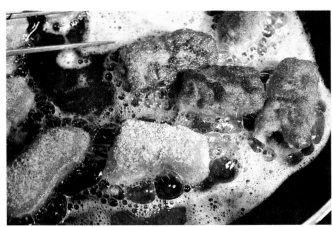

Chapter 5
Individual Hot Dishes

A Wide Range of Savory Dishes

The variety of dishes presented in this chapter will add dimension and choice to the caterer's repertoire.

Grouped in six families, these preparations are ideal as a hearty first course for an elegant dinner or luncheon main course.

Six Families
of Individual Hot Dishes

All of the preparations in this chapter are easy to make and reheat well. Since they can be made in advance, they are ideal to serve at large functions or in a restaurant.

Fresh ingredients give each of these dishes a delicious taste, appreciated by customers.

1 - Individual Pâtés " en Croûte ", " Talmouses " and " Croques "

2 - Cheese Pastries

3 - " Bouchées "

4 - Filled Crêpes and Soufflé Crêpes

5 - Dishes in Scallop Shells

6 - Shellfish with Flavored Butters

Individual Pâtés " en Croûte ", " Talmouses " and " Croques "

Introduction

The dishes in this section are made with a crust and an addition of meats or vegetables.

Cheese adds flavor as well as moistness in several of the preparations.

These classic pastry and bread-based preparations made in individual sizes are a staple in French pastry and take out shops. They are easy to transport and reheat easily at home to make a tasty light meal or elegant first course.

The " croques monsieur ", a refined sandwich made with tender " pain de mie " (milk enriched white bread) are familiar to all who have eaten in a French café.

The selection in this category includes:

1 - Individual Pâtés " en Croûte "

2 - Sausage " en Croûte "

3 - Cheese " Roulades "

4 - " Talmouses "

5 - " Croques "

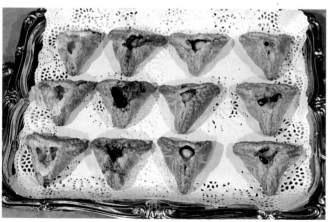

Individual Pâtés " en Croûte "

Introduction

Delicate puff pastry is used to encase the savory forcemeat used to make these pâtés " en croûte " (" in crust ").

They can be shaped two ways:

• Round, using two pieces of pastry forming the top and the bottom and held in place with egg glaze.

• Half moon or turnover, using one round of pastry folded over the filling.

The forcemeat is made with blade end of pork, pork jowl and fat back. The meats are marinated, then ground.

The ground meats are bound with a purée of goose liver and eggs. Marinated strips of veal are incorporated into the mixture.

For pastries the size presented here, the forcemeat is divided into balls weighing 50g (about 1 1/2oz) each and chilled until ready to assemble. It is important that there is ample meat in relation to the pastry.

Equipment

Cutting board, hotel pan, meat grinder, paring knife, thin-bladed flexible knife, chef's knife, pastry scraper, wooden spoon, measuring cup, mixing bowls, rolling pin, plain round pastry cutter, pastry brush, soft-bristled brush, sheet pan, baking sheet, cooling rack

Ingredients

For the Pastry

Puff pastry, with 6 turns
Egg glaze

For the Filling

(For 32 pieces weighing 50g (about 1 1/2oz) each)

Forcemeat

500g (1lb) boneless blade end of pork
500g (1lb) skinned pork jowl
45g (1 1/2oz) skinned fat back
20g (2/3oz) shallots
7g (1/4oz) garlic
15g (1/2oz) salt
Pepper, allspice, saltpeter, thyme, piece of bay leaf
2.5cl (1/8 cup) white wine
1cl (2tsp) madeira
1.5cl (1 tbsp) cognac
1 egg
60g (2oz) goose liver purée

Filet

500g (1lb) trimmed and pared sirloin tip of veal
5g (1tsp) salt
Pepper, allspice, saltpeter, thyme, piece of bay leaf
1cl (2tsp) white wine
5cl (1tsp) cognac

Procedure

One day in advance, make the puff pastry and give it four turns.
Trim the meats, cut them into pieces and mix them with the marinade ingredients.

To Make Round Pâtés

The next day, give the puff pastry two turns and chill in the refrigerator.

Form the forcemeat into balls weighing approximately 50g (1 1/2oz) each and refrigerate.

Roll the puff pastry into a sheet 2-2.5mm (1/16-1/8in) thick and let the dough rest before cutting out the shapes.

Cut out the shapes needed to form the base, top and decoration. For example, for 8 pâtés, cut out 8 8cm (3 1/4in) rounds for the bases, 8 9cm (3 1/2in) rounds for the tops and 8 4cm (1 3/4in) rounds for the decorations.

Assembly

Line up the pastry bases and brush egg glaze around the edge without letting the glaze drip down the sides.

Place a ball of forcemeat in the center of each round.

Place the larger round of pastry on top and carefully press down

around the forcemeat inside, lining up the edges of the base and the top as shown.

Seal the two layers of pastry with the top of the pastry cutter dipped

in flour.

Place the pâtés in even rows on a heavy baking sheet and flute the edges with the back of a paring knife.

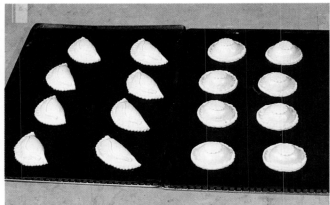

Brush the top with egg glaze. Place the scalloped round of pastry in the center as decoration. Brush the small round with egg glaze and score with a small knife to make an attractive pattern.

Prick the dough in a north-south-east-west pattern with the tip of a skewer to allow steam to escape during cooking, which helps the pastry to rise evenly.

Chill for at least one hour before baking.

To Make a Turnover Shape
Roll out a sheet of puff pastry 2-2.5mm (1/16-1/8in) thick. Cut out rounds using a fluted pastry cutter measuring about 13cm (5 1/4in) across.

Also cut very thin strips of dough (about 6mm (1/4in)) to use as decorations.

Assembly
Line up the rounds of dough and brush egg glaze on half of the circle without letting it drip down the sides of the pastry.

Roll the ball of forcemeat into an oval and place one just off center of each pastry shape, as shown.

Fold the unglazed side of dough over the forcemeat and press to seal the edge. Brush the top with

egg glaze.

Set the strip of dough on top in a curved pattern as decoration.

Brush on a second coat of egg glaze and score the top. Prick the dough to allow the steam to escape during cooking.

Refrigerate at least one hour before baking.

Cooking

Begin baking at 220C (425F) to brown the pastry, then lower the temperature to 190C (370F) to finish baking. Bake for about 35-40 minutes. During cooking, the flavors of the forcemeat are absorbed by the flaky pastry.

Transfer the cooked pastries to a cooling rack immediately so they do not become soggy on the bottom.

Storage

These pâtés will keep in the refrigerator for 1-2 days.

Serving

To serve, reheat in a warm oven.

Chipolatas " en Croûte "

Introduction

These fresh sausage pastries are highly seasoned with onions, parsley, garlic and wine, like the spicy " chipolatas " available throughout Europe.

The forcemeat, made with veal and pork, is bound with eggs and enveloped in puff pastry.

They are not expensive to make and make an excellent light lunch served with a green salad--an ideal addition to a " gourmet " picnic basket.

Equipment

Cutting board, meat grinder, small bowls, plates, mixing bowls, chef's knife, paring knife, palette knife, spatula, pastry scraper, straightedge, pastry brush, measuring cup, pastry bag and plain tip, baking sheet, cooling rack

Ingredients

For the Sausage Meat

500g (1lb) veal
500g (1lb) pork

For the Marinade

45g (1 1/2oz) onions
30g (1oz) shallots
15g (1/2oz) garlic
45g (1 1/2oz) parsley
Sprig of thyme
Bay leaf
1dl (1/2 cup) white wine
Salt
Saltpeter
Pepper
Allspice
Egg

Procedure

The Forcemeat

Pass the meats separately through a meat grinder fitted with a fine disk.

Cut the onions and shallots in very fine dice, crush the garlic and chop it. Rinse the parsley, dry it and chop it finely.

Add these ingredients plus the spices and wine to the ground meats, stir to blend and leave to marinate for one hour.

The Pastry

Roll out a sheet of puff pastry 3-3.5mm (about 1/8in) thick. Cut

The forcemeat can be piped out onto stainless steel baking sheets in advance and refrigerated. To assemble the pastries to order, cut the sausage meat to the length needed.

Fold the unglazed side of dough over the forcemeat and press to seal the edge.

Flutè the edge with the back of a paring knife. Brush the surface with egg glaze and score the top with a paring knife to make an attractive pattern.

Pierce the pastry around the edge as shown. Chill the pastries thoroughly before baking. Baking, storage and serving is identical to individual pâtés en croûte.

in squares about 11cm (4 1/2in)-each square of pastry should weigh about 40g (about 1 1/2oz).

Assembly

Brush egg glaze along three edges of the pastry without letting it drip down the sides.

Using a pastry bag fitted with a large tip, pipe out the forcemeat as shown. The meat for each one will weigh about 35g (about 1oz).

Cheese " Roulades "

Introduction

These " roulades " of puff pastry " rolled " around a metal tube, baked then filled with creamy bechamel, cheese and ham are a classic offering in French specialty food shops. They are easily transported and reheated at home.

The roulades are made in two steps:

1 - Strips of puff pastry are rolled around specially designed aluminum cylinders, chilled, then baked.

2 - The bechamel is mixed with cheese and ham, piped into the hollow rolls, then the ends are covered with grated cheese.

Equipment

Aluminum tubes 2.5cm (1in) in diameter and 12-15cm (5-6in) long, rolling pin, baking sheet, soft-bristled brush, pastry brush, sheet pan, cutting board, large saucepan, mixing bowls, whisk, measuring cup, pastry scraper, chef's knife, pastry bag and plain tip, ladle, cooling rack, spatula

Ingredients

The Roulades

Puff pastry, with 6 turns (or puff pastry with 6 turns and trimmings incorporated)
Butter, egg glaze

The Filling (for 10 roulades)
Bechamel

4dl (1 2/3 cup) milk
75g (2 1/2oz) butter
75g (2 1/2oz) flour

Filling

200g (7oz) boiled ham
45g (1 1/2oz) grated swiss cheese

To Finish

45g (1 1/2oz) grated swiss cheese

Procedure

The Pastry

Roll out a sheet of puff pastry 2mm (about 1/16in) thick and cut strips that are 2.5-3cm (about 1in) wide, and long enough so that one strip will wrap around each cylinder.

Butter the cylinders, and wrap the pastry strips around each one, starting at one end and overlapping the pastry a little as it wraps around. Seal the ends with a touch of egg glaze without dripping any on the cylinder. Make sure that the pastry is well chilled before you start, and do not pull on the strips as you wrap so that they do not shrink out of shape while baking.

Brush on two coats of egg glaze and chill before baking. Bake at 220C (425F) for 20-25 minutes. Remove the metal cylinders as soon as they are done and set the pastry on a cooling rack.

The Filling

Make the bechamel and mix with the ham cut in small dice and the grated cheese.

Assembly

Using a pastry bag fitted with a large plain tip, fill each pastry roulade with the bechamel mixture. Cover the ends with grated cheese

as shown.

Storage

The cheese roulades will keep in the refrigerator for two days.

Serving

Reheat in a warm oven; the roulades should warm through without drying out or browning too much.

" Talmouses "

Ingredients

Basic Bechamel

(For 300g (10oz))
30g (1oz) butter
30g (1oz) flour
3.5dl (1 1/2 cups) milk
Salt, pepper, nutmeg

Mushroom Talmouses

30g (1oz) clarified butter
45g (1 1/2oz) shallots
350g (12oz) mushrooms
Salt, pepper
20g (2/3oz) chopped parsley
300g (10oz) bechamel sauce

Spinach and Quail's Egg Talmouses

30g (1oz) clarified butter
600g (1 1/4lbs) spinach
Salt, pepper, nutmeg
300g (10oz) bechamel sauce
6 quail's eggs

Niçoise Talmouses

2cl (4tsp) olive oil
150g (5oz) red pepper
250g (1/2lb) tuna
Salt, pepper
12 black olives
300g (10oz) bechamel sauce

Ham Talmouses

250g (1/2lb) boiled ham
300g (10oz) bechamel sauce

Introduction

Talmouses are individual pastries that can be filled with an assortment of ingredients which are bound with a bechamel sauce that makes the talmouses moist and delicious.

They are made with rounds of puff pastry that are wrapped around the filling with the edges joined at the top to form the distinctive tri-cornered shape.

The filling and pastry rounds can be prepared in advance and assembled to order.

They are easy to make and the varieties shown here are not expensive to make.

Equipment

Cutting board, small bowl, plates, mixing bowls, large saucepan with lid, sauté pan with lid, paring knife, thin-bladed flexible knife, chef's knife, 2-pronged fork, spatula, whisk, pastry scraper, spoon, fork, measuring cup, rolling pin, soft-bristled brush, pastry brush, pastry cutter (13cm (5 1/4in)), baking sheet, cooling rack

Procedure

The pastry for all talmouses is made and shaped in the same way.

For best results, give four turns to the puff pastry, let it rest overnight and give the last two turns the day you make the pastries.

Roll out a sheet of pastry 2-2.5mm (1/16-1/8in) thick and chill it.

Cut out rounds with a 13cm (5 1/4in) fluted or plain pastry cutter. Each one should weigh about 35g (about 1oz).

Brush egg glaze on the surface, and in the center, place a spoonful of the cooled filling. Bring the edges of the round up around the filling and form a tri-cornered pastry as shown, pinching the edges together to seal.

Brush each talmouse with egg glaze and chill for one hour before baking.

Brush on a second coat of egg glaze and score the sides with a paring knife to make an attractive pattern.

Cooking

All of the talmouses bake at 210C (400F) for 25-30 minutes, until golden brown.

NOTE: as with all pastries, sometimes double baking sheets are necessary to keep the crust from browning too fast on the bottom.

Storage

These talmouses will keep for two days in the refrigerator.

Serving

Reheat for 6-8 minutes in a warm oven (190C (370F)) and serve warm.

Mushroom Talmouses

Make the bechamel sauce.

Cut the shallots into fine dice.

Chop the parsley finely.

Thoroughly wash the mushrooms, drain and slice thinly.

Melt the butter, add the mushrooms, shallots, parsley and season with salt and pepper.

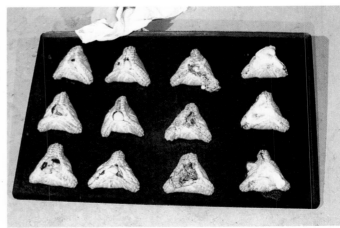

Cover and cook over high heat to draw out the moisture in the mushrooms.

Remove the lid and continue to cook to evaporate the cooking liquid.

Mix the cooked mushrooms with the bechamel and cool.

Niçoise Talmouses

Remove the pits from the olives (small black olives from Nice are traditional) and cut them in small pieces.

Cut the red pepper into small dice and sauté in olive oil without browning, which would make it bitter.

Flake the tuna and mix the olives, peppers, tuna and olive oil into the bechamel. Chill.

Ham Talmouses

Cut the ham into small dice.

Blend the ham into the bechamel and chill.

Talmouses with Spinach and Quail's Egg

Remove the stem from the spinach and wash thoroughly in cold water.

Melt the butter, add the spinach and season with salt and pepper. Cover and cook over high heat to draw out the moisture.

Remove the lid and cook to evaporate the liquid, stirring from time to time with a two-pronged fork. Mix the spinach and bechamel. Cool.

To assemble, place a quail's egg in the center of the spinach mixture.

" Croques "

Introduction

In France, " croque ", which means " crunch ", refers to a family of sandwiches that are toasted in the oven. They are traditionally filled with ham and cheese, with bechamel sauce and cheese baked on top to make the well know "croque monsieur". Other ingredients can be used to make original versions of this elegant sandwich.

They are made with milk enriched " pain de mie ", which is usually baked in a 4-sided mold to create a close-textured, moist interior.

In these variations, the creamy bechamel sauce used to coat the interior of the croques adds flavor and richness.

Before they are toasted, the sandwiches are brushed with melted butter which forms a crispy top and keeps the bread moist on the inside.

A croque is a meal in itself, and makes a nice quick lunch. They can be made ahead and reheated for sale in a specialty food shop.

Equipment

Cutting board, plates, small bowls, mixing bowls, saucepans, serrated knife, palette knife, paring knife, pastry brush, whisk, spatula, frying pan, pastry cutter, baking sheet, cooling rack

Ingredients

Croque Monsieur

(to make one croque)

2 slices (45g (1 1/2oz) each) pain de mie or other enriched white bread
45g (1 1/2oz) bechamel sauce
30g (1oz) slice of boiled ham
30g (1oz) slice of swiss cheese
15g (1/2oz) melted butter
15g (1/2oz) grated cheese

Assembly

Lay one slice of bread on the work surface and brush it with melted butter. Spread a little more than half the bechamel on top. Lay the slices of ham and cheese on top.

Spread the second slice of bread with the remaining bechamel and lay it, sauce side down, on the cheese. Brush the top of the bread with more melted butter and sprinkle with grated cheese.

Place it on a baking sheet and toast it in a hot oven.

Croque Madame

Ingredients

(to make one croque)

2 slices (45g (1 1/2oz) each) pain de mie or other enriched white bread
45g (1 1/2oz) bechamel sauce
45g (1 1/2oz) chicken breast, sliced
30g (1oz) slice of swiss cheese
15g (1/2oz) melted butter
10g (1/3oz) clarified butter 1 egg
Salt, pepper

Assembly

Lay one slice of bread on the work surface and brush it with melted butter. Spread a little more than half the bechamel on top. Lay the slices of cheese and chicken breast on top.

Spread the second slice of bread with the remaining bechamel and lay it, sauce side down, on the cheese. Brush the top of the bread with more melted butter.

Place it on a baking sheet and toast it in a hot oven. Top it with a fried egg before serving.

Croque Niçoise

Ingredients

(to make one croque)

2 slices (45g (1 1/2oz) each) pain de mie or other enriched white bread
45g (1 1/2oz) bechamel sauce
30g (1oz) slice of boiled ham
30g (1oz) slice of swiss cheese
15g (1/2oz) melted butter
1.5cl (1 tsp) olive oil
15g (1/2oz) slice peeled tomato
2 anchovy filets
Salt, pepper
Marjoram, oregano
Black olives, halved and pitted

Assembly

Lay one slice of bread on the work surface and brush it with melted butter. Spread a little more than half the bechamel on top. Lay the slices of ham and cheese on top.

Spread the second slice of bread with the remaining bechamel and lay it, sauce side down, on the cheese. Brush the top of the bread with more melted butter and sprinkle with grated cheese.

To finish, place it on a baking sheet and toast it in a hot oven. Place the slice of tomato in the center, sprinkle it with the herbs and top with half an olive. Lay the anchovy filets on top in a cross.

Cheese Pastries

Introduction

These dishes are all made with a rich sauce augmented with cheese. This sauce is combined with other ingredients and paired with pastry in different forms to create savory delights.

The pastry bases are baked first, the prepared filling is added before serving, which allows the caterer to make sizeable batches of the two elements and assemble the pastries to order.

They are quick and simple to prepare, as well as being easy to transport and reheat, which makes them standard take-home items in French specialty food shops.

Gnocci à la Parisienne

Introduction

In Chapter 2, quenelles made with cream puff pastry were presented. This recipe shows how the quenelles are incorporated into a more complex dish.

These quenelles, made with cream puff pastry, are easy and inexpensive to make. Here they are combined with a rich bechamel and grated cheese, then spooned into pastry shells or spread in a gratin dish and browned.

A hint of grated nutmeg is added to the sauce which enlivens the taste of the cheese without being detected.

These are ideal items to sell in a specialty food shop where the customer can easily reheat them at home for a quick lunch or snack.

The quenelles will expand and lighten a bit when the dish is reheated and the cheese will melt and turn golden brown.

Equipment

Large saucepans, mixing bowls, colander, plates, hotel pan, measuring cup, spatula, skimmer, ladle, whisk, pastry bag and plain tip, metal skewer, pastry scraper, tablespoon, paring knife, palette knife

Ingredients

Cream Puff Pastry

1/4L (1 cup) milk
100g (3 1/2oz) butter
Salt, pepper, nutmeg
150g (5oz) flour
4 eggs

Bechamel Sauce

125g (4oz) butter
125g (4oz) flour
1.5L (6 cups) milk
Salt, pepper, nutmeg
125g (4oz) grated cheese

To Finish

Grated cheese
Butter

Procedure

Making the Gnocchi

Make the cream puff pastry following the classic method. The ingredients here make a dough that is slightly stiffer than that needed to make baked cream puffs.

Season with salt, pepper and nutmeg. Chill the mixture before shaping.

Shaping and Poaching

For the dish here, the mixture is piped out with a pastry bag fitted with a tip measuring 8-10 mm (about 3/8in).

The pastry bag is held over the simmering water and the gnocchis are cut off with a metal skewer as they are extruded, as shown. (These are about 1-2 cm (3/8-3/4in) long.)

Poach the gnocchi in lightly salted, simmering water which is not allowed to boil (this would cause them to expand too quickly).

Do not poach too many at a time, and stir them around so they cook evenly.

Check the cooking by cutting a few of them in half and verifying that the interior is firm.

Cooling the Gnocchis

Plunge the cooked gnocchis into ice water to stop the cooking. As soon as they are cool, drain them in a colander and spread them out on a hand towel to dry completely.

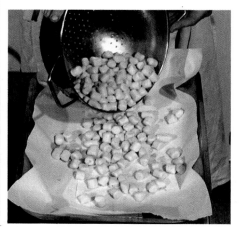

Making the Bechamel Sauce

Melt the butter, stir in the flour and cook the roux a few minutes.

Pour in the milk, whisking constantly and bring the sauce to a boil.

NOTE: If the roux is hot, use cold milk. If the roux has cooled, add hot milk.

Simmer the sauce. Season to taste. Off the heat, stir in the cheese. (With the addition of cheese, the bechamel becomes mornay sauce.)

Serving

Reheat in a medium oven to melt the butter and cheese and brown the top. The gnocchi will expand and lighten a little as they are warmed. Serve immediately.

Assembly

Carefully stir the drained gnocchi into the warm sauce.

Transfer the mixture to a lightly buttered gratin dish. Count on about 120g (4oz) of the mixture per person. Sprinkle the top with grated cheese and place a few pieces of butter on top.

The mixture can also be spooned into prebaked pastry shells made with basic pie pastry or puff pastry. For these individual presentations, it is preferable to cool the mixture so that it can be heaped in an ample dome shape, as shown.

Cover the top with grated cheese and set a curl of butter on top which serves as decoration when the gnocchis are sold in a specialty food shop and adds flavor and moistness when the dish is reheated.

Storage

The gnocchi mixture will keep in the refrigerator for two days covered with plastic wrap. Once assembled, the dishes will keep about 12 hours.

Feuilletées made with Cheese and Ham

Introduction

The two simple dishes presented here are both made with a base of puff pastry which is baked then filled with a savory cheese sauce. A slice of ham augments the second selection.

The puff pastry should be made with butter and the sauce should always be creamy and well seasoned.

They reheat easily, which makes them ideal for a restaurant that specializes in light lunches or for a specialty food shop.

Equipment

Fluted 10cm (4in) pastry cutter, rolling pin, baking sheet, soft-bristled brush, pastry brush, paring knife, sheet pan, large saucepan, mixing bowls, whisk, cheese grater, measuring cup, pastry scraper, serrated knife, chef's knife, pastry bag with plain tip, ladle, cooling rack

Ingredients

3/4L (3 cups) milk
130g (4oz) butter
1/4L (1 cup) milk
100g (3 1/2oz) cornstarch
4 eggs
250g (8oz) grated cheese
Salt, pepper

Puff Pastry

Puff pastry, with 6 turns
Egg glaze, grated cheese

Procedure

Making the Pastry Base

Make the puff pastry a day in advance so that it has a chance to rest and lose its elasticity. It is recommended to give the first four of the total six turns to the pastry at this stage. Cover with plastic wrap and refrigerate.

The next day, give the pastry two more turns and refrigerate if the pastry is elastic. (This often happens if the kitchen is very warm.)

The pastry is easier to roll out if the block of dough is divided in smaller portions first.

Dust the work surface with enough flour to keep the pastry from sticking, but using too much flour will offset the proportion of butter to flour.

Roll out the pastry to a thickness of 6mm (1/4in). Let the dough rest again if necessary.

Shaping the Pastry

Cut out the pastry using a round, fluted pastry cutter measuring about 10-12 cm (4in) for the cheese pastries and cut rectangles with a chef's knife for the ham pastries.

Turn each cut-out pastry over as you place it on a heavy baking sheet so that the smoother side next to the work surface is now the top. Arrange the shapes so that they are evenly spaced on the baking sheet.

Brush the top of each shape with egg glaze. Refrigerate for 15-20 minutes.

Brush on a second coat of glaze, taking care to not let the glaze drip down the sides. Sprinkle the top with grated cheese.

Pierce the pastry shape in a north-south-east-west pattern and in the center with the point of a paring knife or skewer. These " air vents " allow just a little steam to escape from the pastry during baking, which helps it to puff evenly.

Refrigerate again, about 15-30 minutes before baking.

Cooking

Bake in a hot oven preheated to 220C (425F) for about 20-25 minutes until the pastries are golden brown.

Transfer the cooked pastries to a cooling rack immediately so they do not become soggy.

NOTE: The pastry bases can be made several weeks in advance, in sizeable quantities and frozen. For best results, freeze the unbaked shapes and bake to order.

Making the Sauce

In a heavy pot, bring the 3/4L (3 cups) milk and butter slowly to a

boil so that the butter is completely melted.

Meanwhile, whisk together the 1/4L (1 cup) of milk with the cornstarch and blend until smooth.

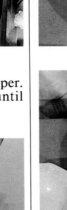

Season with salt and pepper. Add the eggs and blend until smooth.

Pour the milk and egg mixture into the boiling milk and butter, whisking constantly. (The procedure is similar to pastry cream.)

Cook the sauce for 3-5 minutes to thicken it, stirring constantly.

Remove from the heat and stir in the grated cheese.

Taste the sauce and season if necessary.

Transfer the sauce to a stainless steel hotel pan and cover the top with butter so it does not dry out.

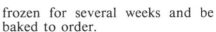

Assembly

Split the cooled pastries in the middle with a small knife.

Stir the cold sauce so that it can be piped onto the base using a pastry bag fitted with a large tip. Cover the base evenly with sauce and replace the top of the pastry. (For the one with ham, lay a slice of ham over the sauce.)

Storage

Once filled, these preparations will keep 24 hours maximum in the refrigerator. The sauce softens the pastry very quickly.

Separately, the sauce will keep 2-3 days covered with plastic wrap in the refrigerator.

The baked pastry bases will keep 2 days in an air tight container or the frozen, shaped dough can be frozen for several weeks and be baked to order.

Serving

Reheat in a medium oven for about 10 minutes and serve warm.

" Gougères "

Parmesan Sauce

3/4L (3 cups) milk
130g (4oz) butter
1/4L (1 cup) milk
100g (3 1/2oz) cornstarch
4 eggs
250g (1/2lb) grated cheese
Salt, pepper

Procedure

Make a classic cream puff dough, with an addition of salt, pepper and nutmeg.

Lightly butter the baking sheet and pipe out shapes that are all the

same size and space them evenly on the sheet. They can be round, oval or piped out in a ring.

Brush the top of each one with egg glaze and flatten the top a bit with the brush or the back of a fork so they do not form cracks in the surface while baking.

Sprinkle the top with grated cheese and bake in medium oven until puffed and golden. Transfer immediately to a cooling rack.

Cut the cooled pastries in half and pipe in the sauce. Replace the top.

Storage

The gougères keep about two days in the refrigerator. Seperately, the sauce and pastry will keep a little longer.

Serving

Reheat in a medium oven for about 10 minutes and serve warm.

Introduction

Cream puff pastry forms the base for this preparation, which is piped out in two different forms.

Gougères are a regional specialty of Burgundy where they are eaten without a filling (with cheese incorporated directly into the dough) and are often served with kir (an apperitif made from white wine and black currant liqueur).

The sauce is identical to the puff pastry dishes in the previous section.

These are not expensive to make, can be made in various sizes to suit the occasion and are therefore very popular with customers.

Equipment

Large saucepan, measuring cup, spatula, mixing bowls, pastry brush, baking sheet, pastry bag with plain top, whisk, pastry scraper, cheese grater, hotel pan, serrated knife, chef's knife, cutting board, ladle, cooling rack, triangular spatula

Ingredients

Cream Puff Pastry

1/4L (1 cup) water
1/4L (1 cup) milk
200g (7oz) butter
300g (10oz) flour
8 eggs
Salt, pepper, nutmeg
Egg glaze
300g (10oz) grated cheese (to finish)

Bouchées

Introduction

A "bouchée", which means "mouthful" in French, can also be made in bite-size shapes to serve as finger food. On the other end of the scale, the pastry can be formed to hold enough filling for a main course for eight. For this dramatic presentation, the sauce and pastry are reheated seperately, and each guest is served a spoonful of sauce and a piece of the crust.

The size presented here is just right for an elegant starter to a multi-course dinner or a light main course. The individual portions are lovely as well as practical for large occasions.

The base of puff pastry should be made with great care to achieve maximum lightness and height.

The ingredients in the sauce can vary to take advantage of seasonal foods when they are at their best. In all cases the sauce should be well seasoned and thickened just enough to coat and not run out of the pastry base.

In addition to the classic round and rectangular shapes, the pastry can be cut to resemble a fish or mushroom to coordinate with the filling. For maximum height, two layers of dough are used to form the bottom and the rim on top.

These individual bouchées can be assembled a few hours in advance and warmed through just before serving.

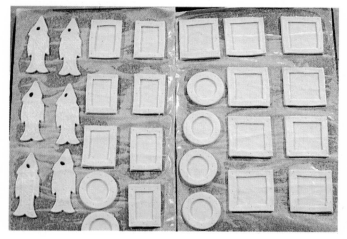

Bouchées " à la Reine "

Introduction

This is the most popular of the classic bouchées. La " reine " (" queen " in French) indicates that this is an elegant dish fit for royalty.

The sweetbreads are often very expensive and could be replaced with brains or veal. The delicate veal quenelles are a good example of how the recipes in Chapter 2 of this volume can be incorporated into more complex dishes.

The sauce is made with a veal stock that is reduced to concentrate the taste and mushrooms add flavor to the sauce as well as complementing the veal and sweetbreads in the filling.

Equipment

Cutting board, mixing bowls, small bowls, measuring cup, paring knife, vegetable peeler, thin-bladed flexible knife, 2-pronged fork, tablespoon, plates, skimmer, ladle, frying pan, fine-meshed conical sieve, whisk, sauté pan, large saucepan with lid, colander, pastry scraper

Ingredients

Cooked puff pastry cases

Braised Sweetbreads

400g (14oz) sweetbreads
15g (1/2oz) clarified butter
45g (1 1/2oz) onions
45g (1 1/2oz) carrots
10g (1/3oz) celery
45g (1 1/2oz) leek, white part only
1 bouquet garni (parsley, thyme bay leaf)
1.5dl (2/3 cup) white wine
1.5dl (2/3 cup) madeira
250g (1/2lb) veal quenelles

Sauce

Roux, made with
    75g (2 1/2oz) butter and
    75g (2 1/2oz) flour
3/4L (3 cups) light stock
1dl (1/2 cup) reduced mushroom cooking liquid
1.5dl (2/3 cup) reduced sweetbread braising liquid

Liaison

3 egg yolks
1.5dl (2/3 cup) heavy cream
Salt, pepper

Mushrooms

400g (14oz) mushrooms – 2dl (3/4 cup) water – 15g (1/2oz) butter – juice of 1/4 lemon – salt, pepper

Procedure

The Sweetbreads

Degorge the sweetbreads in cold running water for about one hour to draw out blood and impurities. Drain them and trim the thin skin that covers them and remove nerves and spots of blood.

Braising the Sweetbreads

Peel the vegetables (carrot, onion, leek, celery) and cut them in small dice. Make a bouquet garni with thyme, bay leaf and parsley tied with kitchen twine.

In a heavy pan, sauté the vegetables in clarified butter until they are light brown.

In a heavy skillet, sear the sweetbreads in clarified butter with a little oil. Place the seared sweetbreads on the bed of sautéed vegetables in the other pan, add the bouquet garni and season with salt and pepper.

Pour off the fat from the skillet, deglaze with white wine and add these juices to the sweetbreads. Add the madeira, cover the pan and braise in the oven.

Braise for 15-30 minutes, basting from time to time with the braising liquid. Reserve the liquid for the sauce.

The Veal Quenelles

Follow the instructions for veal

quenelles in Chapter 2 and shape them as shown. For extra flavor, poach them in simmering veal stock (do not let the poaching liquid boil) for 5-10 minutes. Drain the quenelles on a hand towel.

The Mushrooms

Trim the sandy stem of the mushrooms and wash them in a large basin of cold water, changing the water several times to remove all the sand and dirt.

Drain and sprinkle with lemon juice.

To keep them firm and white, bring the water, butter, lemon juice, salt and pepper to a boil and add the mushrooms to this liquid.

Cover the pot and cook over high heat for 3-5 minutes. Reserve the liquid for the sauce.

Preparing the Filling

Cut the sausage-shaped quenelles into 1cm (3/8in) slices. Cut the mushrooms into small pieces.

Cut the braised sweetbreads in small pieces.

Making the Sauce

Melt the butter, whisk in the flour and cook the roux for a few minutes until light brown.

Pour in the full-flavored veal stock and simmer the sauce, whisking constantly. Skim the surface of impurities if necessary.

Strain the juice from the mushrooms and the braising liquid into

the sauce through a conical sieve. Bring the sauce back to a boil and cook until it reduces and thickens enough to coat a spoon.

Whisk together the egg yolk and cream, and off the heat whisk them into the hot sauce. Taste and season with salt and pepper if necessary.

Pour the finished sauce through a conical sieve over the prepared filling ingredients as shown. Cool the mixture in a stainless steel hotel pan. It will keep in the refrigerator for two days.

Assembly and Serving

Spoon the cooled filling into the baked bouchées, counting on about 110g (4oz) of filling for a pastry case that weighs about 45g (1 1/2oz).

Reheat in a medium oven so that it slowly warms throughout and serve immediately.

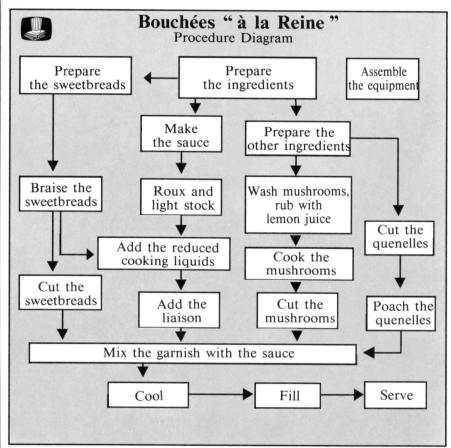

Bouchées " à la Reine "
Procedure Diagram

Prepare the ingredients → Prepare the sweetbreads

Assemble the equipment

Prepare the ingredients → Make the sauce

Prepare the ingredients → Prepare the other ingredients

Prepare the sweetbreads → Braise the sweetbreads

Make the sauce → Roux and light stock

Prepare the other ingredients → Wash mushrooms, rub with lemon juice

Prepare the other ingredients → Cut the quenelles

Braise the sweetbreads → Add the reduced cooking liquids

Roux and light stock → Add the reduced cooking liquids

Wash mushrooms, rub with lemon juice → Cook the mushrooms

Braise the sweetbreads → Cut the sweetbreads

Add the reduced cooking liquids → Add the liaison

Cook the mushrooms → Cut the mushrooms

Cut the quenelles → Poach the quenelles

Mix the garnish with the sauce

Cool → Fill → Serve

Bouchées " Financières "

Introduction

The " financièrs " or " bankers " were among the few who could afford this delicacy of classic cooking.

The cock's combs and testicles may be hard to obtain and expensive. They can be replaced by chicken breast, which would lower the price of these bouchées.

Sweetbreads and veal quenelles round out the delicious meats used. The dark brown sauce is more assertive than in the previous recipe, and olives add another strong accent. Truffles, which are optional, make the dish truly elegant if the budget allows.

Equipment

Cutting board, mixing bowls, small bowls, plates, measuring cup, paring knife, vegetable peeler, thin-bladed flexible knife, 2-pronged fork, tablespoon, ladle, frying pan, fine-meshed conical sieve, whisk, sauté pans, large saucepans, colander, pastry scraper

Ingredients

Sweetbreads

400g (14oz) sweetbreads
15g (1/2oz) clarified butter
45g (1 1/2oz) onions
45g (1 1/2oz) carrots
45g (1 1/2oz) leek, white part only
10g (1/3oz) celery
1 bouquet garni (parsley, thyme, bay leaf)
1.5dl (2/3 cup) white wine
1.5dl (2/3 cup) madeira
Full-flavored brown stock

Mushrooms

400g (14oz) mushrooms
2dl (3/4 cup) water
15g (1/2oz) butter
Juice of 1/4 lemon
Salt, pepper

250g (1/2lb) *veal quenelles*

100g (3 1/2oz) *green olives*

Cock's Combs and Testicles

" Blanc " for cooking the cock's combs, made with 1L (1qt) water, 45g (1 1/2oz) flour, juice of 1/4 lemon, 5cl (1/4 cup) oil, salt, pepper
200g (7oz) cock's combs
150g (5oz) cock's testicles

30g (1oz) *truffles* (optional)

Sauce

Roux made from 100g (3 1/2oz) butter and 100g (3 1/2oz) flour
1L (1qt) reduced veal stock
1.5dl (2/3 cup) reduced mushroom cooking liquid
1.5dl (2/3 cup) reduced sweetbread braising liquid
5cl (1/4 cup) truffle juice
15g (1/2oz) butter
Salt, pepper

Procedure

The Sweetbreads

Degorge the sweetbreads under

cold running water for 1 hour to remove blood and impurities. Drain them and trim the thin skin around them, nerves and spots of blood.

Braising the Sweetbreads

Peel the vegetables (carrot, onion, leek, celery) and cut into small dice. Make a bouquet garni with thyme, bay leaf and parsley tied together with kitchen twine.
Sauté the vegetables in clarified butter.
In a skillet, brown the sweetbreads in clarified butter mixed with a little oil. Place the seared sweetbreads on the bed of sautéed vegetables, add the bouquet garni and season with a little salt and pepper.
Pour off the fat from the skillet and deglaze with white wine. Add this liquid to the sweetbreads and add the madeira. Cover the pan and braise in the oven for 15-30 minutes, basting and turning them over after a few minutes.

The Cock's Combs and Testicles

Blanch the cock's combs in cold water brought to a boil for 2 minutes which softens the skin so that it can be removed easily. Trim the thin skin from the testicles as well.

To keep the combs from discoloring while cooking, simmer them in water with an addition of flour, lemon juice, oil, salt and pepper for 1 hour.

The testicles can be gently poached for 10 minutes or sautéed in clarified butter.

The Veal Quenelles

Make the veal quenelles following the instructions in Chapter 2. Poach them for 5-10 minutes in full-flavored veal stock that is simmering but never boiling. Drain them on a hand towel.

The Mushrooms

Trim the sandy stem of the mushrooms and wash in a large basin of cold water, changing the water several times to remove all the sand and dirt. Drain them and sprinkle with lemon juice.

To keep them firm and white, bring the water, butter, lemon juice, salt and pepper to a boil and add the mushrooms to this liquid. Cover the pot and cook over high heat for 3-5 minutes. Reserve the liquid for the sauce.

Preparing the Filling

Cut the sausage-shaped quenelles into 1cm (3/8in) slices. Cut the mushrooms, sweetbreads, cock's combs and testicles into small pieces.

Blanch the olives to draw out a little salt and cut them in half and remove the pit.

Making the Sauce

Melt the butter, whisk in the flour and cook the roux until it is light brown. Add the full-flavored veal stock and bring the sauce to a boil, whisking constantly.

Pour in the mushroom juice, braising liquid and truffle juice if using. Bring back to a boil, whisking constantly. Reduce until it thickens and coats a spoon. Whisk in the pieces of cold butter to add body and flavor to the sauce.

Taste and season with salt and pepper if necessary. Pour the finished sauce through a conical sieve onto the prepared filling ingredients.

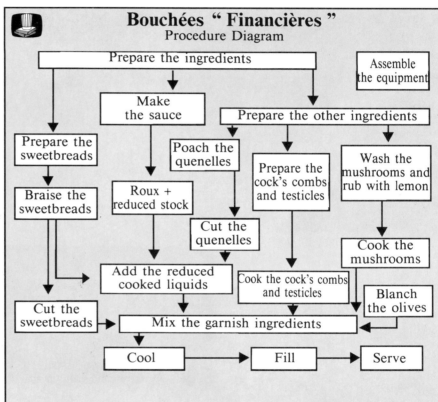

Bouchées " Financières "
Procedure Diagram

```
Prepare the ingredients                          Assemble
                                                 the equipment

            Make                      Prepare the other ingredients
         the sauce

Prepare the          Poach the        Prepare the        Wash the
sweetbreads          quenelles        cock's combs       mushrooms and
                                      and testicles      rub with lemon

Braise the           Roux +
sweetbreads          reduced stock                       Cook the
                                      Cut the             mushrooms
                                      quenelles

                     Add the reduced              Cook the cock's combs    Blanch
Cut the              cooked liquids               and testicles            the olives
sweetbreads

                     Mix the garnish ingredients

            Cool              Fill              Serve
```

Cool the mixture in a stainless steel hotel pan.

Assembly and Serving

Spoon the cooled filling into the baked bouchées, counting on about 110g (4oz) of filling for a pastry case that weighs about 45g (1 1/2oz).

Reheat in a medium oven so that it slowly warms throughout and serve immediately.

Mushroom Bouchées

Introduction

These bouchées are quick and easy to prepare. The food cost is low and they can be made in any season. In addition, the delicious taste of mushrooms marries well with meat or fish so that these bouchées could be part of any menu.

It is very important to choose firm, white mushrooms. It is recommended to cook them soon after they are purchased when their taste and appearance are fresh.

To keep them from darkening, sprinkle them with lemon juice before they are sliced and add lemon juice to the cooking liquid as well. However, just add enough to keep them white without overwhelming the sauce with lemon.

For the caterer who wishes to add bouchées to his repertoire, this simple recipe is a good place to start.

Equipment

Cutting board, mixing bowls, small bowls, plates, large saucepan with lid, sauté pan, paring knife, thin-bladed flexible knife, chef's knife, whisk, spatula, measuring cup, fine-meshed conical sieve, pastry scraper, colander

Ingredients

500g (1lb) mushrooms
1/4L (1 cup) water
45g (1 1/2oz) butter
Juice of 1/2 lemon
Salt and pepper

Sauce

Roux made from 45g (1 1/2oz) butter + 45g (1 1/2oz flour), 4dl (1 2/3 cup) mushrooms cooking liquid, 2dl (3/4 cup) light stock, 1dl (1/2 cup) port, 3 egg yolks 2dl (3/4 cup) heavy cream, 30g (1oz) parsley, salt, pepper

Procedure

The Mushrooms

Trim the sandy stem of the mushrooms and wash them in a

large basin of cold water, changing the water several times to remove all sand and dirt. Drain and sprinkle with lemon juice.

To keep them firm and white, bring the water, butter, lemon juice, salt and pepper to a boil and add the mushrooms to this liquid. Cover the pot and cook over high heat for 3-5 minutes. Reserve the liquid for the sauce.

The Sauce

Melt the butter, whisk in the flour and cook the roux until it is light brown. Pour the mushroom juice into the roux, whisking constantly. (If there is not enough mushroom juice, add veal stock.)

Add the port and simmer the sauce to thicken it.

Blend together the egg yolk and cream and off the heat, whisk into the hot sauce. Return to low heat and stir the sauce as it thickens slightly; do not let the sauce boil, which would curdle the yolks. Taste and season if necessary.

Pour the sauce through a conical sieve onto the cooked mushrooms, add the chopped parsley and cool in a stainless steel hotel pan.

The sauce will keep for 2 days in the refrigerator.

Assembly and Serving

Spoon the cooled filling into the baked bouchées and reheat slowly in a warm oven to warm them throughout without drying them out.

Seafood Bouchées

Introduction

These bouchées can be made with whatever seafood is freshest; the sauce will go with any combination of fish and shellfish.

The least expensive choices include mussels and shrimp. Scallops and monkfish would be very good if available, and the salmon quenelles in Chapter 2 would be a nice addition as well.

It is important to remember that seafood is naturally salty, therefore the seasoning should be added with care so that when the sauce is reduced it is not too salty.

The pastry bouchées can be shaped to resemble fish or scallop shells to coordinate with the filling.

Equipment

Cutting board, mixing bowls, small bowls, plates, paring knife, thin-bladed flexible knife, chef's knife, mixing bowl, measuring cup, fine-meshed conical sieve, large saucepan with lid, colander, whisk, spatula, sauté pans, spoon, fork, ladle, skimmer, pastry scraper

Ingredients

Mushrooms

300g (10oz) mushrooms
1.5dl (2/3 cup) water
15g (1/2oz) butter
Juice from 1/4 lemon
Salt, pepper

Mussels " Marinières "

1kg (2lb) mussels
30g (1oz) clarified butter
45g (1 1/2oz) onions
45g (1 1/2oz) shallots
1.5cl (2/3 cup) dry white wine
Pepper
Bouquet garni (parsley stems, thyme, bay leaf)

Scallops and Monkfish

10 scallops, with their coral
300g (10oz) monkfish filets
15g (1/2oz) clarified butter
45g (1 1/2oz) shallots
45g (1 1/2oz) mushrooms
Bouquet garni (chervil, thyme, bay leaf)
1dl (1/2 cup) dry white wine
1dl (1/2 up) white vermouth 1/2L (2 cups) fish stock
Salt and pepper

200g (7oz) shrimp

Sauce

Roux made from 100g (3 1/2oz) butter + 100g (3 1/2oz) flour
1/2L (2 cups) fish stock
2dl (3/4 cup) scallop and monkfish poaching liquid
2dl (3/4 cup) mussel cooking liquid
1dl (1/2 cup) mushroom cooking liquid
Liaison (4 egg yolks + 2dl (3/4 cup) heavy cream)
Salt and pepper

Procedure

The Mushrooms

Follow the directions for preparing the mushrooms in the previous recipe.

The Seafood

The Shrimp

If using raw shrimp, plunge them into boiling salted water and cook for a few minutes. Plunge them

into ice water to stop the cooking. Remove the shells.

The Mussels

Scrape the shells to remove seaweed and barnacles. Rinse in a large basin of cold water, changing the water several times to remove all the sand.

Cut the onions and shallots into fine dice and sauté them in clarified butter without browning. Add the mussels, the bouquet garni and a little white wine.

Cover the pot and cook over high heat until the shells open. Transfer the mussels to a stainless steel hotel pan to cool and reserve the cooking liquid.

The Monkfish

Prepare the " nage "--a full flavored poaching liquid that the fish " swims " in as it cooks. Cook the chopped shallots and mushrooms stems in clarified butter without browning. Add the chervil, thyme, bay leaf, white wine and vermouth and reduce by half. Add the fish stock and cool. Add the filet of monkfish to cold poaching liquid and bring slowly to a simmer and cook about 5-10 minutes until the fish is firm to the touch. Cool in the liquid.

The Scallops

The scallops are simply added to hot fish stock off the heat and left in the liquid until cool.

Preparing the Filling

Ideally, all the ingredients are cut so that they are about the same size. (In this case, about the size of a mussel) Cut the scallops in two or three slices depending on the size. Cut the shrimp in half if necessary. Cut the mushrooms in small pieces. Remove the mussels from the shells and pull off the dark rim or " beard " around each one.

Making the Sauce

Melt the butter, whisk in the flour and cook the roux until it browns a little. Pour in the fish stock, whisking constantly, bring to a boil and skim any impurities that rise to the surface in the form of a foam.

Using a conical sieve to strain, add the cooking liquids from the fish and mushrooms. Simmer the sauce, skimming if necessary.

Stir the egg yolk and cream together and whisk into the hot sauce off the heat. Return to low heat and simmer very gently to thicken the sauce slightly without overcooking the egg. Taste and season if necessary.

Pour the sauce through a fine-meshed conical sieve over the filling ingredients and cool in a stainless steel hotel pan.

Assembly and Serving

Follow the instructions in the previous recipe.

147

Bouchées with Filets of Sole

Introduction

These bouchées are made with a delicate combination of sole and crayfish paired with a classic Nantua sauce.

The presentation in fish-shaped bouchées with bright crayfish shells as decoration is sure to please customers.

Other fish can used if the sole is not available or too expensive. Brill and flounder are also fine-fleshed fish and are also expensive. For more reasonably priced bouchées, whiting or other mild white fish could be used.

Equipment

Cutting board, mixing bowls, small bowls, plates, paring knife, thin-bladed flexible knife, large saucepan with lid, sauté pans, measuring cup, colander, fine-meshed conical sieve, ladle, skimmer, spoon, fork, pastry scraper, whisk, spatula

Ingredients

The Mushrooms

200g (7oz) mushrooms
1dl (1/2 cup) water
15g (1/2oz) butter
Juice from 1/8 lemon
Salt and pepper

Crayfish

18 crayfish
4cl (1 2/3 cups) olive oil

Filets of Sole

3 filets of sole (75g (2 1/2oz) each)
15g (1/2oz) clarified butter, 15g (1/2oz) shallots, 30g (1oz) mushrooms, 1 bouquet garni (chervil, thyme, bay leaf), 5cl (1/4 cup) dry white wine, 5cl (1/4 cup) white vermouth, 1/4L (1 cup) fish stock, salt and pepper

Sauce

Roux made from 45g (1 1/2oz) butter + 45g (1 1/2oz) flour
1.5dl (2/3 cup) fish stock
1.5dl (2/3 cup) mushroom cooking liquid
1dl (1/2 cup) reduced " Américaine " sauce
8cl (1/3 cup) heavy cream
Salt, cayenne pepper
1cl (2 tsp) cognac
15g (1/2oz) shellfish butter (for the sauce)

Procedure

The Mushrooms

Follow the instructions described in this chapter.

The Sole

Prepare a " nage " (" nager " means " to swim " in French), which is flavored cooking liquid that the fish " swim " in as they poach. Cook the chopped shallots and mushroom stems in clarified butter without browning. Add the chervil, thyme and bay leaf, wine and vermouth and reduce by half. Add the fish stock, season and cool. Add the filets of sole to the cool liquid and poach gently for about 3 minutes. Cool in the liquid.

Drain the filets on a hand towel, then cut into small slices. Strain the poaching liquid and reserve for the sauce.

The Crayfish

If using fresh crayfish, it is necessary to pull out the intestine which will impart a bad flavor during cooking. To do this, hold the crayfish flat against the work surface so that it cannot move, firmly grasp the center tail fin, twist and pull out the vein-like intestine.

Sauté the crayfish in olive oil with a little salt, until they turn bright red.

While still warm, remove the shells without damaging the tail meat. The shells can be used to make a sauce, flavored butter or as a colorful decoration.

Add the poaching liquid and the mushroom cooking liquid, bring to a boil and skim impurities that rise

to the surface. Reduce to thicken slightly until the sauce coats a spoon. Season with salt and a little cayenne pepper.

Whisk in the cream and crayfish butter and pass the sauce through a fine-meshed conical sieve.

Assembly and Serving

Heat all the elements separately. Pour a little sauce in the bottom of the bouchées.

Place a layer of cooked mushrooms in the bottom, then arrange the sole and crayfish on top. Pour sauce over the top and serve.

Making the Sauce

Melt the butter, whisk in the flour and cook the roux until it is light brown. Add the fish stock and reduced " Américaine " Sauce and simmer the sauce, whisking constantly.

Filled Crêpes and Soufflé Crêpes

Introduction

Crêpes are a versatile wrapper for a wide range of ingredients that can rotate with the seasons and provide the customer with an ever-changing choice of flavors and prices.

An array of sauces complements the taste of the fillings and makes them rich and moist. The crêpes themselves can be personalized with an addition of herbs or other flavorings. Some fillings can be made even more elegant with an addition of beaten egg whites, which transforms a sauce or purée into a delicate soufflé which puffs as it cooks to open the folded crêpe.

The crêpes and the fillings can be made in advance in sizeable quantities so that large orders and last-minute requests can be accommodated easily and quickly.

The filled crêpes can be sold in a specialty food shop with the sauce packaged separately to be reheated at home by the customer.

Crêpes Filled with Mussels and Spinach

Introduction

A fine dice (mirepoix) of sautéed vegetables added to the batter makes crêpes that are delicious and original.

The cooked crêpes are filled with sautéed spinach and steamed mussels.

They are accompanied by a sauce made with the cooking juice from the mussels combined with cream and accented with chopped chives.

In addition to being easy to prepare, these crêpes are not expensive to make.

Equipment

Cutting board, mixing bowls, crêpe pan, large saucepans with lids, sauté pans with lids, colander, fine-meshed conical sieve, measuring cup, plates, platter, whisk, palette knife, chef's knife, paring knife, skimmer, ladle, spatula, 2-pronged fork, tablespoon, fork

Ingredients

Crêpe Batter

60g (2oz) flour
1 egg
1.5dl (2/3 cup) milk
20g (2/3oz) melted butter
Salt, pepper

Spinach

30g (1oz) clarified butter
400g (14oz) spinach
Salt, pepper, nutmeg

Vegetable Mirepoix

10g (1/3oz) clarified butter
60g (2oz) carrots
45g (1 1/2oz) mushrooms
45g (1 1/2oz) leeks, white part only
Salt, pepper

Mussels " Marinières "

20g (2/3oz) clarified butter
30g (1oz) chopped onions
15g (1/2oz) chopped shallots
500g (1lb) mussels
1 small bouquet garni (thyme, bay leaf, parsley)
5cl (1/4 cup) white wine
1dl (1/2 cup) heavy cream
Pepper

Cream Sauce

1/4L (1 cup) mussel cooking liquid
2dl (3/4 cup) heavy cream
45g (1 1/2oz) roux
8 sprigs chives
Salt, pepper, saffron

Procedure

Make a classic crêpe batter by whisking eggs, milk and melted butter into the sifted flour, seasoning with salt and pepper, then passing the batter through a fine-meshed conical sieve.

Preparing the Vegetable Mirepoix

Cut the colorful vegetables into very small dice. Melt the butter, add the vegetables, cover the pot and cook over medium heat until tender. Season with salt and pepper; cool.

Stir these vegetables into the crêpe batter.

Cooking the Crêpes

Use a seasoned crêpe pan or non-stick pan to cook the crêpes. Use just enough batter to cover the bottom of the pan and brown both sides without overcooking.

Stack them on a plate and cover with plastic wrap.

Preparing the Filling

Pull the stem from each leaf of spinach and wash them in a large basin of cold water, changing the water several times to rinse away all sand and dirt.

Melt the clarified butter, add the spinach, cover and cook over high heat to draw out the moisture in the spinach.

Remove the cover and cook to evaporate the liquid. Season with salt and pepper.

The Mussels

Scrape the shells of the mussels to remove seaweed and barnacles.

Melt the clarified butter and sauté the chopped shallots without

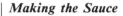

browning them. Add the bouquet garni, white wine and cream. Season with pepper, cover and cook over high heat until the mussels open.

Reserve the cooking liquid for the sauce. Remove the mussels from the shells, and pull off the dark rim or "beard" around the edge of each mussel.

Making the Sauce

Strain the mussel juice through cheesecloth if there is any sand in the bottom of the pot.

Reduce the cooking liquid from the mussels a little.

Pour in the cream and bring to a boil, whisking constantly.

Stir in the cooked roux to obtain a velvety sauce and simmer for a few minutes.

Season to taste with pepper and a pinch of saffron. The sauce will be naturally salty because of the mussel juice.

Assembly

Lightly butter the serving dish and place the crêpes in the middle.

Place some cooked spinach down the center and place a few mussels on top of the spinach.

Spoon a little sauce over the mussels, fold over the edges of the crêpe and gently turn it over so the seam is on the bottom.

Serving

Brush the surface of the crêpe with melted butter and warm the filled crêpe in a medium oven, without drying it out.

Surround the warm crêpes with heated sauce, sprinkle chopped chives over the surface of the sauce and serve immediately.

Alternatively, the filling, crêpes and sauce can be kept warm, separately and filled to order for service in a restaurant.

For sale in a specialty food shop, fill the crêpes, cover with plastic wrap and sell the sauce separately in small containers.

Crêpes with Wild Mushrooms and Breast of Guinea Hen

Introduction

This combination of wild mushrooms and guinea hen is a delicious dish to offer in the fall, when fresh wild mushrooms are most plentiful.

The assertive taste of the guinea hen marries well with the woodsy flavor of the mushrooms.

If guinea hen is not available, substitute other poultry such as pheasant, duck or chicken.

This is an expensive dish to make, given the high price of game birds and wild mushrooms, but highly appreciated by customers who enjoy new and different combinations.

Equipment

Cutting board, mixing bowls, plates, small bowls, colander, measuring cup, sauté pans with lids, crêpe pan, skimmer, ladle, whisk, spatula, pastry scraper, paring knife, chef's knife, palette knife, pastry brush, tablespoon, fork

Ingredients

The Crêpe Batter

60g (2oz) flour
1 egg
1.5dl (2/3 cup) milk
20g (2/3oz) melted butter
Salt, pepper
10g (1/3oz) chopped fresh herbs (chervil, tarragon, chives)

Filling

160g (5oz) guinea hen filets

Mushroom Filling

10g (1/3oz) clarified butter
15g (1/2oz) shallots
1 clove garlic, salt, pepper
45g (1 1/2oz) horn of plenty
45g (1 1/2oz) chanterelles
45g (1 1/2oz) oyster mushrooms
45g (1 1/2oz) cèpes

Brown Sauce

2cl (4tsp) white wine
5cl (1/4 cup) madeira
4dl (1 2/3 cups) reduced veal stock
30g (1oz) butter
Salt, pepper

Procedure

Making the Crêpes

Make a classic crêpe batter by whisking eggs, milk and melted butter into the sifted flour, seasoning with salt and pepper, then passing the batter through a fine-meshed conical sieve.

Stir the chopped herbs into the batter.

Cooking the Crêpes

Use a seasoned crêpe pan or non-stick pan to cook the crêpes. Use

just enough batter to cover the bottom of the pan and brown both sides without overcooking.

Stack them on a plate and cover with plastic wrap.

Preparing the Filling

The Mushrooms

Prepare each type of mushroom separately.

Trim the stems of the mushrooms and wash them in a large basin of cold water, changing the water several times to remove all sand and dirt.

Drain them, slice the white mushrooms and cut the others into pieces if necessary.

Melt the clarified butter. Sauté each mushroom separately with some of the chopped shallots and garlic. Season with salt and pepper and remove from the pan with a slotted spoon.

Reserve the pan with the cooking liquid to make the sauce.

Preparing the Guinea Hen

For maximum flavor and moistness, roast the guinea hen in the oven, taking care not to dry it out.

Cut away the breast meat and remove the skin. (For this recipe, only the breast meat is used, but the cooked meat from the legs could also be used.) Cut the meat into small cubes or strips.

Making the Sauce

Deglaze the pan used to sauté the mushrooms with white wine and madeira.

Reduce by half and add the reduced full-flavored stock and reduce by half.

If meat juices have adhered to the sides of the pan, deglaze with a pastry brush dipped in water.

Whisk pieces of cold butter into the sauce to make it rich and give it body. Pass through a fine-meshed conical sieve. Season to taste with salt and pepper.

Assembly

Lightly butter the serving dish and place a crêpe in the middle. Spoon some mushrooms down the center and place the pieces of meat on top.

Spoon a little sauce over these ingredients and fold over the edges of the crêpe; gently turn it over so the seam is on the bottom.

Serving

Brush the surface of the crêpe with melted butter and warm the filled crêpe in a medium oven, without drying it out.

Surround the warm crêpes with heated sauce and serve immediately.

Crêpes with Belgian Endive and Ham

Introduction

This classic filling of endive and ham is very easy to make.

Belgian endives are usually most plentiful and of better quality in the winter months, which is the best time to offer this crêpe. Choose endives that are white and tightly closed.

Grated cheese marries well with the endive and ham adds flavor and moistness.

These tasty ingredients are rolled inside a crêpe made with chopped sautéed mushrooms.

The food cost is not high, allowing the caterer to offer a delicious dish to customers for a reasonable price.

Equipment

Cutting board, measuring cup, plates, small bowls, pastry scraper, palette knife, paring knife, chef's knife, mixing bowls, whisk, ladle, spatula, fine-meshed conical sieve, frying pan, crêpe pan, sauté pan, tablespoon, fork

Ingredients

The Crêpes

60g (2oz) flour
1 egg 1.5dl (2/3 cup) milk
20g (2/3oz) melted butter
Salt, pepper

Filling

150g (5oz) boiled ham
30g (1oz) grated swiss cheese

The Mushroom Duxelle

15g (1/2oz) clarified butter
20g (2/3oz) shallots
100g (3 1/2oz) mushrooms
Few drops lemon juice
Salt, pepper

The Endives

20g (2/3oz) clarified butter 250g (1/2lb) endives Few drops lemon juice
Salt, pepper, sugar

Sauce

3dl (1 1/4 cups) heavy cream
6 sprigs chives

Procedure

Making the Crêpes

Make a classic crêpe batter by whisking eggs, milk and melted butter into the sifted flour, season with salt and pepper, then passing the batter through a fine-meshed conical sieve.

Making the Mushroom Duxelles

Select white firm mushrooms for the most attractive duxelles. Chop them very finely.

Cut the shallots into fine dice and cook them in clarified butter until soft but not brown.

Add the chopped mushrooms with a few drops of lemon. Season with salt and pepper.

Cook covered at first to draw out the water from the mushrooms, then continue cooking uncovered until the mixture is very dry. Leave to cool.

When cool, add the mushroom duxelles to the crêpe batter and whisk to combine.

Preparing the Fillings

Julienne of Ham

Use a good quality boiled ham. Trim away any fat, then cut the ham into short julienne strips, about 3-4mm (1/8in) thick.

Grated Cheese

Use a good quality swiss cheese, such as Emmenthaler or Gruyère.

Endives

Wash the endives, discarding

any discolored leaves. Drain them, then cut into thick crosswise slices as shown.

Cook the endive in clarified butter. Season with salt and pepper and a little sugar, which will caramelize and give a lovely golden color.

Remove the endives from the pan and set aside. Reserve the pan to use for making the sauce.

Making the Sauce

Deglaze the pan in which the endives were cooked with the heavy cream.

Season to taste with salt and pepper. Bring to a boil, whisking constantly.

Whisk the butter into the sauce, a little at a time. Pass the sauce

through a fine-meshed conical sieve. Add the chopped chives.

Assembly

Place the crêpe in a lightly but-tered heatproof serving dish. Spoon the endives down the center of the crêpe. Add the julienne of ham and sprinkle with cheese. It is not necessary to add the sauce to the inside, as the cheese will melt and bind the filling ingredients. Fold over the edges of the crêpe; gently turn it over so the seam is on the bottom.

Serving

Brush the surface of the crêpe with melted butter and warm the filled crêpe in a medium oven, without drying it out. Serve with warm sauce.

For sale in a specialty food shop, wrap the crêpes in plastic wrap and package the sauce separately.

Soufflé Crêpes with Cheese

Introduction

The two soufflé crêpe recipes in this section replace the precooked vegetable and meat filling with a soufflé mixture that puffs slightly inside the crêpe " envelope ".

Since these crêpes must be assembled at the last moment, they do not adapt to all methods of sale. They can be served in restaurants or at a catered event where the chef is present to supervise their preparation.

These make an excellent first course or light luncheon dish and the food cost is quite low.

Equipment

Cutting board, plates, small bowls, mixing bowls, measuring cup, frying pan, sauté pan, large saucepan, cheese grater (optional), copper bowl for egg whites, balloon whisk, whisk, baking sheet, chef's knife, paring knife, pastry scraper, spatula, pastry brush, palette knife

Ingredients

Crêpes

60g (2oz) flour
1 egg
1.5dl (2/3 cup) milk
20g (2/3oz) melted butter
Salt, pepper

Soufflé Mixture

Roux (made with 45g (1 1/2oz) butter and 45g (1 1/2oz) flour)
4dl (1 2/3 cups) milk
5 eggs, separated
100g (3 1/2oz) grated swiss cheese
Salt, pepper, nutmeg

To finish:
20g (2/3oz) grated swiss cheese

Sauce

3dl (1 1/4 cup) heavy cream
30g (1oz) butter
20g (2/3oz) truffles (optional)
Salt, pepper, nutmeg

Procedure

Making the Crêpe Batter

Make a classic crêpe batter by whisking eggs, milk and melted butter into the sifted flour, seasoning with salt and pepper, then passing the batter through a fine-meshed conical sieve.

Cooking the Crêpes

Use a seasoned crêpe pan or non-stick pan to cook the crêpes. Use just enough batter to cover the bottom of the pan and brown both sides without overcooking.

Stack them on a plate and cover with plastic wrap.

Making the Soufflé Mixture

The base of this mixture is a classic béchamel sauce.

Melt the butter, add the flour and cook the roux a little. Bring the milk to a boil and pour it into the roux, whisking constantly. Simmer the thick sauce for a few minutes. Season with salt, pepper and nutmeg.

Separate the eggs and incorporate the yolks into the warm sauce and stir until smooth. Mix in the grated cheese and check the seasoning, remembering that the beaten egg whites are quite bland.

Beat the egg whites until stiff peaks are formed.

Whisk a little beaten egg white into the béchamel to lighten it, then transfer the sauce into the egg whites and gently fold the two mixtures together.

Fill the center of each crêpe with soufflé mixture as shown.

Transfer them to the serving dish, sprinkle with grated cheese.

Cooking and Serving

Cook the crêpes in an oven preheated to 220C (425F) for about 15 minutes.

Serve immediately.

NOTE: the crêpes can be accompanied by a light cream sauce made by reducing heavy cream and whisking in cold pieces of butter. Season with salt and pepper and chopped truffles, if available.

With a plastic scraper, scrape down the sides of the bowl so the mixture that adheres does not dry out.

Assembly

Brush the ovenproof serving dish with butter.

Soufflé Crêpes with Crayfish

Introduction

This soufflé crêpe features the delicious taste of crayfish. The base of the soufflé mixture is also a béchamel sauce with an addition of fish-based " Américaine " sauce to reinforce the flavor of the shell-fish.

Crayfish tail meat augments the filling and the bright red shells make a lovely decoration. A cream sauce made with " Américaine " sauce adds color to the presentation as well.

The crayfish are usually expensive, which is reflected in the price of the crêpe.

Equipment

Cutting board, plates, small bowls, mixing bowls, measuring cup, sauté pan, large saucepan, copper bowl for egg whites, balloon whisk, whisk, tablespoon, pastry scraper, spatula, platter, pastry brush, sheet pan

Ingredients

Crêpes

60g (2oz) flour, 1 egg, 1.5dl (2/3 cup) milk, 20g (2/3oz) melted butter
Salt, pepper

Filling

2cl (4tsp) olive oil 20 crayfish
Salt

Sauce

2dl (3/4 cup) " Américaine " sauce
1dl (1/2 cup) heavy cream
Few drops cognac
Salt, pepper, cayenne

Soufflé Mixture

Roux (made with 45g (1 1/2oz) butter and 45g (1 1/2oz) flour)
2dl (3/4 cup) milk
2dl (3/4 cup) " Américaine " sauce, slightly reduced
5 eggs, separated
Salt, pepper, cayenne

Procedure

Making the Crêpes

Make a classic crêpe batter by whisking eggs, milk and melted butter into the sifted flour, seasoning with salt and pepper, then passing the batter through a fine-meshed conical sieve.

Cooking the Crêpes

Use a seasoned crêpe pan or non-stick pan to cook the crêpes. Use just enough batter to cover the bottom of the pan and brown both sides without overcooking.

Stack them on a plate and cover with plastic wrap.

Making the Soufflé Mixture

Melt the butter, add the flour and cook the roux a little. Bring the milk to a boil and pour it into the roux, whisking constantly. Simmer the thick sauce for a few minutes. Season with salt, pepper and nutmeg.

Whisk in the " Américaine " sauce and cook a few more minutes. Separate the eggs and incorporate the yolks into the warm sauce and stir until smooth.

Beat the egg whites until stiff peaks are formed.

Whisk a little beaten egg white into the béchamel to lighten it, then transfer the sauce into the egg whites and gently fold the two mixtures together.

With a plastic scraper, scrape down the sides of the bowl so the

mixture that adheres does not dry out.

Preparing the Crayfish

Deveining

To remove the dark "vein" from the crayfish, pinch the center tail fin and carefully pull it out, pulling the vein along with. Do this before cooking the crayfish to avoid a bitter flavor.

Sautéing the Crayfish

Cook the crayfish in lightly salted olive oil over high heat, shaking and stirrring constantly until they turn bright red. This should take only 1-2 minutes; take care not to overcook them.

Shelling the Crayfish

Remove the tailmeat from the shells while the crayfish are still warm. Set the meat aside and reserve the shells for garnishing the platter.

Making the Sauce

Make a full-flavored "Américaine" sauce and add some heavy cream and a dash of cognac.

Taste and correct seasoning with salt, pepper and cayenne.

Assembly

Brush the ovenproof serving dish with butter.

Using the pastry scraper, put some soufflé mixture on each crêpe. Place the crayfish tails on the soufflé mixture and cover with more mixture.

Fold the crêpes over in half. Transfer the crêpes to the lightly buttered platter and place the crayfish shells around in a decorative manner.

Cooking

Cook the crêpes for about 15 minutes in a 220C (425F) oven, until puffed and brown. Spoon some warm sauce around the crêpes and serve immediately.

Dishes Served in Scallop Shells

Introduction

Scallop shells are natural containers in which to present seafood dishes.

Porcelain ones are available that resemble scallop shells for use in a restaurant. Aluminum shells are also available for take out dishes, but they are not recommended because the thin metal becomes too hot during reheating and foods tend to stick on the bottom.

These convenient individual portions can be made in advance and reheated to order in a restaurant or sold in a specialty food shop for the customer to take home.

These preparations can be served from a chafing dish for a buffet dinner as well.

The final presentation can be augmented with a traditional crescent of puff pastry called a "fleuron" in French, or with duchess potatoes piped around the edge with a star tip.

Another finishing touch is to place the filled shells under the broiler. This is usually done when the potato garnish is used, to make it crisp and pretty. Also lovely is to gratinee the surface of the sauce under the broiler (best accomplished when there is an egg yolk in the sauce) just before serving.

Scallops in Normande Sauce

Introduction

The best cream in France comes from the northern region of Normandy, therefore sauces rich in cream are often called "normande".

Fresh scallops are the star of this dish, which includes shrimp, mushrooms and slices of pike quenelles as well.

Scallops are most plentiful in the winter months and can often be found with their bright orange coral attached. Even though the coral adds a splash of color, the true taste is in the round "nut" of the scallop itself.

If only frozen scallops are available, thaw them slowly in the refrigerator.

Since this is an expensive dish to make, it is important to make a sauce that is flavorful and velvety which makes the most of the expensive ingredients.

For a more modest dish, replace the scallops with slices of firm fleshed white fish.

These elegant dishes are always popular and are often served for special occasions.

Easy to reheat and serve, they are ideal for a fancy dinner.

Equipment

Cutting board, empty scallop shells, small rings, plates, small bowls, mixing bowls, measuring cup, hotel pan, paring knife, thin-bladed flexible knife, sauté pans with lids, spatula, whisk, fine-meshed conical sieve, pastry scraper, spoon, skimmer, ladle, colander

Ingredients

(For 6 shells)

Scallops

9 scallops with coral

Schrimps

150g (5oz) cooked shrimp

Poaching liquid ("nage") for scallops

15g (1/2oz) clarified butter
45g (1 1/2oz) shallots
45g (1 1/2oz) mushrooms (may use trimmings or stems)
1 bouquet garni (1 small bay leaf, 1 sprig thyme, 5 parsley stems)
1dl (1/2 cup) dry white wine
1dl (1/2 cup) white vermouth
1/4L (1 cup) fish stock
Salt, pepper

Quenelles

3 pike quenelles (150g (5oz))
1/4L (1 cup) fish stock
Salt

Mushrooms

150g (5oz) mushrooms
1dl (1/2 cup) water
15g (1/2oz) butter
Salt, pepper
1/2 lemon

The Sauce

45g (1 1/2oz) butter
45g (1 1/2oz) flour
1/2L (2 cups) fish stock
1/4L (1 cup) scallop poaching liquid
5cl (1/4 cup) mushroom cooking liquid
3 egg yolks
1.5dl (2/3 cup) heavy cream
Salt, pepper
45g (1 1/2oz) butter

Decoration

6 fleurons (for decoration)

Procedure

The Shrimp

Remove the shell, then pull out the dark vein that runs the length of each shrimp. Rinse them, drain and cut them in half if necessary so that each piece is bite-size.

The Scallops

Prepare the "nage" ("nager" means "to swim" in French)--a

full-flavored poaching liquid that the fish "swims" in as it cooks. Cook the chopped shallots and mushrooms stems in clarified butter without browning. Add the bouquet garni, white wine and vermouth and reduce by half. Add the fish stock, season to taste with salt and pepper and cool.

In contrast to the poaching of the other fish in this chapter, which starts in cold liquid, the scallops are put directly into the hot nage, taken off the heat and left to cook as the liquid cools.

Drain the scallops on a hand towel and slice them in two, depending on the size. Reduce the poaching liquid by half.

The Mushrooms

Trim the sandy stem of the mushrooms and wash them in a large basin of cold water, changing the water several times to remove all the sand and dirt.

Drain and sprinkle with lemon juice.

To keep them firm and white, bring the water, butter, lemon juice, salt and pepper to a boil and add the mushrooms to this liquid.

Cover the pot and cook over high heat for 3-5 minutes. Remove the mushrooms and drain them, reserving the liquid for the sauce.

Dry on a hand towel and cut the mushrooms into small even pieces and set aside.

The Quenelles

Follow the instruction in Chapter 2 for Pike Quenelles.

Pipe them out in a long "éclair" shape and poach in simmering fish stock.

Drain them on a hand towel, then cut in 1cm (3/8in) slices. Reduce the poaching liquid by half and reserve for making the sauce.

Making the Sauce

Melt the butter, whisk in the flour and cook the roux until light brown.

Add the fish stock, whisking constantly. Add the reduced poaching liquids and the mushroom liquid, bring to a boil and skim off any impurities that rise to the surface.

Simmer the sauce until it thickens and coats a spoon.

Blend the egg yolks and cream and off the heat, whisk them into the hot sauce.

Return to a low heat and cook briefly to thicken.

Pass the sauce through a fine-meshed conical sieve. Season if necessary.

The sauce can be further enriched with butter. Cut the cold butter into small pieces and off the heat, whisk them into the hot sauce.

Assembly

1. Spoon a little sauce into the bottom of each shell.

2. Place two slices of quenelles on the sauce.

3. Cover the quenelles with mushrooms.

4. Place three shrimp on the mushrooms.

5. On top, place three slices of scallop with a coral in the center.

6. Ladle sauce over the ingredients.

7. Decorate with a pastry crescent ("fleuron").

Serving

Reheat at 150C (300F) for about 15 minutes. Serve immediately.

Scallops in "Normande" Sauce
Procedure Diagram

```
Assemble                          Prepare the ingredients
the equipment

                          The scallops        Prepare the
                                              different garnishes
    Make the
    Normande sauce       Make
                         the "nage"    Shell,        Poach,
    Cook the roux                      wash,         drain,
    (butter + flour)     Poach the     drain,        cut the
                         scallops      cut the       quenelles
    Add stock, "nage"                  shrimp
    and cooking liquid   Drain
                                              Trim, wash,
    Cook      Add the    Slice              Cook, with cover,
    the sauce  egg yolk                     Drain and
                                            cut the mushrooms
    Enrich with butter   Fill the shells
                                      Decorate
    Coat with                        with "fleuron"
    sauce              Reheat                Serve
```

165

Monkfish with Duglére Sauce

Introduction

The velvety sauce that is served here with the monkfish was first served with sole by Chef Adolphe Duglére in Paris at the Café Anglais, a famous 19th century restaurant.

The monkfish can be replaced by other fish to take advantage of what is freshest at the market. Therefore this is a dish that can be made year-round.

Duchess potatoes are piped around the edge of the shell to decorate the dish and keep the sauce from running over.

Equipment

Cutting board, small bowls, plates, measuring cup, mixing bowls, colander, casserole, large saucepan with lid, sauté pan with lid, fine-meshed conical sieve, drum sieve, paring knife, thin-bladed flexible knife, pastry bag with star tip, 6 empty shells, 6 small rings, spatula, pastry scraper, tablespoon, skimmer, ladle, hotel pan

Ingredients

(For 6 shells.)

Main Ingredient

250g (1/2lb) monkfish, trimmed and pared (may substitute turbot or sole)

The Mussels

15g (1/2oz) clarified butter
30g (1oz) onions
15g (1/2oz) shallots
1 bouquet garni (thyme, bay leaf, parsley stems)
600g (1 1/4lb) mussels
5dl (2 cups) dry white wine
Pepper

The Mushrooms

15g (1/2oz) clarified butter
200g (7oz) mushrooms
1/2 lemon
Salt, pepper

The Sauce

650g (1lb 5oz) tomatoes
5cl (1/4 cup) olive oil
45g (1 1/2oz) onions
45g (1 1/2oz) shallots
30g (1oz) garlic
1 bouquet garni (thyme, bay leaf, parsley stems, leek green)
1dl (1/2 cup) fish stock
2dl (3/4 cup) heavy cream
Salt, pepper

The Duchess Potatoes

500g (1lb) potatoes
45g (1 1/2oz) butter
1/2 egg
2 yolks
Salt, pepper, nutmeg

Procedure

The Mushrooms

Trim the sandy stem of the mushrooms and wash them in a large basin of cold water, changing the water several times to remove all the sand and dirt.

Drain and sprinkle with lemon juice.

Trim the thin skin from the monkfish and cut in 1cm (3/8in) slices.

The monkfish will be poached in the sauce.

Making the Sauce

To keep them firm and white, bring the water, butter, lemon juice, salt and pepper to a boil and add the mushrooms to this liquid.

Cover the pot and cook over high heat for 3-5 minutes.

Remove the mushrooms and drain them.

The Mussels

Scrape the shells of the mussels to remove seaweed and barnacles. Rinse them in a large basin of cold water, changing the water several times to remove all the sand.

Peel the onions and shallots and cut into fine dice and cook in clarified butter without browning.

Add the mussels, bouquet garni and white wine and season with pepper.

Cover the pot and cook over high heat until the shells open.

They will cook very quickly and will become dry and chewy if cooked too long.

Drain and remove the shells. Pull off the dark rim or " beard " around the edge of each mussel.

Reserve the cooking liquid for the sauce.

The Monkfish

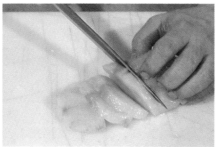

Cut out the stem end of the tomatoes and slit the skin on the other end. Plunge them in boiling water for a few seconds to loosen the skin. Drain, pull off the skin and cut the tomato in half.

Squeeze out the seeds and cut in small dice.

Peel the shallots and onions and cut into fine dice.

Peel the garlic, remove the green sprout, crush with the side of a chef's knife and chop finely.

Cook the shallots, onions and garlic in the olive oil until soft but not brown.

Reduce the sauce over high heat.

Pour in the cream and reduce again to thicken.

Whisk in enough cooked roux to achieve a velvety sauce that will coat the spoon.

Season with salt and pepper and set aside to cool.

The Duchess Potatoes

Peel the potatoes, rinse and drain them.

Place them in a pot of cold lightly salted water, bring to a boil and cook until tender. Drain the cooked potatoes, spread them on a baking sheet and dry them out a little in a low oven.

Add the diced tomatoes and bouquet garni. Cover and cook for a few minutes.

Add the cooking juice from the mussels and let cool.

Place the slices of monkfish in

the cooled sauce and poach gently over low heat.

Remove with a slotted spoon and drain the poached monkfish on a hand towel.

Purée the potatoes by passing them through a sieve with a pastry scraper. Scrape the underside of the sieve to recover all the purée, put it in a pot and dry it out a little more on the stove, stirring constantly.

Off the heat, stir in a little butter to loosen the purée, beat in the egg yolks and whole eggs. Season to taste with salt, pepper and nutmeg.

Assembly

Pour a little sauce in the bottom of each shell as shown. Add a few mushrooms and place three mussels on top. Finish with three slices of monkfish.

Cover these ingredients with the sauce to the rim of the shell. Pipe a decorative border of duchess potatoes using a pastry bag fitted with a medium star tip.

Storage

Once assembled, these preparations will keep one day in the refrigerator, covered with plastic wrap. (It is recommended to add the potato decoration just before serving.)

Serving

Reheat at 150C (300F) for about 15 minutes. (Use the small rings to hold the shells.) Serve immediately.

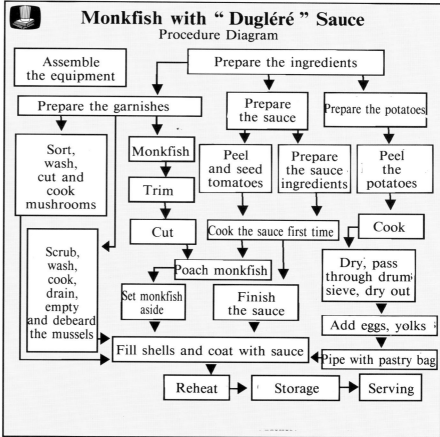

Monkfish with " Dugléré " Sauce
Procedure Diagram

Assemble the equipment

Prepare the ingredients

Prepare the garnishes

Prepare the sauce

Prepare the potatoes

Sort, wash, cut and cook mushrooms

Monkfish → Trim → Cut

Peel and seed tomatoes

Prepare the sauce ingredients

Peel the potatoes

Scrub, wash, cook, drain, empty and debeard the mussels

Cook the sauce first time

Cook

Poach monkfish

Set monkfish aside

Finish the sauce

Dry, pass through drum sieve, dry out

Add eggs, yolks

Fill shells and coat with sauce

Pipe with pastry bag

Reheat → Storage → Serving

Shellfish with Flavored Butters

Introduction

The small shells of clams, mussels and snails are perfect for holding single bites of these seafoods in hot savory butters.

The natural containers make advance preparation easier and facilitate sale in a specialty food shop.

If the actual shells are not available, bite-size variations of these three preparations can be made in tiny bouchées or tartelette shells. Special plates, with indentations to hold the sauce, and porcelain " shells " are available for service in a restaurant.

If customers are going to reheat these at home, they should be advised to warm them slowly and not let the butter boil which would separate the butter and ruin the dish.

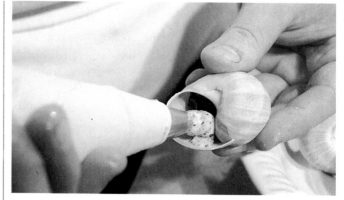

Snails in Garlic Butter

Introduction

Different kinds of snails are available on the market from all over the world. In France the best variety is the " Bourgogne " which has a creamy white shell and is large and meaty. They are highly regarded in France and are ideal for use in this recipe.

The butter for these dishes is garlicky and full of fresh parsley. A hint of anise-flavored liquor accents all the flavors.

Equipment

Cutting board, plates, small bowls, mixing bowls, chef's knife, paring knife, spatula, snail plate, pastry bag and tip, pastry scraper, colander

Ingredients

(For butter to fill 2 dozen large snails)

250g (1/2lb) butter
30g (1oz) flat parsley
15g (1/2oz) garlic
15g (1/2oz) shallots
Salt, pepper, nutmeg
Few drop anise-flavored liquor

Procedure

Preparing the Snails

If using fresh snails it is necessary to starve them so they will eliminate any toxins in their digestive system. The plants they have eaten may not hurt them, but could make a human sick.

Next, degorge the snails in coarse salt and a little vinegar for 2-3 hours. Rinse them in several changes of cold water.

Blanch the degorged snails in boiling water for 5 minutes, plunge them into ice water to stop the cooking, then drain.

Pull the blanched snails from the shells and trim each one thoroughly to remove unsightly black bits.

To cook them, cover with equal quantities of white wine and stock. Add diced vegetables (carrots, onions, shallots) and a bouquet garni. Season with salt and pepper and simmer gently for about 3 hours, until tender. Add a little stock if necessary to keep the snails covered while cooking.

To clean the shells, boil them for 1/2 hour in a solution of water and bleach. Rinse them thoroughly, then finish the cleaning process by scrubbing them inside and out with a small brush. Dry them in a low oven.

NOTE: If using canned snails, purchase the best quality available, and drain them before using. Clean shells are also available.

Making the Garlic Butter

Let the butter soften at room temperature, then stir until creamy without incorporating air.

Pluck the leaves from the parsley, wash in cold water and squeeze dry in a hand towel. Chop finely with a chef's knife.

Peel the garlic, remove the green sprout in the center which is bitter, crush with the side of a chef's knife, then chop finely.

Peel the shallots and cut into very fine dice.

Stir these ingredients into the butter. Season with salt, pepper, a little nutmeg and a few drops of anise-flavored liquor (Pastis).

Assembly

Using a pastry bag fitted with a small plain tip, pipe a little garlic butter into the bottom of the shell. Press the snail into the hollow of the shell (do not "bury" the snail too deep or it will be difficult for the customer to retrieve).

Pipe in more butter to the rim of the shell and smooth the surface with a small knife.

Storage

Once assembled, the snails keep for 48 hours in the refrigerator.

Serving

Warm the snails in a low oven to heat the snails through and to melt the butter without boiling it, which would cause the butter to separate from the delicious seasonings. Serve immediately.

Mussels with Garlic Butter

Introduction

Choose the largest, freshest mussels available. Tightly shut shells are an indication of freshness; when tapped, the shells should not sound empty.

The shells should be carefully scraped to remove the seaweed and barnacles that are often attached. To flush out the sand inside and wash the exterior of the shells, soak them briefly in a large basin of cold water, changing the water several times to remove all the sand and impurities.

The garlic butter for this dish includes chopped dill and the reduced cooking juices from the mussels.

Mussels are usually available year-round so this reasonably-priced dish can be served any-time.

Equipment

Cutting board, plates, small bowls, mixing bowls, colander, measuring cup, paring knife, chef's knife, pastry scraper, pastry bag with plain tip, sauté pan with lid, saucepan, spatula, spoon, cooling rack.

Ingredients

The Mussels

2 dozen large mussels, 30g (1oz) clarified butter, 45g (1 1/2oz) shallots, 30g (1oz) onions, 1 bouquet garni, 1dl (1/2 cup) white wine, 5cl (1/4 cup) heavy cream, pepper

Flavored Butter

200g (7oz) butter
5cl (1/4 cup) reduced cooking
 liquid
15g (1/2oz) chopped flat parsley
45g (1 1/2oz) chopped dill
15g (1/2oz) shallots
15g (1/2oz) garlic
Pepper

Dry bread crumbs, to finish

Procedure

The Mussels

Scrape the shells and rinse in several changes of cold water. Discard any mussels that do not close when you squeeze the shell.

Steam open the mussels "à la marinière". Sauté the chopped shallots and onions in clarified butter, add the bouquet garni and the mussels.

Add the white wine and cream. Season with pepper but no salt because the mussels are naturally salty.

Cover the pot and cook over high heat just long enough to open the shells.

The mussels will cook again in the oven, so they must not be cooked too much at this stage. Transfer them immediately from the hot liquid to cool. Reserve the liquid for the butter.

Remove the mussels from the shells and pull off the dark rim or " beard " around each one.

Rinse the shells thoroughly. Set aside the half with the deeper hollow to serve the prepared mussels.

Making the Garlic Butter

Reduce the cooking liquid from the mussels. (Reduce 1.5dl (2/3 cup) to 5cl (1/4 cup).) Set aside to cool.

Pluck the leaves from the parsley and dill, rinse, squeeze dry and chop finely.

Peel the garlic, remove the green sprout in the center that is bitter, crush with the side of chef's knife and chop finely. Peel the shallots and cut into very fine dice.

Soften the butter at room temperature, stir until creamy, then incorporate the flavorings without beating in too much air.

Taste and season with pepper.

Assembly

Pipe a little butter in the bottom of each shell using a pastry bag fitted with a small tip. Press a mussel into the butter. Pipe in more butter to the rim of the shell and smooth the surface with a small knife. Cover the top with dried breadcrumbs.

Storage

The assembled mussels keep for 48 hours in the refrigerator.

Serving

Reheat in a low oven so the mussels are warm and the butter does not separate. The mussels, in their flat shells, reheat more quickly than the snails.

Clams with Garlic Butter

Introduction

The garlic butter for the clams is personalized with the addition of chopped walnuts and a few drops of vermouth.

Like the mussels, they are steamed just long enough to open the shells so they do not become too tough when cooked again in the oven.

Equipment

Cutting board, plates, small bowls, mixing bowls, colander, measuring cup, paring knife, chef's knife, pastry scraper, pastry bag and tip, sauté pan with lid

Ingredients

The Clams

2 dozen clams
30g (1oz) clarified butter
1dl (1/2 cup) white wine
Pepper

Flavored Butter

200g (7oz) butter
5cl (1/4 cup) heavy cream
30g (1oz) chopped flat parsley
20g (2/3oz) garlic
45g (1 1/2oz) chopped walnuts
1cl (2tsp) white vermouth
Salt and pepper

Procedure

The Clams

Brush the outside of the shells to clean them and rinse the clams in a large basin of cold water, changing the water several times to remove all the sand inside the shells.

Melt the butter, add the clams and white wine and season with pepper. Cover the pot and cook over high heat just long enough to open the shells.

The cooking time will be a little longer than the mussels because the shells are thicker and like the mussels, they must not be overcooked at this stage because they will be reheated later.

Transfer immediately and cool a little. Remove the clams from the shells, using a small knife to detach them. They do not need to be " debearded ".

Reserve the liquid for another seafood dish, choose the nicest, deepest shells and rinse and dry them.

Making the Garlic Butter

Soften the butter at room temperature and stir until creamy.

Pluck the leaves from the parsley, rinse, squeeze dry in a hand towel and chop finely.

Peel the garlic and remove the bitter green sprout from the center. Crush with side of a chef's knife and chop finely.

Chop the walnuts finely and stir all these ingredients into the butter without incorporating too much air. Add the vermouth and season with salt and pepper.

If the butter is too stiff (the walnuts may absorb liquid), stir in a little cream so the mixture is loose enough to pipe.

Assembly

Pipe a little butter in the bottom of each shell with a pastry bag fitted with a small tip.

Press the clams into the butter, pipe more butter on top and cover with dried breadcrumbs.

Storage

The assembled clams keep for 48 hours in the refrigerator.

Serving

Reheat in a low oven to warm the clams without boiling the butter. Serve immediately.

Chapter 6
Mixed Salads

Freshness and Variety

Salads are more popular than ever and have become an important item for the professional caterer.

The possibilities are endless, combining the best ingredients in each season to offer the customers an ever-changing selection.

It is important to consider taste and color when marrying different greens, meats and vegetables to make these exciting mixed salads.

General Advice

The six key points about salads

Different Methods of Sale

Mixed salads adapt to many methods of sale, and it is important to consider how the salad will be served when it is prepared. For example, ingredients that soften quickly will not last well enough in the refrigerated case of a specialty food shop.

In some cases, the ingredients can be prepared in advance, stored separately in covered containers and the salad can be assembled to order.

Mixed salads brighten the selection in a specialty food shop and customers enjoy a rotating selection that allows them to try different taste combinations.

The salads can be pre-portioned in small disposable containers or natural bowls like a grapefruit or avocado shell.

They are also lovely arranged in a larger salad bowl, decorated with nicely shaped elements of the salad, then weighed out freshly to order. They are always sold by weight. (It is wise to supply disposable forks to customers who are planning to eat the salads in the office.)

For a dinner buffet, they add a fresh note to a selection including terrines, fish in aspic and meat dishes.

In a restaurant, the ingredients can be arranged in a lovely pattern on the plate to be served in small portions as a first course or in larger portions for a light main course.

The dressing and seasonings should always be blended with the ingredients before being served to coat the entire salad evenly for a delicious flavor.

Excite All the Senses

A mixed salad should be pleasing to look at as well as exciting to taste. Choose ingredients with colors and flavors that are complementary.

Add a finished touch to each salad by arranging some of the ingredients on the top in a decorative pattern; spears of asparagus or shrimp in a pinwheel, or strips of lettuce around the edge.

Choose Seasonings Carefully

Mixed salads are even more interesting and fresh with seasonings that are selected to complement the taste of the other ingredients.

The choice of seasonings can personalize your salads and set them apart from the ordinary.

To make a basic dressing, dissolve the salt and pepper in the lemon juice or vinegar. Add the mustard and whisk to combine, then gradually add the oil, whisking constantly to emulsify the mixture.

To keep the ingredients crisp and to avoid diluting the seasonings, always dry all ingredients on a hand towel before combining with the dressing.

Select
Top Quality Ingredients

Mixed salads can vary from simple to luxurious using ordinary as well as exotic ingredients.

In all cases, the ingredients should be top quality--vibrant vegetables, fresh meats and seafood.

The canned ingredients should always be the best quality available.

It is recommended to buy ingredients when they are in season and most plentiful. Not only are they usually fresher and better tasting, but the price is usually more reasonable as well.

Know How
to Combine Ingredients

Do not combine ingredients haphazardly. You can draw inspiration from classic " taste marriages " that work well, like nuts and cheese or foie gras and truffles. Also remember the importance of color and texture.

The Chinese salad, for example, is a mixture of foods and seasonings found in well-known oriental dishes that are combined in this chapter to make a fresh, zesty salad.

Another interesting touch is to mix different greens with different tastes and textures.

Each salad in this chapter combines eight to ten ingredients.

Limited Shelf Life

Once assembled, these salads stay fresh 4-8 hours maximum and ideally should be served immediately.

In a specialty food shop, the individual salads should be dressed just before the " luncheon rush ". If the customer takes the salad home to eat later in the day, the dressing can be packaged separately with instructions for mixing it with the other ingredients before serving.

For a catered event, the salad and dressing can be transported separately and combined at the last moment.

For best results in a restaurant, the separate elements of each salad can be stored separately covered with plastic wrap and assembled to order.

18 Salads in Three Families

*The selection in this chapter has been divided into three groups
to help the caterer make choices according to style and cost.*

A. – Simple, light salads

B. – Exotic salads

C. – Sophisticated, expensive salads

1 - *Chef's Salad*

2 - *Mediterranean Salad*

3 - *" Méli-Mélo " Salad*

4 - *Chinese Salad*

5 - *Cinderella Salad*

6 - *Vegetables*
   " à la Grecque "

7 - *Russian Salad*

8 - *Exotic Salad*

9 - *Brazilian Salad*

10 - *Japanese Salad*

11 - *Mediterranean Taboulé*

12 - *Seafood Salad with Pink Peppercorns*

13 - *Haddock and Pine Nut Salad*

14 - *Pasta and Seafood Salad*

15 - *Salad with Chicken and Sweetbreads*

16 - *Foie Gras Salad Gourmand*

17 - *Duck Salad*

18 - *Country-style Beef Salad*

Chef's Salad

Ingredients

(For about 6 portions)
250g (1/2lb) endive
45g (1 1/2oz) mâche
100g (3 1/2oz) red leaf lettuce
100g (3 1/2oz) green leaf lettuce
2 hard-boiled eggs (cut in quarters)
200g (7oz) tomatoes (cut in quarters)
100g (3 1/2oz) julienne of swiss cheese (4cm (1 3/4in long and 8mm (about 3/8in) wide)
45g (1 1/2oz) chopped walnuts
10g (1/3oz) chives (20 sprigs)

Dressing

1 1/2 tablespoons vinegar
1 teaspoon mustard
8 tablespoons corn oil
Salt and pepper

Procedure

Trim the greens, wash thoroughly in cold water and spin dry.

Tear or cut in small pieces and mix together in a salad bowl.

Cut the tomatoes and hard-boiled eggs in quarters, chop the walnuts into large pieces and cut the cheese into julienne strips. Cut the chives.

Whisk together the dressing ingredients, then toss dressing and salad ingredients thoroughly just before serving.

Introduction

The base of this salad is an assortment of greens that can change with the season and provide a blend of tastes and textures. Here the greens include Belgian endive, red and green leaf lettuce and " mâche ", or lamb's lettuce.

Tomatoes, hard-boiled eggs, walnuts and cheese complete this easy-to-make salad.

Advice

Choose firm, ripe tomatoes that will make neat wedges.

The type of cheese can vary, some good choices are Cantal, Beaufort, Comté and Emmenthal.

Mix the salad with the dressing just before serving.

Decorate the top with undressed ingredients of the salad as shown.

Mediterranean Salad

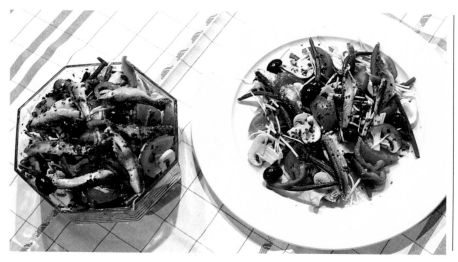

Remove the seeds and white ribs from inside the pepper and cut into thin julienne strips.

Trim the sandy stems of the mushrooms. Wash in a large basin of cold water, drain, slice thinly and sprinkle with lemon juice.

Cut away the peel of the celeriac with a stiff bladed stainless steel knife.

Cut into very thin slices, preferably using a mandoline, and then into very thin strips with a stainless steel chef's knife. Sprinkle with lemon juice.

Introduction

Olives, tomatoes and anchovies give this salad its Mediterranean flavor. This salad is zesty and refreshing as well as colorful.

Ingredients

(For about 10 portions)
650g (1 1/4lb) tomatoes
175g (6oz) green pepper
175g (6oz) green beans
200g (7oz) mushrooms
100g (3 1/2oz) celeriac
60g (2oz) olives
100g (3 1/2oz) anchovies
15g (1/2oz) parsley leaves

Dressing

1 1/2 tablespoons wine vinegar
4 tablespoons olive oil
4 tablespoons corn oil
1 teaspoon mustard
Salt and pepper

Advice

Set aside a few anchovies, olives and a little chopped parsley for the decoration.

The mushrooms and celeriac must be rubbed with lemon to keep them from darkening. The olives and anchovies are naturally salty, so the dressing will need less salt.

Preparation

Trim the green beans and plunge them into rapidly boiling salted water. Cook them until tender but still slightly crunchy. Plunge them into ice water to stop the cooking and dry on hand towels.

Rinse the tomato, cut out the stem end, and cut into quarters.

Drain the olives and anchovies.

Rinse the parsley, squeeze dry and chop finely with a chef's knife.

Whisk together the dressing ingredients, then toss dressing and salad ingredients thoroughly just before serving.

" Méli-Mélo " Salad

Introduction

Green peppercorns in brine add a spicy accent to this bright, mixed (méli-mélo) salad. A blend of many colors gives this salad a festive appearance.

Ingredients

(For about 7 portions)
250g (1/2lb) carrots, cut in julienne
100g (3 1/2oz) celeriac
150g (5oz) mushrooms
150g (5 oz) apples
200g (7oz) peeled tomatoes
150g (5oz) corn kernels
45g (1 1/2oz) pistachios
15g (1/2oz) green peppercorns in brine

100g (3 1/2oz) cooked shrimp
45g (1 1/2oz) sliced lettuce

Dressing

1/2 lemon
4 tablespoons olive oil
4 tablespoons peanut oil
1 teaspoon Worcestershire sauce
10g (1/3oz) chervil sprigs
Salt and pepper

Advice

The mushrooms, celeriac and apples must be sprinkled with lemon juice to prevent them from darkening. Mix this salad with the dressing a little bit in advance so the acid can soften the raw, crunchy ingredients slightly.

Preparation

Peel the carrots and celery root. Slice them thinly with a mandoline, then cut into very thin strips with a chef's knife.

Trim and wash the mushrooms, then cut them into thin strips.

Peel the apples, remove the seeds and cut into small dice.

Peel the tomatoes, squeeze out the seeds and cut into small dice.

Peel the shrimp if necessary and cut into small pieces.

Drain the corn and peppercorns.

Shell the pistachios, if necessary.

Whisk together the dressing ingredients, then toss dressing and salad ingredients thoroughly.

Chinese Salad

Sunflower oil is blended with sesame oil, which is too strong and nutty to be used on its own.

Preparation

Trim the beans sprouts and rinse them. If using fresh " flageolets ", soak them the night before and cook them in advance.

Soak the shiitake mushrooms and cook in salted water.

Remove the seeds and white ribs from the green pepper, rinse and cut into small dice.

Peel the carrots, rinse and cut into very thin strips.

Peel the shrimp, leaving the tail on a few of them for decoration, cut the rest into small pieces.

Drain the ginger and cut into small pieces.

For a nuttier taste, lightly toast the sesame seeds.

Make the sauce and mix together all the ingredients.

Decorate the top with some pieces of ginger and whole shrimp.

Introduction

The fresh taste of preserved ginger combined with sesame and bean sprouts makes this salad fresh and crunchy. Shrimp and green peppers add a bright splash of color.

Ingredients

(For about 8 portions)

300g (10oz) bean sprouts
175g (6oz) carrots cut in julienne
90g (3oz) green pepper
20g (2/3oz) dried shiitake mush-
    rooms
200g (7oz) cooked white beans or
    " flageolets "
30g (1oz) preserved ginger
10g (1/3o) sesame seeds
150g (5oz) unshelled shrimp

Dressing

1 tablespoon soy sauce
2 tablespoons sesame oil
3 tablespoons sunflower oil
Salt, pepper

Advice

The sesame oil, preserved ginger and shiitake are available in shops specializing in Oriental products.

Cinderella Salad

Introduction

Asparagus and artichoke bottoms are the featured ingredients in this salad, that also includes potatoes and celeriac.

A dice of apples adds a light sweet taste.

Ingredients

(For about 12 portions)
250g(1/2lb) artichoke bottoms (about 8 artichokes)
500g (1lb) potatoes
750g (1 1/2lb) asparagus (about 15)
300g (10oz) raw apple (about 2 apples)
75g (2 1/2oz) celeriac

Decoration

4 lettuce leaves
15 asparagus tips
15g (1/2oz) truffle
1 tomato rose

Dressing

1 tablespoon wine vinegar
1 teaspoon mustard
4 tablespoons corn oil
Salt, pepper

Advice

Make this salad when fresh artichokes and asparagus are available.

The truffle garnish, which adds a contrast of color as well as flavor, is an optional ingredient.

Preparation

Peel the stems of the asparagus, rinse, plunge into boiling salted water and cook until tender but

slightly crunchy. Plunge them into ice water to stop the cooking, then drain.

Cut the tips of the asparagus to use as decoration and cut the stems into pieces.

Trim the leaves from the base of the artichokes, cook them in acidulated water, cool and cut in strips.

Peel and rinse the potatoes. Cook them in salted water, cool and cut in slices.

Peel and seed the apples. Cut in small dice and sprinkle with lemon juice.

Peel the celeriac, rinse, rub with lemon, cut into very fine strips and sprinkle with lemon juice.

Chop the truffles, if using. Whisk together the sauce ingredients. Mix the salad ingredients.

Decorate the top with asparagus tips, a tomato rose and diced truffles.

Vegetables " à la Grecque "

Introduction

This salad must be made in advance and so it is ideal for specialty food shops and catered events. The coriander and olive oil add a Greek accent to this salad.

Ingredients

(For about 8 portions)
400g (14oz) mushrooms
1.5kg (3 1/4lbs) artichokes
20 pearl or spring onions
45g (1 1/2oz) currants
Approx. 2dl (3/4 cup) water
6dl (2 1/2 cups) white wine
5cl (1/4 cup) tomato paste
20g (2/3oz) parsley sprigs
1 tablespoon coriander seed
Bouquet garni (thyme, bay leaf, leek green)
1dl (1/2 cup) olive oil
Salt, pepper

Advice

Cut all the vegtables about the same size so they cook evenly and so the salad is attractive.

Do not overcook the vegetables; taste the cooked vegetables and add more seasoning if necessary.

The salad will taste better if made 24 hours in advance.

Preparation

Peel the onions. Trim the leaves off the artichokes, scoop out the choke and cut the bottoms in large dice.

Clean the mushrooms and cut them in half or quarters. Combine all of the seasonings, vegetables and olive oil, wine and water to cover in a heavy pan. Cover and cook over medium heat until the vegetables are tender. Transfer to a stainless steel hotel pan to cool.

Serve after 24 hours.

Russian Salad

Drain well, then bind them with the mayonnaise. Frozen peas may be substituted for fresh peas if necessary.

Preparation

Peel and rinse the carrots and turnips. Cut them into small dice, then cook them separately in boiling salted water. Refresh in cold water and drain well.

String the green beans. Cut them into short pieces the size of the diced vegetables and cook them in salted boiling water. Refresh in cold water and drain well.

Shell the peas. Cook them in boiling salted water. Refresh in

Introduction

This blend of cooked diced vegetables in mayonnaise is a fresh accompaniment to cold meat or fish dishes. Once assembled, it must be served immediately.

Ingredients

(For about 12 portions)

300g (10oz) green beans
500g (1lb) peas
500g (1lb) peeled carrots
500g (1lb) peeled turnips
200g (7oz) tomatoes, cut in quarters (about 2 tomatoes)
2 hard-boiled eggs
45g (1 1/2oz) black olives (about 10 olives)
4-5 lettuce leaves
Salt, pepper

Mayonnaise

5dl (2 cups) oil
2 egg yolks
1 tablespoon mustard
Salt, cayenne pepper

Advice

Do not let the vegetables soak in the cold water when refreshing them or they will absorb liquid and become soggy.

cold water and drain well.

Carefully combine all the vegetables with the mayonnaise. Season to taste with salt and pepper.

Exotic Salad

Another tart pickle can be substituted if cornichons are not available.

Preparation

Trim the bean sprouts, rinse and drain. Remove the seeds and white ribs from the red pepper and cut in small dice about the size of a pea or kernel of corn.

Shell the peas and cook in boiling salted water, refresh in cold water and drain.

Cut the cornichons in thin slices. Drain the corn and capers.

Trim the lettuce, wash and spin dry.

Introduction

The variegated leaves of curly red leaf lettuce frame this colorful salad when arranged on a plate. Capers and tart pickles add tang to this tasty salad.

Ingredients

(For about 10 portions)
300g (10oz) bean sprouts
150g (5oz) corn kernels
100g (3 1/2oz) red pepper
45g (1 1/2oz) capers
75g (2 1/2oz) cornichons (small sour gherkins)
250g (1/2lb) peas
100g (3 /2oz) celeriac

Decoration

45g (1 1/2oz) curly red leaf lettuce

Dressing

1/2 lemon
6 tablespoons olive oil
1 tablespoon mustard
Salt, pepper

Advice

The small pickles used here are "cornichons" which are crunchy French gherkins flavored with tarragon and mustard seed.

Whisk together the dressing ingredients, then toss dressing and salad ingredients thoroughly just before serving.

Brazilian Salad

Cooking the Rice

Bring the water to a boil. Add the salt, oil and rice and stir as the water comes back to a boil. Stir from time to time as the rice cooks. When tender, drain and rinse with cold water.

Preparation

Peel the sausage and slice it thinly. Blanch the bacon, then sauté it until brown. Drain the corn and the kidney beans.

Shell the peas and cook them in boiling salted water. Refresh in cold water and drain.

Introduction

This salad made with brown rice and spicy sausage is a meal in itself. The colors of this dish are as lively as the taste. Sherry vinegar and tabasco add zest to the dressing.

Ingredients

(For about 10 portions)

400g (14oz) raw brown rice
120g (4oz) corn kernels
200g (7oz) peas
100g (3 1/2oz) cooked red kidney
  beans
130g (4oz) carrots
100g (3 1/2oz) slab bacon
90g (3oz) chorizo sausage
4-5 lettuce leaves
10g (1/3oz) parsley sprigs

Dressing
2 tablespoons sherry vinegar
10 tablespoons olive oil
1/2 tablespoon mustard
Few drops tabasco

Advice
Brown rice takes longer to cook

than white rice and benefits from an addition of oil to keep it from sticking.

The bacon should be smoked and is best if the "lardons" (thick, short strips) are cut from a slab.

Sort, wash and spin dry the salad. Chop the parsley.

Whisk together the dressing ingredients, then toss dressing and salad ingredients thoroughly just before serving.

Japanese Salad

Drain the grapefruit well before mixing with other ingredients.

Preparation

Boil the rice in salted water until tender. Drain crab and remove bits of shell.

Cut the peel from the grapefruit, cut out the sections and cut in half.

Scoop out the avocado, cut in dice and sprinkle with lemon juice.

Peel and seed the apples, cut in dice and sprinkle with lemon juice.

Remove the seeds and white ribs from the red pepper and cut in small dice.

Trim, wash and spin dry the lettuce. Remove the shells from the

Introduction

This delicate salad combines the pastel colors of shrimp, avocado and grapefruit.

The refreshing taste is accented with a hint of tabasco. The combination of ketchup and cream in the dressing makes it rosy pink and full of flavor.

This salad would be appropriate served in a hollowed out grapefruit shell.

Ingredients

(For 10-12 portions)
300g (10oz) raw rice
200g (7oz) drained crabmeat
900g (2lbs) grapefruit (2)
350g (12oz) avocados (1 1/2)
150g (5oz) apples (2)
90g (3oz) red pepper (1/2)
5-6 lettuce leaves
150g (5oz) cooked shrimp (7)
45g (1 1/2oz) black olives (10)

Dressing
2dl (3/4 cup) heavy cream, whipped
1 teaspoon mustard
2 tablespoons ketchup
Tabasco (Few drops)
Salt, pepper

Advice

The rice should be firm and not mushy for a good taste and a neat presentation.

Check the crabmeat for little bits of shell.

Choose avocados that are ripe, but not too soft so they can be cut into neat pieces.

shrimp and save the heads for decoration.

Pit the olives.

To make the sauce, whip the cream and stir in the other ingredients.

Mix the dressing and salad ingredients and decorate with olives and shrimp.

Mediterranean Taboulé

First, soak the couscous in an equal weight of water, separating the grains with the palms of your hands as the couscous absorbs the water and forms lumps.

Season with salt and pepper and add a little oil, incorporating it with your hands. Place the couscous in the top of a "couscousière" (a double decker steamer) and steam it.

Spread the couscous on a tray, soak with water, separate the grains using a little oil, then steam again.

Preparation

Soak the raisins in hot water.

Trim, wash, dry and chop the herbs. Remove the seeds and white ribs from the peppers, cut into small dice.

Introduction

This sweet and salty combination flavored with fresh mint and lemon is the perfect summertime salad.

A classic dish in Mediterranean countries, taboulé is gaining popularity in other parts of the world.

Ingredients

(For about 12 portions)
500g (1lb) medium couscous
275g (9oz) cucumber
60g (2oz) green pepper
450g (15oz) tomatoes
200g (7oz) onions
100g (3 1/2oz) white raisins
45g (1 1/2oz) mint leaves
30g (1oz) parsley sprigs
200g (7oz) lemons
Mint leaves
3-4 sliced lettuce leaves

Dressing
Juice of 1 lemon
Olive oil
Salt, pepper
Few drops tabasco
Advice

Couscous is found in specialty stores specializing in Middle Eastern foods and even in certain large supermarkets.

Peel and seed the tomatoes, cut them in small dice. Cut away the peel of the lemon, cut out the sections and cut into small dice. Trim the lettuce, wash it, spin it dry and slice. Whisk together the dressing ingredients, then toss dressing and salad ingredients thoroughly just before serving.

Seafood Salad with Pink Pepppercorns

Advice

Choose perfectly fresh seafood to ensure good results. For extra flavor, poach the seafood in fish stock or well-seasoned court bouillon.

Preparation
Preparing the Vegetables

Cut carrots into thin strips, cook until tender but firm. String the beans and cook until tender but firm. Wash the mushrooms, cut in strips, sprinkle with lemon juice. Peel, seed cucumber and cut into strips. Peel the mango and cut into strips. Cut the zest from the orange, cut out the sections. Trim wash and spin dry the lettuce.

Preparing the Seafood

Wash the mussels, steam them open and remove the dark rim or " beard ". Remove the shell of the prawns and poach them in fish stock.

Introduction

This is an elegant salad that would make an ideal luncheon main course. The spicy pink peppercorns marry well with the shellfish and the assortment of vegetables add color and crunch.

Ingredients
(For about 12 portions)
250g (1/2lb) turnips
250g (1/2lb) carrots
100g (3 1/2oz) green beans
100g (3 1/2oz) mangoes
300g (10oz) oranges
150g (5oz) mushrooms
200g (7oz) tomatoes
45g (1 1/2oz) shallots
150g (5oz) cucumber
Red leaf lettuce
12 mussels
2 filets of sole (120g (4oz))
6 langoustines
6 cooked shrimp
4 scallops
10g (1/3oz) basil
Julienne of orange zest
10g (1/3oz) chives
10g (1/3oz) pink peppercorns (2 tsp)

Dressing
Juice of 1 lemon
Salt, pepper
1/2 tablespoon mustard
12 tablespoons corn oil

If the shrimp are raw, poach them with the langoustines; otherwise simply peel them. Poach the scallops and cut in half. Cut the sole filets in strips and poach. Mix the vegetables with the sauce. Arrange the seafood on top.

Haddock and Pine Nut Salad

Preparation
Cook the potatoes in their skins.

String the green beans, and cook until tender but still firm.

Trim the artichokes, cook in acidulated water, cut in quarters.

Trim, wash and spin dry the salad.

Introduction
This a a rustic salad with a lot of character. The haddock and bacon provide a woodsy, smoky flavor which marries well with the potatoes boiled in their skins.

The dressing has a dash of fish based " Américaine " sauce, which adds a delicious flavor.

Ingredients
(For about 8 portions)
800g (1lb 10oz) potatoes
200g (7oz) green beans
300g (10oz) artichokes (6)
480g (1lb) tomatoes, cut in quarters
200g (7oz) curly endive
300g (10oz) smoked haddock filet
100g (3 1/2oz) slab bacon
45g (1 1/2oz) pine nuts
Milk for poaching

Dressing
2 tablespoons reduced " Américaine " sauce
2 egg yolks
Salt, pepper
1/2 tablespoon mustard
1 tablespoon heavy cream
4 tablespoons oil

Advice
The potatoes can be boiled in salted water or baked in the oven, covered with aluminum foil. The smoked haddock is usually quite salty, so the poaching liquid should have little or no salt added.

Poach the haddock in milk and water and cut it into strips.

Blanch, then sauté the bacon. Toast the pine nuts in the oven.

Whisk together the dressing ingredients, then toss dressing and salad ingredients thoroughly just before serving.

Pasta and Seafood Salad

Preparation

Poach the squid and cut it in strips. Poach the bay scallops. Wash the mussels, then steam them " à la marinière ", remove the shells and pull off the dark rim or " beard ".

Peel and seed the tomatoes and cut them into small dice.

Cook the broccoli in boiling salted water, plunge into ice water to stop cooking, and drain. Trim, wash and sauté the chanterelles.

Rinse and dry the basil and cut into thin strips.

Rinse and dry the chives and cut into tiny pieces.

Whisk together the dressing ingredients, then toss dressing and salad ingredients thoroughly just before serving. Decorate the top of the salad with some of the seafood.

Introduction

This is a copious yet refreshing salad. Tricolor pasta harmonizes with the green broccoli and orange mussels. The dressing is appropriately made with olive oil and basil, giving it an Italian accent as well.

Ingredients

(For about 12 portions)
100g (3 1/2oz) tri-color pasta
150g (5oz) squid
150g (5oz) bay scallops
100g (3 1/2oz) mussels
250g (1/2lb) tomatoes, cut in dice
250g (1/2lb) broccoli
150g (5oz) chanterelle mushrooms
10g (1/3oz) basil
10g (1/3oz) chives

Dressing

1 egg yolk
Pinch mustard
1dl (1/2 cup) heavy cream
6 tablespoons olive oil
3 tablespoons corn oil
Salt, pepper

Advice

The three seafoods are cooked separately as they each have a different texture.

Serve this salad when fresh basil is in season, as dried is a poor substitute in this recipe.

The chanterelles can be replaced by another type of mushroom.

Carefully cook the broccoli to keep the bright color and individual flowerets intact.

Cooking the Pasta

Bring a large pot of salted water to a rapid boil, add a little olive oil and the pasta. Cook the pasta " al dente ", firm and not mushy.

Rinse it in cold water to stop the cooking, drain thoroughly and toss with olive oil so it does not stick together.

Salad with Chicken and Sweetbreads

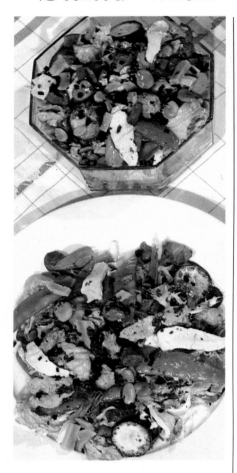

Introduction

This is an elegant salad with many lovely shades of green. The chicken breasts are poached in a well-seasoned stock and the sweetbreads are sautéed for a deep, rich flavor.

A touch of honey in the vinaigrette dressing brings out the best in the other ingredients.

Ingredients

Dressing
1 tablespoon vinegar honey
3 tablespoons hazelnut oil
3 tablespoons corn oil
Salt and pepper

(For about 10 portions)
200g (7oz) zucchini
Oil for cooking
200g (7oz) snow peas
200g (7oz) artichoke bottoms (4)
100g (3 1/2oz) chanterelles
200g (7oz) fava beans
100g (3 1/2oz) lettuce
45g (1 1/2oz) mâche (lamb's lettuce)
100g (3 1/2oz) curly endive
200g (7oz) boneless chicken or turkey breast
200g (7oz) sweetbreads
10g (1/3oz) truffle
10g (1/3oz) chervil

Advice

For moistness and flavor, allow the chicken to cool in the well-seasoned stock in which it is poached.

The salad greens can vary according to availability.

Preparation

Cut the unpeeled zucchini into 1/2cm (about 1/4in) slices and sauté them in oil until tender but still firm.

Shell the fava beans, blanch and remove skins.

Trim the leaves of the artichokes, cook in acidulated water until tender but firm, cut in slices.

Trim the ends of the snow peas and steam them.

Chop the truffles.

Pluck the leaves of the chervil, chop finely.

Poach the chicken breasts in stock.

Degorge the sweetbreads in cold running water, trim away the thin membrane, slice and sauté them in a non-stick pan with a little butter. Trim, wash and spin dry the greens.

Whisk together the dressing ingredients, then toss dressing and salad ingredients thoroughly just before serving.

Foie Gras Salad Gourmand

Introduction

Smooth and rich foie gras is delicious when contrasted with crisp greens and a tart vinaigrette.

Truffles, often paired with foie gras in terrines or hot dishes, are added to this salad in the form of decorative julienne and the juice of the truffles augments the vinaigrette.

Ingredients

(For about 8 servings)
300 g (10 oz) green beans
300 g (10 oz) artichoke bottoms (6)
750 g (1 1/2 lb) asparagus tips (12)
130 (4 oz) mushrooms
10 g (4 oz) truffle
150 g (5 oz) foie gras " en bloc "
130 g (4 oz) hearts of lettuce

Dressing

1/2 tablespoon sherry vinegar
7 tablespoons corn oil
1 tablespoon truffle juice
Salt, pepper

Advice

The foie gras should be " en bloc ", that is not puréed or mixed with other ingredients. For the best results, make a terrine using raw livers (instructions in Volume 2 of this series) or purchase foie gras " semi-conserve "--which is a refrigerated product that comes in cans or jars and retains the creamy quality of the foie gras.

Preparation

Make the terrine of foie gras several days in advance.

Cook the asparagus tips in rapidly boiling salted water until tender but firm.

Cut away the leaves of the artichokes with a stiff bladed stainless steel knife. Cook in acidulated water. Slice thinly.

Trim the sandy stems of the mushrooms, slice thinly and sprinkle with lemon juice.

Slice the truffles into very thin julienne.

Whisk together the dressing ingredients, then toss dressing and salad ingredients thoroughly just before serving.

Decorate the salad with asparagus tips, julienne of truffle and slices of foie gras.

Duck Salad

Preparation
Cut the duck breasts crosswise into very thin slices.

Gently heat the gizzards to melt the fat. Drain on paper towels, and cut into small pieces if they are large.

Shell and peel the fava beans. String the green beans, then cook them in boiling salted water.

Peel the celeriac, rub it with lemon juice, then cut it into fine julienne.

Peel the avocado, rub with lemon juice and cut into thin strips.

Peel, flute and slice the carrots, then cook them in boiling salted water.

Introduction
Smoked duck breast and preserved duck gizzards are rich and tasty ingredients of the cooking in southwest France.

Hazelnut oil and sherry vinegar in the vinaigrette go exceptionally well with the duck.

breasts often have a thick fatty skin which will make the salad too greasy and hard to digest.

Good quality canned gizzards are available, and they are also easy to prepare. Refer to a recipe for " confit de canard ".

`Sort, wash and spin dry the lettuce.

Chop the chervil finely.

Whisk together the dressing ingredients, then toss dressing and salad ingredients thoroughly just before serving.

Ingredients
(For about 8 portions)
220g (7 1/2oz) avocado (1)
200g (7oz) green beans
100g (3 1/2oz) celeriac
150g (5oz) carrots
200g (7oz) fava beans
150g (5oz) smoked duck breast
180g (6oz) preserved gizzards
200g (7oz) lettuce
10g (1/3oz) chervil

Dressing
1/2 tablespoon sherry vinegar
7 tablespoons hazelnut oil
Salt and pepper

Advice
Choose medium size, lightly smoked duck breasts. Larger

Country-style Beef Salad

Introduction
This rustic salad is ideal for a casual buffet or picnic lunch. The beef is cooked in a broth and teams up with the well-aged Cantal to form a hearty combination.

Ingredients
(For about 10 portions)
1.8kg (4lbs) ox tails or shin
150g (5oz) onions
100g (3 1/2oz) currants
350g (12 oz) celery stalks
250g (1/2lb) aged Cantal
   (or swiss or cheddar)
10g (1/3oz) chervil sprigs
220g (7 1/2oz) lettuce

Dressing
1/2 tablespoon vinegar
9 tablespoons corn oil
1/2 tablespoon mustard
Salt and pepper

Advice
Use a tender, gelatinous cut of beef which will pull apart easily when cooked. (Oxtail and shin are good choices.) For moist and flavorful meat, poach the meat in a well-seasoned meat stock, start in cold liquid, simmer gently until very tender when pierced with a fork, and leave to cool in the liquid.

For best results, prepare the meat 2 days in advance.

Choose a well-aged cheese, that blends with the other ingredients.

Preparation
Tie the beef for even cooking, poach as described; when cool, cut into strips.

Peel and cut the onions into small dice.

Pluck the leaves of the chervil, rinse and chop finely.

Peel the celery to eliminate the strings, rinse and cut into small dice.

Soak the currants in hot water to soften them.

Cut the wax coating off the cheese, cut into strips.

Trim, wash and spin dry the salad.

Whisk together the dressing ingredients, then toss dressing and salad ingredients thoroughly just before serving.

Chapter 7
Fish in Aspic

Beautiful and Delicious

This chapter covers the variety of fish in aspic dishes, ranging from individual preparations to large centerpieces, which are very impressive on a buffet table.

Though the finished presentations are different, the techniques used are basically the same.

The accompanying garnishes are versatile and should be selected to harmonize with the flavor and texture of the fish.

A sauce may be served on the side and should always marry well with the ingredients of the dish.

General Advice

Ingredients

Always choose the best quality and freshest ingredients, especially when it comes to fish.

How to Recognize a Fresh Fish

- bright shiny scales
- clear bright eyes
- very red gills
- clean fresh smell
- firm flesh

How to Store the Fish

Store the fish in ice until ready to use; wrap the fish in a hand towel or heavy duty paper to prevent direct contact with the ice.

Procedure

Preparing the Fish

To prepare fish for poaching, begin by cutting off the fins.

Next scrape off the scales.

Cut out the gills, then remove the entrails through the gill opening. Pull them out carefully in one piece.

Rinse the inside of the fish with cold water and verify that all the entrails have been removed. Rinse the outside of the fish as well to clean away scales and impurities.

Cover and refrigerate until ready to bone. The fish in this chapter are presented four ways:

- Whole, with head and tail; bones left in or bones removed.

- Whole with the bones removed then filled with a mousse.

- Filets filled with a mousse.

- Filets reshaped like a ballotine.

Poaching the Fish

The ingredients for the poaching liquid, or court bouillon, may vary according to the type of fish. For all fish, begin the poaching in cold liquid. This court bouillon should be cooked, strained and cooled in advance. Always use a thermometer to control the temperature so that it stays about 80-85 °C (175-185F).

Poaching time will vary greatly according to the size of the fish, the texture of its flesh and whether or not it is stuffed. A larger fish should be poached for a longer time at a slightly lower temperature.

Always let the fish cool in the poaching liquid so it stays moist.

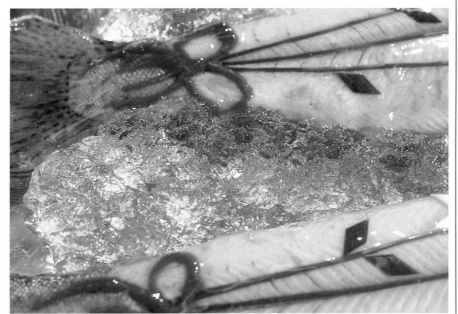

The poaching liquid can be clarified to make the aspic glaze. Aspic is also used to make the delicate mayonnaise-based chaud-froid sauce that is used to glaze some of the presentations in this chapter.

Assembly

Carefully remove the skin from the poached and cooled fish.

Coat with the first layer of aspic

or chaud-froid sauce and arrange the decorations. Cover with a second coat of aspic. Place on a serving platter and add the garnishes in a decorative pattern.

Storage

When carefully prepared, the fish may be kept up to 24 hours at 4 °C (40F).

Individual Servings

Trout in Aspic

These attractive fish are a good size for a single serving. Their pretty color and eye-catching decoration make them always popular as part of a buffet.

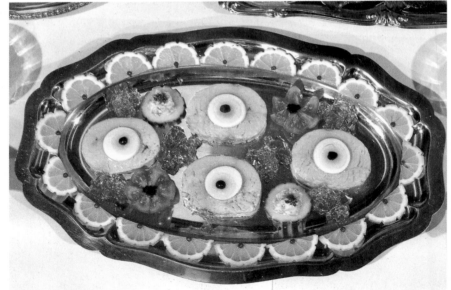

Salmon Steaks in Aspic

Pink and moist, these salmon steaks look inviting on a buffet table. The fact that all the bones have been removed is an added plus.

Stuffed Filets of Sole

The beautiful presentation highlights to best advantage the fine flavor of fresh sole, made all the more delicious by the combination with salmon and truffles.

Large Centerpieces

Sea Bass in Chaud-Froid

The fine texture and flavor of sea bass makes it one of the most prized of fish. Its large size creates a stunning presentation, completed by a light coating of chaud-froid sauce.

Salmon in Aspic

Always use the finest quality salmon for this dish, such as Scottish salmon with deep red flesh. Careful poaching will leave the salmon moist and flavorful. A light coating of crystal clear aspic shows off the salmon's sleek silhouette.

Hake in Chaud-Froid

Hake has slightly fragile flesh, but it is delicious and not very expensive. It is therefore appropriate for all occasions.

The hake is boned then stuffed, which enhances both flavor and presentation.

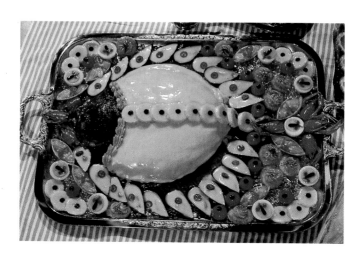

Turbot with Salmon Mousse

The shape of this flat fish lends itself to beautiful presentations. The turbot is made even more delicious by a filling of salmon mousse-the perfect partner for the delicate flavor of the turbot.

Trout in Aspic

Introduction

Trout is an inexpensive fish that is popular with everyone. The most frequently used varieties are rainbow trout and salmon trout.

The techniques required for this dish are simple. The fish is poached in a light court bouillon.

Clear fish aspic coats the fish, gives it is brilliant shine and keeps the decorations in place.

The dish can be augmentd with a light mayonnaise-based sauce.

Equipment

Cutting board, hotel pan, roasting pan, fish shears, paring knife, teaspoon, sheet pan, cooling rack, plates, mixing bowls, thermometer, pastry brush, large pot, skimmer, serving platter, truffle cutter

Ingredients

Main Ingredient
6 trouts (150-180g (5-6oz) each)

Decoration

Leek green
3cl (2 tbsp) tomato paste
2 hard-boiled egg whites
1 black olive
30g (1oz) lumpfish eggs
30g (1oz) salmon eggs

Aspic Glaze

1/2L (2 cups) fish aspic

Garnishes

1 tomato
15g (1/2oz) lumpfish eggs
1 lemon
Curly parsley
3/4L (3 cups) chopped aspic

Court Bouillon

3L (3 qts) water
1L (1qt) dry white wine
400g (14oz) onions
75g (2 1/2oz) parsley stems
1 sprig thyme
1/2 bay leaf
45g (1 1/2oz) coarse salt
10g (1/3oz) black peppercorns

Procedure

Preparing the Trout

It is not necessary to scale the trout. To clean them, cut out the gills, make a small incision in the belly as shown, then pull out the entrails through the gill opening. Remove all the entrails and rinse thoroughly.

With a small spoon, scrape along the inside of the backbone to remove the pocket of blood on either side. Check that the trout are perfectly clean.

The Court Bouillon

Combine all the ingredients. Cook briefly, let cool, then pass through a fine-meshed conical strainer or a cheesecloth.

Poaching

For a 180g (6oz) trout, count on about 20 minutes poaching time.

Carefully lay the trout side by side in a roasting pan. They may touch each other, but do not overlap them.

Pour on cold court bouillon to cover, and lay a piece of buttered parchment paper on top to keep them moist during cooking.

Season with salt and pepper and cook over low heat or preferably in an oven at 180 °C (350F), using a thermometer to check the temperature. The poaching liquid should remain between 80-85 °C (175-185F).

Cooling

Leave the trout to cool in the poaching liquid so they stay moist and tender. The trout should be poached the day before they are to be used.

Draining

Carefully drain the trout on a hand towel.

Removing the Skin

Remove the skin carefully using a flexible, stainless steel knife. Remove the skin completely or leave on some skin to form a decoration, as shown.

Making the Aspic

Use a fish aspic made either from the clarified court bouillon or clarified fish stock. The liquid should be clarified in the classic manner using egg whites, leek greens and some puréed whiting filets to enhance the flavor of the aspic.

In hot weather, use 20-24g (2/3-3/4oz) gelatin per liter (quart) of court bouillon or stock. In colder weather, only 16-20g (1/2-2/3oz) will be necessary for the aspic to set properly.

Soften the gelatin in cold water, then stir it thoroughly into the warm liquid. Test the consistency by pouring a little in a shallow dish and chilling to set.

Decorating the Trout

There are numerous ways to decorate the trout. For the decoration shown here, blanched leek greens are used for the stems and leaves.

Wash the leeks carefully and select only straight, evenly colored leaves. Plunge them in boiling water, then remove them immediately with a skimmer and put them in ice water to stop the cooking and to set the bright green color.

Many other ingredients can be used to make colorful designs on the fish and platter, including chopped aspic, hard-boiled egg white, hard-boiled egg yolk, salmon eggs and lump fish eggs.

Colored butter, mayonnaise or tomato paste can be piped through a paper cone to make floral designs as well.

Baskets cut from tomatoes, fluted lemon slices or lemons cut in saw-tooth complete the decor.

Glazing

Stir the aspic over ice until it thickens slightly. Take the trout from the refrigerator.

Brush on a first coat of aspic, which will smooth out the surface of the fish. Chill to set and arrange the decorations on the fish.

Chill again so the next layer of aspic will set correctly. Brush on a second coat and, if needed, a third coat.

Presentation

The trout can be presented on individual plates or large serving platters.

Chopped aspic can complement any of the presentations. An aspic containing a bit more gelatin will work better.

To make chopped aspic, pour the aspic in a shallow pan and chill to set.

When set, unmold it onto a hand towel, then place it on a cutting board and cut into very small dice.

Arrange the chopped aspic using a spoon or by piping it through a lightly moistened pastry bag fitted with a large tip.

Service

Several sauces would make good accompaniments to the trout: classic mayonnaise, mousseline sauce (mayonnaise lightened with whipped cream), green sauce (mousseline sauce flavored with chopped fresh herbs).

The trout may also be accompanied by little barquettes filled with diced vegetables (macedoine).

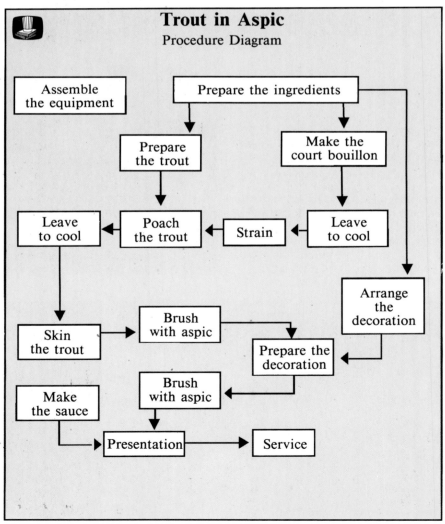

Trout in Aspic
Procedure Diagram

Assemble the equipment

Prepare the ingredients

Prepare the trout

Make the court bouillon

Leave to cool → Poach the trout → Strain → Leave to cool

Arrange the decoration

Skin the trout → Brush with aspic → Prepare the decoration

Make the sauce

Brush with aspic

Presentation → Service

Salmon Steaks in Aspic

Introduction

These individual-sized portions are prepared from slices of a boned whole salmon, which has been rolled up in a cylinder and poached like a ballotine.

The salmon is poached in court bouillon and left to cool in its poaching liquid so that it retains its moisture and stays firm. Therefore, it is necesesary to allow enough time to poach and completely cool the fish before it is needed.

To finish the dish, cut the ballotine into thick slices and decorate each slice. Coat the slices with fish aspic to give them a clear shine and to prevent them from drying out.

Arrange on platters, plates or disposable containers according to the method of sale.

The fish may be accompanied by a variety of sauces and garnishes.

Equipment

Cutting board, mixing bowl, fish poaching pan, fish shears, scaler, paring knife, thin-bladed flexible knife, tweezers, ballotine wrapper, cheesecloth, kitchen twine, plastic wrap, cooling rack, sheet pan, thermometer, hotel pan, serrated knife, egg slicer, channel cutter, serving platter, palette knife, pastry brush

Ingredients

Main Ingredients

1 Scottish salmon
Salt, powdered gelatin

Court Bouillon

5L (5 qts) water
2dl (3/4 cup) vinegar
60g (2oz) salt
450g (1lb) carrots
350g (12oz) onions
1 sprig thyme
1 bay leaf
75g (2 1/2oz) parsley stems
15g (1/2oz) black peppercorns
1 leek
1L (1qt) white wine

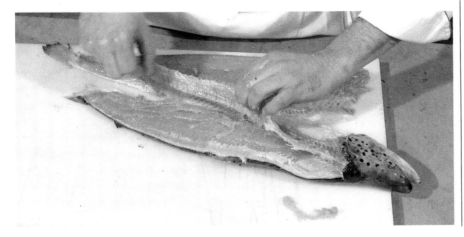

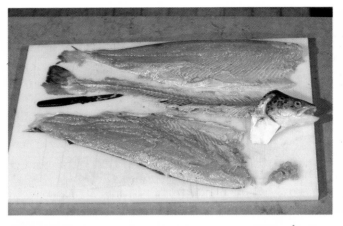

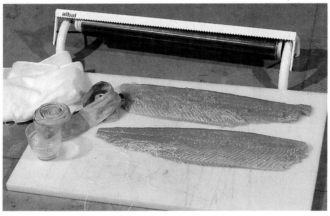

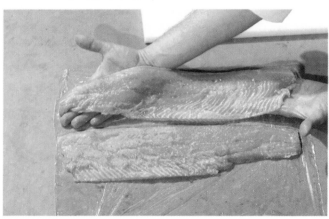

Glaze

1/2L (1/2qt) fish aspic

Decoration

3 eggs
3 black olives

Garnishes

3/4L (3 cups) chopped aspic
1 cucumber
Parsley
7 tomatoes
2cl (4tsp) tomato paste
45g (1 1/2oz) lumpfish eggs
2 lemons

Procedure

Preparing the Salmon

Scrape off the scales and rinse under cold running water.

Cut off the fins, using a pair of fish shears.

Make a small incision in the belly, then cut out the gills and pull out the entrails through the gill opening. Make sure the cavity is empty, then rinse with cold water.

Boning the Salmon

Using a small well-sharpened knife, cut along the backbone from head to tail. Carefully cut away the top filet, keeping the knife angled toward the central bones in order not to cut into the flesh.

Turn the fish over and repeat the process to remove the other filet.

Using small pincers or a pair of tweezers, pull out the small bones that run vertically along the center of the filet. These are located by feeling gently with your finger.

Check again that all the bones have been removed. This not only makes for better eating, but it allows for a cleaner slice; any remaining bones could tear the flesh when the fish is sliced.

Cut away the skin with a sharp

knife, starting at the tail end and always angling the knife toward the skin. Hold the end of the skin taut and use a sawing motion to remove the skin neatly without damaging the flesh.

Rinse the filets gently under cold running water to wash away any bits of skin, scale and bones.

Blot away excess moisture using a hand towel.

Rolling the Salmon

Lay the filets on a large sheet of plastic wrap, cut side up. Season with salt and pepper and sprinkle lightly with powdered gelatin. This will help seal the filets together so they will keep their form when rolled into the ballotine shape.

Lay one filet on top of the other, cut sides together and so the wide end of the top filet is on the narrow end of the bottom filet, as shown.

Using the plastic wrap, roll up the filets lengthwise into a tight "sausage" shape. Roll this cylinder tightly in a piece of cheesecloth or a thin hand towel.

Twist the ends closed and tie very tightly with a double knot.

Wrap a ballotine band tightly and evenly around the ballotine, beginning at one end and overlapping slightly with each wrap. Repeat with a second band, working in the opposite sense, so that the salmon is securely wrapped. Tie up with kitchen twine, as for a roast, as shown.

Cooking

Place the ballotine in a fish poaching pan filled with court bouillon that has already been cooked, cooled and strained. Add the white wine.

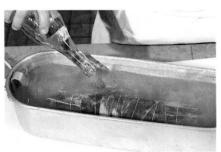

Put the fish poaching pan in the oven to poach at 200 °C (375F). For a 1.5-2kg (3 1/2-4lb) fish, count on 45 minutes to 1 hour.

Checking the Cooking

- by touch, however, this requires an experienced cook.

- using a thermometer, which must register about 82 °C (about 180F) at the center of the fish.

Cooling

Leave the ballotine to cool in its poaching liquid. As with all these preparations, allow enough time for poaching and completely cooling the fish before preparing the final presentation.

Carefully remove the ballotine wrappers and the cheesecloth.

Remove the plastic wrap and blot the surface of the salmon with a paper towel.

Assembly

With a sharp knife, cut the salmon into slices 1.5-2cm (1/2-3/4in) thick.

If the slices are too thin, they will be too fragile and will break easily. If they are too thick, they will lack finesse in taste and appearance.

Place a cooling rack on a large stainless steel sheet pan to catch the dripping aspic, then place the salmon slices on the rack.

Brush on a first coat of aspic, made from the clarified court bouillon or clarified fish stock. This will make a smooth surface.

Be sure to brush the sides of the slices as well as the tops.

Chill until set.

Decoration

Boil the eggs and peel them. Using an egg slicer, or a sharp knife, cut them into even slices.

Lay a slice of egg on each salmon steak and decorate it with a bit of tomato, pepper, black olive or even truffle. If truffles are used, the sale price must be adjusted.

Presentation

The salmon steaks may be sold by the piece in a disposable carry out container or they may be arranged on plates or platters.

Garnishes

There are many possibilities for platter garnishes. Always try to achieve a nice color contrast.

Cucumber slices topped with diced vegetables (macedoine) bound in mayonnaise are fresh and colorful; tomatoes cut in a sawtooth pattern dotted with a bit of lumpfish eggs look stunning, as do fluted slices of lemon, accented with a dot of tomato paste piped from a paper cone.

Sauces

The salmon steaks can be served with classic mayonnaise, mousseline sauce (mayonnaise lightened with whipped cream), or green sauce (mousseline sauce flavored with chopped fresh herbs).

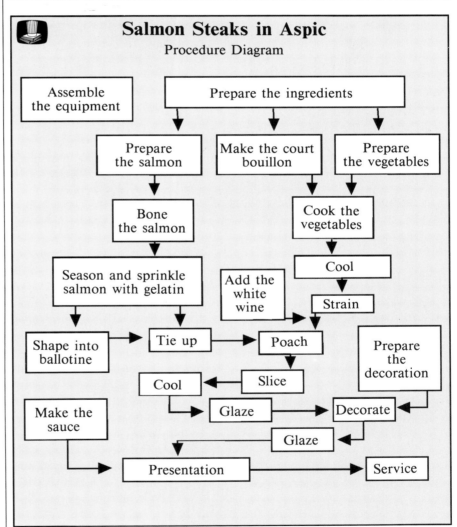

Salmon Steaks in Aspic
Procedure Diagram

- Assemble the equipment
- Prepare the ingredients
  - Prepare the salmon
  - Make the court bouillon
  - Prepare the vegetables
- Bone the salmon
- Cook the vegetables
- Season and sprinkle salmon with gelatin
- Add the white wine
- Cool
- Strain
- Shape into ballotine
- Tie up
- Poach
- Prepare the decoration
- Slice
- Cool
- Make the sauce
- Glaze
- Decorate
- Glaze
- Presentation
- Service

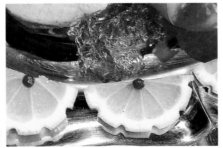

Stuffed Filets of Sole with Salmon Mousse

Introduction

This is a delicate and delicious dish made from filets of sole filled with a salmon mousse accented with truffles.

The filets are filled with the mousse, then folded over to enclose the filling and make an attractive shape.

It is best to poach the filled filets one day in advance to allow enough time for complete cooling.

The filets are glazed with a chaud-froid sauce made from fish aspic and mayonnaise.

Designs cut from truffles provide a contrast against the white filets. The whole dish is highlighted by a dome of vegetables in aspic, tomato roses and bright pink shrimp.

Equipment

Cutting board, small bowls, mixing bowls, food processor, chef's knife, paring knife, thin-bladed flexible knife, palette knife, pastry scraper, plastic wrap, drum sieve, pastry brush, pastry bag with plain tip, sheet pan, cooling rack, roasting pan, skimmer, ladle, thermometer, truffle cutter, serving platter, dome-shaped mold

Ingredients

Main Ingredients (filets and stuffing)

8 filets of sole, 75g (2 1/2oz) each
Salt, pepper
Salmon mousse made from 225g
    (7 1/2oz) salmon filets, 2 eggs,
    1 egg white, 75g (2 1/2oz) cream,
    75g (2 1/2oz) butter, 15g (1/2oz)
    truffles, salt and pepper

Court Bouillon

2L (2qts) water
7dl (1/4 cup) white wine
280g (9oz) onions
60g (2oz) parsley stems
1 sprig thyme, 1/2 bay leaf
30g (1oz) salt
8g (1/4oz) pepper

Chaud-froid

1/4L (1 cup) mayonnaise
1/2L (2 cups) fish aspic

Decoration

Truffles

Glaze

1/4L (1 cup) aspic

Garnish

For the vegetable dome

75g (2 1/2oz) carrots
75g (2 1/2oz) turnips
45g (1 1/2oz) green beans
45g (1 1/2oz) peas
3dl (1 1/4 cup) aspic

Other elements

8 tomatoes
8 shrimp
1/4L (1 cup) mayonnaise
1/2L (2 cups) chopped aspic

Procedure

Fileting the Fish

As a rule, the sole are not scaled. Cut off the fins, then remove the four filets and cut away the skin from each filet. It is not necessary to gut the fish.

Choose sole weighing between 500-600g (1-11/4lbs). The filets from smaller soles will not be big enough and filets from larger fish will be too big and thick.

Wrap the filets in a hand towel and chill until ready to use.

Preparing the Salmon Mousse

The flavors of salmon and sole marry well together and the contrast in colors is very attractive, especially with the addition of the chopped truffles. For a lower food cost, the truffles could be replaced by chopped pistachios or fresh herbs.

Keep the salmon cold until ready to use.

Work the salmon filets in the food processor until the purée forms a ball. Add the whole eggs and egg white and process again; add the heavy cream, process a few seconds, then finish by adding the butter and processing a few more seconds.

Pass the mixture through a drum sieve to make it smooth and to remove any bits of skin, scale or bone.

Combine the chopped truffles with the mousse. Season with salt and pepper. Poach or pan-fry a spoonful of mousse, taste and correct the seasoning if necessary.

Filling the Filets

Season the filets lightly with salt and pepper.

Lay them on the work surface with the skin side up.

Using a pastry bag and a plain medium tip, pipe the salmon mousse over half the length of the filet, as shown.

Fold the filet neatly in half. Press lightly to seal.

With a small palette knife, smooth the edges.

Wrap each prepared filet in several layers of plastic wrap. Make sure the wrapping is even and tight so the fish keep their shape during poaching.

Poaching

Lay the fish in a shallow roasting pan and pour over the court bouillon or fish stock just to cover.

Lay a piece of buttered parchment paper on top to keep them moist while they are cooking.

Poach the filets in an oven at 180 ⁰C (350F) or over low heat for about 25-30 minutes. Take care to monitor the temperature and cooking in order to have perfect results.

Cooling

Leave the filets to cool in their poaching liquid.

For this reason, it is best to do this step one day ahead.

If the filets are accidentally poached for too long, remove them immediately from the poaching liquid and let them cool in their wrappers.

Making the Chaud-froid Sauce

The chaud-froid is made with 2/3 fish aspic and 1/3 mayonnaise. The aspic can be made from the court bouillon or fish stock.

Whisk cold liquid aspic into the mayonnaise.

Chill the chaud-froid over crushed ice until it is thick and creamy, stirring constantly with a whisk or spatula.

Do not stir too vigorously, however, or air bubbles will become incorporated in the sauce and will ruin the appearance with tiny bubbles or a dull finish. If this happens, start over by gently melting the chaud-froid again and thickening over ice.

Glazing

The chaud-froid is applied in two steps.

First, use a thick creamy sauce. Brush the sauce evenly over the filets, filling in any holes and making a smooth surface. Chill the filets to set. Meanwhile, thin the chaud-froid a little by heating it gently in a bain-marie. Apply a second coat, using a pastry brush, ladle or a spoon.

Always work with the filets on a cooling rack placed over a stainless steel sheet pan in order to catch all the drips. To reuse, simply melt it in a bain-marie, pass it through a fine-meshed conical sieve.

Decorating

Cut the truffle into very thin slices then stamp out designs using the truffle cutter. In the example presented here, the simplicity of the black and white design is stunning, however bits of red, such as cooked red pepper, would be appropriate as well. Press lightly on the decoration to make it stick. Chill again before glazing with aspic.

Adding an Aspic Glaze

Coat each piece with clear fish aspic to give it a shine and to protect it from drying out.

Presentation

The filled filets of sole may be served individually on plates for an elegant dinner or sold in disposable containers in a specialty food shop.

221

They may also be arranged on serving platters garnished with chopped aspic, tomato roses, shrimp and little barquettes filled with diced vegetables for presentation on a buffet.

Alternatively, garnish the platter with a dome shaped vegetable aspic, as shown. Use turnips, carrots, green beans, peas. No sauce is served with this dish as it is quite rich on its own.

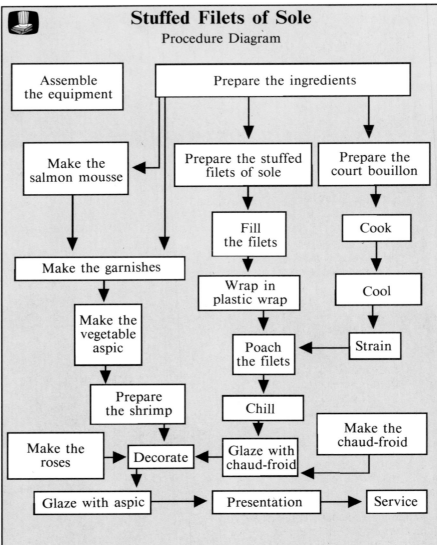

Stuffed Filets of Sole
Procedure Diagram

Assemble the equipment

Prepare the ingredients

Make the salmon mousse

Prepare the stuffed filets of sole

Prepare the court bouillon

Make the garnishes

Fill the filets

Cook

Make the vegetable aspic

Wrap in plastic wrap

Cool

Prepare the shrimp

Poach the filets

Strain

Make the roses

Chill

Decorate

Glaze with chaud-froid

Make the chaud-froid

Glaze with aspic

Presentation

Service

Sea Bass in Chaud-froid

Introduction

There are many members of the sea bass family; different varieties are available in different geographic regions. They all share the same fine sweet flesh.

The typical markings are a silvery gray-blue back and white belly.

Bass is prized by food-lovers for its delicate flavor and fine-textured, firm flesh. It ranks among the most sought-after of fish. Unfortunately, it is becoming rarer and therefore more costly.

The bass can be served whole or cut in filets and cooked "en papillote" (in a paper case). Use a light court bouillon for poaching this fish.

The ideal size is 2-3kg (about 4-6 lb). Much larger than that and the flesh is too firm, with a less delicate taste.

When well-prepared and expertly glazed, the bass in chaud-froid is a beautiful and impressive dish.

Equipment

Cutting board, cooling rack, sheet pan, plates, small bowls, mixing bowls, fish shears, paring knife, scaler, chef's knife, serrated knife, fine-meshed conical sieve, measuring cup, pastry brush, pastry scraper, spatula, whisk, ladle, truffle cutter, pastry bag and star tip, serving platter

Ingredients

For a bass weighing approximately 2.5kg (5 1/2lb).

Court Bouillon

8L (8qts) water
3dl (1 1/4 cup) wine vinegar
75g (2 1/2oz) salt
600g (1 1/4lbs) onions
1 sprig thyme
1 bay leaf
100g (3 1/2oz) parsley stems
20g (2/3oz) black peppercorns
1 leek

Chaud-froid

1/4L (1 cup) mayonnaise
1/2L (2 cups) aspic
1/4L (1 cup) aspic for final glazing

Garnishes

5 hard-boiled eggs
100g (3 1/2oz) mayonnaise
Salt, pepper
4 black olives
5 tomatoes
45g (1 1/2oz) lumpfish eggs
2 lemons
Tomato paste
Chopped aspic

Decoration for Fish

1 tomato
1 hard-boiled egg
1 truffle
Food coloring
Curly parsley
1 lemon

Procedure

Preparing the Fish

Lay the fish on a work surface and scrape with a fish scaler or the back of a knife to remove the scales. This is best accomplished under running water, which keeps the scales from scattering too far.

Feel the fish to make sure it is thoroughly scaled.

Cut out the gills. Gut the fish by making a small incision in the lower belly. Hold the fish up by its tail, and use your fingers to pull out all the entrails through the gill openings.

Using the handle of a small spoon, scrape along the interior of the backbone to remove the pockets of blood or dark skin.

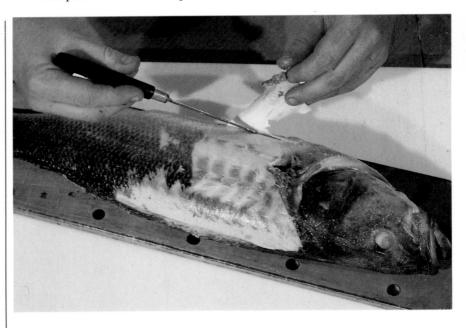

Carefully rinse the inside of the fish.

Drain it and dry carefully on a hand towel or with paper towels.

Lay the fish on a cutting board or hand towel. With a very sharp knife, cut along the backbone, from head to tail.

Keeping the blade of the knife angled toward the central bones, cut away the filet, but do not cut through the belly skin.

Repeat the procedure on the other side. Cut the central bone at each end with the fish shears. Check to see that no bits of bone are remaining, then fold the filet closed again to reshape the whole fish.

Wrap the fish tightly in cheese-cloth or a hand towel, then tie up securely.

Poaching

Put the fish in a fish poaching pan and cover with court bouillon. Always start with cold poaching liquid that has been made in advance, cooled and strained.

Poach the fish in a 190 °C (375F) oven or over low heat. Estimate 1-1 1/4 hours for a 2kg (4 1/2lb) fish.

Check the temperature of the court bouillon during cooking; it should register 80-85 °C (175-185F) on a thermometer. Using a thermometer is recommended because proper poaching is crucial to the success of this dish.

The fish must be left in its poaching liquid to cool, therefore it is best to complete the poaching the day before.

The poached fish may be kept like this in its liquid at 4 °C (40F) for 48-72 hours.

Preparing the Bass for Glazing

Once completely cooled, remove the fish from the liquid, drain it, and remove the cheesecloth.

Lay it on a work surface and carefully blot it dry with a hand towel or paper towels.

With a paring knife, carefully peel away all the skin from the head to the tail, taking care not to nick the skin.

Carefully turn the fish over and repeat the process.

NOTE

As a rule, a whole fish is positioned on a platter with its head left and tail right, with the belly toward the diner when the platter is presented from the right.

On a square or rectangular platter, lay the fish at a slight angle.

Dry the fish again with a hand towel or paper towels. Chill until ready to glaze.

Lay the fish on a rack set on a sheet pan. Be sure the best side is up and will therefore be the side presented on the platter.

Prepare the chaud-froid using the same techniques, as in the preceding recipe for Filet of Sole with Salmon Mousse.

Apply the first coat in a thick layer. Generally, the head and tail are not coated.

Chill to set, then apply a second thinner coat of chaud-froid to obtain a smooth shiny finish.

The chaud-froid may be thinned by heating gently in a bain-marie. Chill again to set.

Decorate the chilled, glazed fish using decorations of your choice.

For the decorations shown here, a colored mayonnaise was piped through a paper cone and shapes were cut out of hard-boiled egg white.

Once the decoration is firmly in place, apply a coat of clear aspic to protect the fish from drying out and to give it a brilliant shine.

Chill to set.

Carefully set the glazed bass on the platter with the head to the left and belly facing you.

A decorative rim of mayonnaise can be piped around the fish using a star tip.

Garnishes

The caterer can have free rein with the choice of garnish that decorates the platter.

They should always be chosen to complement the taste and texture of the fish.

Assembly

The platter shown here is decorated with "mimosa" eggs.

These are made by cutting the hard-boiled egg in half lengthwise, removing the yolk, which is sieved then mixed with mayonnaise, salt and nutmeg, then piped back into the white, in a rosette pattern.

A bit of black olive on top of the rosette adds color contrast.

Tomatoes cut in a saw-tooth pattern with lumpfish eggs in the center are another decorative garnish.

The base of the platter can be garnished whith chopped aspic, which may be spooned on or piped from a pastry bag fitted with a star tip, for a different look.

Additionally, tomato roses, baskets cut from lemons and fresh parsley inserted into the gill openings are decorative possibilities.

The other edge of the platter is decorated with half slices of fluted lemon, dotted with tomato paste piped from a paper cone.

The decorated platter is chilled and the garnishes are reglazed with a thin coat of clear fish aspic which keeps them shiny and prevents them from drying out.

The sauces suggested for the other fish in aspic in this chapter would be appropriate for the bass as well.

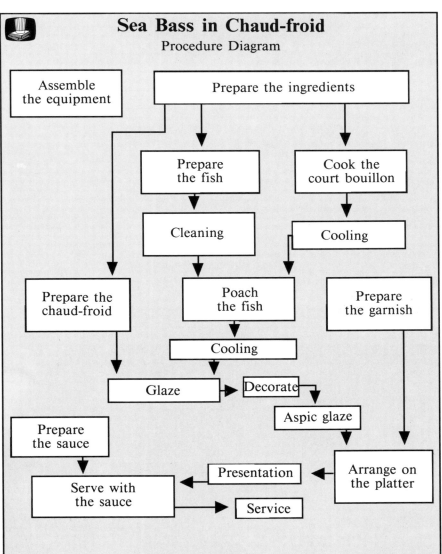

Sea Bass in Chaud-froid
Procedure Diagram

Assemble the equipment

Prepare the ingredients

Prepare the fish

Cook the court bouillon

Cleaning

Cooling

Prepare the chaud-froid

Poach the fish

Prepare the garnish

Cooling

Glaze

Decorate

Aspic glaze

Prepare the sauce

Presentation

Arrange on the platter

Serve with the sauce

Service

Salmon in Aspic

Introduction

Salmon's fine qualities are well-known and much appreciated by all fish lovers. The firm flesh has a silky texture and a distinctive taste.

There are two main categories of Atlantic salmon:

• Norwegian salmon, which has lighter flesh that is less attractive and more often is used for smoking.

• Scottish salmon, with pinker flesh which looks lovely in presentations such as this salmon in aspic.

Choose a salmon that will yield the required number of portions; you may need to use two smaller salmons instead of one very large one, depending on the size of the poaching pan.

Equipment

Cutting board, fish poaching pan, small bowls, paring knife, sheet pan, cooling rack, mixing bowls, pastry brush, plates, channel cutter, barquette molds, oval pastry cutter, small spoon, serving platter, scaler, fish shears

Ingredients

For a 2-2.5kg (4 1/2-5 1/2lb) salmon, serving 10 people.

8L (8qts) water
3dl (1 1/4 cups) vinegar
75g (2 1/2oz) salt
600g (1 1/4lb) carrots
500g (1lb) onions
1 sprig thyme
1 bay leaf
100g (3 1/2oz) parsley stems
20g (2/3oz) peppercorns
1 leek (about 150g (5oz))

Decoration

4 round firm tomatoes
1 leek green
2 lemons
5cl (1/4 cup) tomato paste

Garnishes

10 pastry barquettes
10 green asparagus tips
100g (3 1/2oz) mayonnaise
1/2 cooked red pepper
1 sprig dill
1 cucumber
150g (5oz) macedoine of vegetables (turnip, carrots, peas, green beans)
75g (2 1/2oz) mayonnaise
1 sprig chervil
1 small truffle or 3 black olives

Procedure

The techniques used to prepare the salmon are the same as those used for the sea bass, the only difference being the use of clear aspic for the salmon instead of chaud-froid for the final glaze.

The clear aspic allows the lovely color and texture of the salmon to show through whereas the bass has slightly fragile flesh which may not look perfectly smooth, and the chaud-froid helps to mask any imperfections.

Therefore the choice of a perfectly fresh and rosy salmon is of prime importance.

Prepare the fish and poach it following the guidelines in the preceding recipes.

Summary of Preliminary Steps

Scale the salmon

Cut off the fins

Wash the salmon

Cut into the rear belly

Empty the entrails through the gill openings

Scrape out any pockets of blood

Rinse the inside thoroughly

Wipe and dry off the salmon

Cut along the backbone

Detach the filets from the bones, leaving the belly skin intact

Cut the backbone at each end and remove

Close and reshape the fish

Wrap it in cheesecloth

Tie up to keep its shape

Lay the fish in the fish poaching pan, head to the left

Cover with cold court-bouillon

Poach in a 190 °C (370F) oven

Monitor the time and temperature

NOTE:

Always double check for bones with your finger tips. The bones run along the center of the filet, especially at the thick end.

Remove them with a special pincer or a pair of tweezers.

Poaching

Poaching time varies according to the size of the fish. For a 2kg (4 1/2lb) salmon, count on 1 hour at 190 °C (370F). For a larger salmon, poach it longer at a slightly lower temperature.

Leave to cool in the poaching liquid.

Storage

The fish may be kept in its poaching liquid 48-72 hours at 4 °C (40F).

231

Glazing the Salmon

Remove the cold salmon from the poaching liquid and drain it.

Untie the string and remove the cheesecloth. Blot it dry with a hand towel or paper towels.

Carefully remove the skin on both sides of the fish, leaving it on the head and tail.

Lay the fish on its right side on the cooling rack, so it is in the correct position for platter presentation, i.e. head to the left and belly to the diner.

Chill thoroughly.

Chill the aspic to thicken slightly and brush on a thick coat, filling in any holes to make a smooth surface.

Chill to set.

Brush on a second thinner coat to make it shine. Chill to set again before decorating.

Decorating

Any number of decorations can be used depending on the caterers' available time and artistic inclination.

Leek Greens

Blanch the leek green for a few seconds in boiling water, then refresh in ice water to stop the cooking and set the color. Drain and dry on a hand towel. Use a sharp paring knife to cut out shapes--stems, leaves for example.

Tomato Roses

Use firm, small evenly shaped tomatoes. With a sharp paring knife, cut away the skin in a spiral, keeping the shape thin and even. Twist the pared skin back up to form the rose, which will be placed on the glazed fish. If necessary, secure the rose with a small toothpick, which can be removed once the aspic is set.

Glaze the roses generously with thick aspic. If the aspic is too liquid, it will not adhere to the tomato and the rose will soon darken and go limp.

Garnishes

The garnishes on the platter should harmonize in color and flavor with the fish.

Asparagus Tips

Use bright green evenly shaped asparagus about 1cm (3/8in) thick.

Wash well to remove any sand.

Cook in boiling salted water. Check for doneness using the tip of a knife. The asparagus should stay slightly firm.

Remove the asparagus and plunge into ice water to stop the cooking and set the color.

Dry the cold asparagus on a hand towel or paper towel. Trim the tops if necessary so they are all an even length that fits neatly into the barquette.

The barquette is made from basic pie pastry or from puff pastry trimmings that have been blind baked ahead of time in a boat-shaped mold.

A little mayonnaise in the bottom of the barquette will hold the asparagus in place, as well as flavor it. The asparagus can be decorated with a tiny line of tomato paste piped through a paper cone or with a blanched leek green.

Blanched chive, thin slices of cooked pepper or a sprig of dill complete the decoration.

Chill the barquettes, then brush aspic on the asparagus to keep them fresh and shiny.

Cucumber Slices

Choose an evenly shaped cucumber; cut off the ends, then flute with a channel cutter.

Cut the cucumber into slices about 2cm (3/4in) thick. With a small melon baller or spoon, hollow out the center of each slice without cutting all the way through.

This will form a little "bowl" in which to put the macedoine of vegetables. Choose a variety of vegetables in contrasting colors (carrot, peas, corn, green beans, turnips).

Cut the vegetables so all the pieces are the size of the peas, in small dice, then cook each vegetable separately in boiling salted water.

Drain the vegetables, season with salt and pepper, then bind with a bit of liquid aspic. Mound a little macedoine on each cucumber round. Chill before glazing.

Decorate the tops with a sprig of dill, parsley or pieces of olive or truffle, depending on the color scheme.

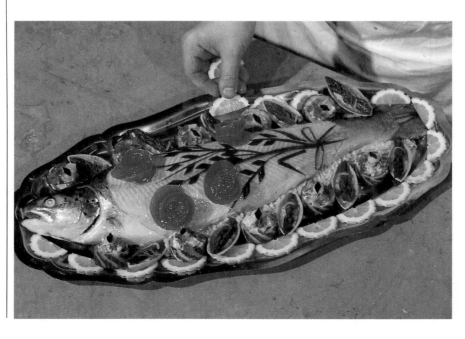

Assembly

The platter can be covered with liquid aspic then chilled to set or chopped aspic applied with a spoon or pastry bag.

Carefully lay the fish on the platter. For this presentation, mayonnaise is piped around the salmon using a star tip.

Arrange the garnishes on the platter, but do not overcrowd. If necessary, fill in with tomatoes or lemons cut in saw-tooth or slices of fluted lemon.

Coat the garnishes with a thin coat of aspic.

Keep the platter chilled, covered with a sheet of plastic wrap.

Always "touch up" the aspic finish on the salmon and garnishes with a pastry brush and new aspic just before serving.

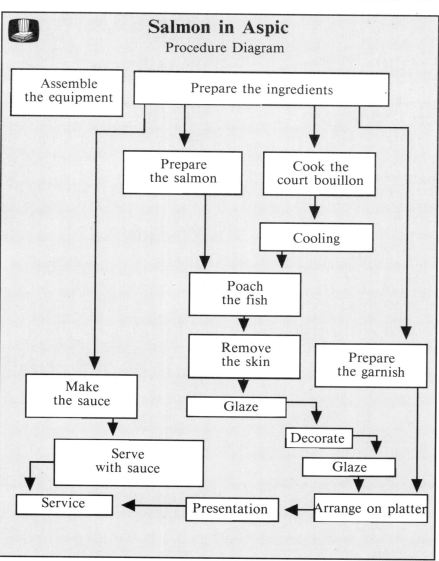

Salmon in Aspic
Procedure Diagram

Assemble the equipment

Prepare the ingredients

Prepare the salmon

Cook the court bouillon

Cooling

Poach the fish

Remove the skin

Prepare the garnish

Make the sauce

Glaze

Decorate

Serve with sauce

Glaze

Service ← Presentation ← Arrange on platter

Hake in Aspic

Introduction

The hake has fragile flesh that is delicious and marries well with the flavor of other fish, which is why it is shown stuffed with a mousse.

This preparation is appropriate for sophisticated menus and for special buffets.

The fish may be decorated and accompanied according to the caterer's artistic talents.

Equipment

Cutting board, fish shears, scaler, paring knife, thin-bladed flexible knife, chef's knife, fish poaching pan, sheet pan, cooling rack, plastic wrap, aluminum foil, cheesecloth, kitchen twine, galantine wrapper, presentation platter, pastry brush, food processor, drum sieve, pastry scraper, channel cutter, mixing bowls, small bowls, frying pan, large saucepan with lid, stainless steel sheet pan

Ingredients

Court Bouillon

8L (8qts) water
3dl (1 1/4 cups) vinegar
75g (2 1/2oz) salt
600g (1 1/4lb) carrots
500g (1lb) onions
1 sprig thyme
1 bay leaf
100g (3 1/2oz) parsley stems
Black peppercorns
1 leek (150g (5oz))

Main Ingredients

(For 12-14 people)
2.5kg (5 1/2lb) hake

Filling

200g (7oz) fish filets (whiting or pike)
2 egg whites
1 egg
75g (2 1/2oz) butter
Salt, cayenne pepper
10g (1/3oz) truffles
20g (2/3oz) pistachios

Decoration

3/4L (3 cups) fish aspic
4 round firm tomatoes

Garnishes

2 lemons
6 quail's eggs
45g (1 1/2oz) cooked red pepper
2 zucchinis
5cl (1/4 cup) olive oil
45g (1 1/2oz) salmon eggs
12 mushroom caps
100g (3 1/2oz) smoked salmon mousse
10 cherry tomatoes
Truffles
45g (1 1/2oz) corn kernels
Few green peppercorns in brine
100g (3 1/2oz) salmon filet
100g (3 1/2oz) green beans
12 sprigs chives
1/4L (1 cup) fish aspic

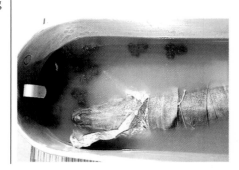

Procedure

Preparing the Fish

Scale, gut and clean the hake using the same method as described in the recipe for Sea Bass in Chaud-froid.

Boning the hake requires special care because the hake's backbone is shaped like an inverted "Y", and therefore the filets must be carefully cut from each branch. Be sure to leave the belly skin intact, especially since the fish is to be stuffed.

Open out the filets and with a paring knife, cut away the dark skin that lines the interior and which, if not removed, would ruin the appearance of the slices of fish.

Making the Stuffing

The stuffing can be made with many kinds of fish, according to budget and availability. However, because the hake has a very delicate flavor, the flavor of the fish used in the stuffing should not be too strong so that it does not overwhelm the hake. Good choices would be whiting, pike or sole.

Regardless of the choice of fish, the mousse is made following similar techniques. (Volume 2 of this series includes a chapter featuring fish mousse.)

Carefully remove the filets and cut away the skin, using a very sharp knife with the blade angled toward the skin to avoid cutting into the flesh.

Put the filets in the freezer until they are very cold, but not quite frozen. This will give better results because the flesh will not overheat when it is ground in the food processor.

Cut the filets into large dice.

Work the filets in the food processor until they form a compact ball.

Pass the puréed fish through a drum sieve to remove any scales, skin or bones and to give it a very smooth consistency.

In a mixing bowl, combine the fish with the cream, eggs, softened butter and seasoning. Stir with a wooden spoon until smooth. Poach or pan-fry a spoonful of the mousse, taste and correct seasonings if necessary.

Filling the Hake

Spread open the filets of the prepared chilled fish and with a pastry

bag, pipe the mousse evenly into the cavity.

The mousse may be accented with chopped truffles, pistachios or a mixture of the two, which will make the sliced fish very colorful.

Close the fish without applying too much pressure, which might squeeze out the mousse.

Wrap the fish in plastic wrap, so it keeps its original shape. Wrap the fish completely in the galantine wrappers or strips of handtowel.

This step requires a lot of attention, as the fish must be wrapped tightly enough so it keeps its shape, but loosely enough that the mousse stays in place and has a little room to swell during cooking.

If necessary, tie the fish with kitchen twine.

Lay the prepared hake in the fish poaching pan. Cover with court-bouillon. Because the hake's flesh is fragile and because the mousse is quite dense, it is best to poach this at a slightly lower temperature and for longer than the other fish presented in this chapter.

Poach in the oven at about 170 °C (340F) for approximately 1 hour for a 2kg (4 1/2lb) hake.

The prepared hake should weigh about the same as the whole unprepared hake, because the weight of the mousse replaces the weight lost through cleaning and boning.

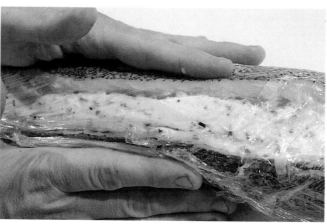

Use a thermometer to test the temperature.

Even more than for unfilled fish, fish filled with a stuffing must be poached one day in advance and cooled in their poaching liquid in order for it to cool completely and allow for easy slicing.

Glazing

Many presentations are possible with this fish; here the fish is partially sliced with the slices arranged in an attractive pattern between the head and tail.

Lay the cooled and unwrapped fish on a cutting board and with a very sharp large knife, cut 1.5cm (1/2in) slices from the middle of the fish, leaving a few inches at the head and tail ends uncut.

Lay the steaks on a cooling rack, chill and glaze them with fish aspic. The clear aspic allows the pretty colors in the mousse to show through, however a chaud-froid sauce could be used as well.

Brush two or three coats of aspic on the head and tail to give them a smooth brilliant shine.

Making the Garnishes

Five garnishes are used to decorate the platter for this presentation.

Salmon Paupiettes

Cook the green beans in boiling salted water, leaving them slightly crunchy. Refresh them in cold water and drain well.

Trim the beans evenly to about 4cm (1 3/4in) and assemble them in little bunches of about 7 beans each.

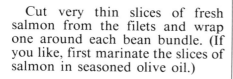

Cut very thin slices of fresh salmon from the filets and wrap one around each bean bundle. (If you like, first marinate the slices of salmon in seasoned olive oil.)

Tie up the bundles with a blanched chive sprig. Alternatively use blanched leek green, which is less tasty.

Chill this and any other garnishes before glazing them two or three times with aspic.

Lemon Wedges

The lemon is cut lengthwise into 8 wedges. The bottom of each wedge is leveled off so that it sits flat on the platter, and the top is hollowed out a little to hold the quail's egg.

Quail Eggs

The quail's eggs are cut in half and fixed in place on each wedge of lemon with a dab of butter or fish mousse.

The eggs are further decorated with a star shape cut out of cooked red pepper.

Zucchini Slices with Corn

The zucchini are fluted with a channel cutter, then sliced and topped with corn kernels and a few contrasting green peppercorns in brine.

Mushrooms

Select nicely formed, white mushrooms. Use only the caps.

The mushroom caps are carefully rinsed, then cooked in water, lemon juice and butter.

The mushroom caps are then drained, dried on paper towels and filled with crab or salmon mousse. The mousse is piped into a rosette shape with a star tip. A cherry tomato is placed on the mousse rosette, and the tomato is topped with a tiny round cut from a slice of truffle.

Assembly

Carefully arrange the fish and garnishes on the platter in an attractive pattern.

The bottom of the platter may be decorated with chopped aspic as described in previous recipes. Other decorations include tomato roses, parsley, and sliced lemons.

Cover the platter with plastic wrap and refrigerate. Brush on a thin coat of aspic just before serving.

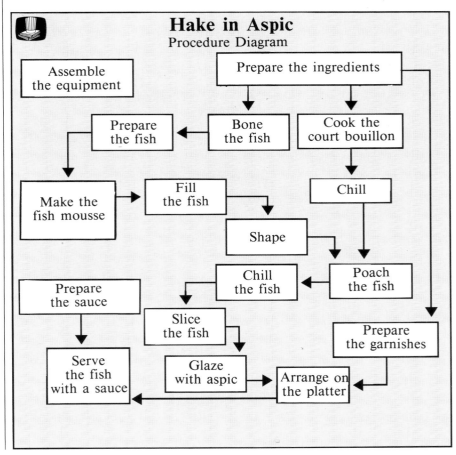

Hake in Aspic
Procedure Diagram

Assemble the equipment

Prepare the ingredients

Bone the fish → Prepare the fish

Cook the court bouillon

Make the fish mousse → Fill the fish

Chill

Shape

Prepare the sauce

Chill the fish

Poach the fish

Slice the fish

Prepare the garnishes

Serve the fish with a sauce

Glaze with aspic → Arrange on the platter

241

Turbot with Salmon Mousse

Introduction

Turbot is a flat fish with a slightly diamond shape; it is found in the Mediterranean and in some parts of the Atlantic. The turbot may reach 80cm (32in) in length, but smaller fish are easier to cook and look much nicer when presented.

The turbot is delicious, with firm, flaky white flesh. Its scales are so small that they do not need to be removed. The fish's eyes are on the left side of its flat body.

The skin on this side will be gray or brownish yellow, with little white and black spots and knobbly protrusions. The skin on the other side is white.

Turbot is a luxurious fish, prized by food connoisseurs. It can be served hot or, as in the recipe presented here, cold. Whatever form it takes, turbot is a very special fish that signals to the diners that they are being offered a notable meal.

Equipment

Cutting board, presentation platter, pastry brush, sheet pan, cooling rack, mixing bowls, paring knife, fish shears, barquette mold, oval pastry cutter, tablespoon, plastic wrap, aluminum foil, truffle cutter, small bowls, round pastry cutter, turbot pan or rectangular roasting pan, parchment paper

Ingredients

(For 15-18 people)

3kg (6 1/2lb) turbot

Poaching Liquid

2dl (3/4 cup) fish stock
1L (1qt) white wine
Salt, pepper

Chaud-froid

1/4L (1 cup) mayonnaise
1/2L (2 cups) fish aspic

Decoration

45g (1 1/2oz) truffles

Salmon Mousse

300g (10oz) salmon filets
3 egg whites
2 eggs
125g (4oz) cream
125g (4oz) butter
Salt, cayenne pepper

Garnishes

12 mussels "marinières"
2dl (3/4 cup) curry chaud-froid
3 green olives stuffed with pimiento
5cl (1/4 cup) aspic
12 white bread croutons
100g (3 1/2oz) salmon or crab mousse
5cl (1/4 cup) aspic
2 sprigs dill
12 pastry barquettes
12 crayfish
100g (3 1/2oz) mayonnaise
45g (1 1/2oz) julienne of red pepper
5cl (1/4 cup) aspic
12 cherry tomatoes
10g (1/3oz) truffles
5cl (1/4 cup) aspic

Procedure

Preparing the Turbot

The turbot is prepared differently from the other fish in this chapter. Its size and shape makes it impossible to roll up in galantine wrappers or cheesecloth, as for the hake and salmon.

Gut the fish, using basically the same techniques as for the other fish. Make a small incision in the belly and remove the gills. Insert your fingers to loosen the contents, then pull them out through the gill opening.

Rinse the interior cavity thoroughly with cold water. With fish shears, cut off the side fins.

Do not cut off the dorsal and ventral fins that run around the perimeter of the fish, as they contribute much to the fish's appearance.

Lay the prepared fish on a cutting board.

Removing the Bones

The turbot has four filets--2 top and 2 bottom. In this case, the filets from the left side are cut loose and opened out (the side of the fish with the dark skin).

With a sharp knife, cut the skin down the central backbone from head to tail. Insert the blade of a thin-bladed flexible knife and cut away the filet, working with the blade always angled toward the bone.

Do not cut through the skin at the edges.

Open out the two filets as shown and cut the ends of the bones to release them from the fish. This is a bit tricky.

Slide the small blade of the fish shears underneath each bone and snip it, taking care not to cut skin or flesh. Cut all the bones free, following the contour of the fish.

Next, cut the central bone at top and bottom and pull away all the bones in one piece.

Rinse the fish with cold water. Dry it thoroughly with a hand towel or paper towels.

Making the Salmon Mousse

The salmon mousse may be made from fresh or frozen salmon. The following instructions are for fresh salmon.

Cut off the salmon's fins, make an incision in the belly and remove the contents.

Throughly rinse the inside with cold water.

Wipe the salmon dry, then remove the filets using the techniques described in the recipe for salmon steaks in aspic.

Feel along the center of the filets, especially at the wider end, to locate the row of tiny bones. Pull these out with a pair of tweezers or special fish pincers.

With a long, sharp flexible knife, cut the skin from the flesh, angling the knife toward the skin to avoid cutting into the flesh.

Chill the filets for a few minutes to firm them up. If using frozen filets, thaw them only partially and use them while still partly frozen.

Cut the salmon into large dice. Work them in the food processor until the flesh forms a compact ball.

Gradually add the eggs and egg whites to the mixture, processing between each mixture, then add the cream and the softened butter and process again. Do not overwork, because too much mixing might cause the butter to melt and separate out of the mixture, making the mousse heavy.

Pass the mixture through a drum sieve to remove any bits of skin, scale or bone and to make it smooth and homogeneous.

Put the mousse in a stainless steel bowl set over ice and stir the mixture until it is very smooth and creamy.

Season with salt and cayenne pepper. Poach or pan-fry a spoonful of mousse, taste and correct the seasoning if necessary. Chill until ready to use.

Filling the Turbot with Mousse

Lay the prepared turbot on the work surface. Open out the filets.

Using a spoon, a pastry scraper or a pastry bag and plain tip, fill the cavity of the turbot with a thick layer of the mousse, enough so that when the filets are closed, they do not quite meet and there is a strip of mousse down the center.

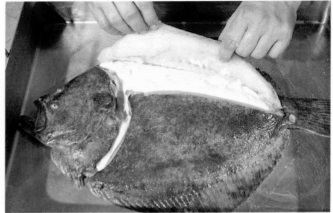

Gently close up the filets without applying too much pressure, which would displace the mousse.

Poaching

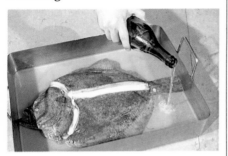

Place a rack in the bottom of the turbot pan or roasting pan and carefully lay the turbot on top.

Add the court-bouillon to half cover the turbot. Do not let the level of the court-bouillon reach the mousse, because the mousse would absorb the liquid and become watery.

Poach the fish over low heat or in an oven at 160-170 °C (325-340F). Estimate about 1-1 1/4 hours for a 2kg (4 1/2lb) turbot.

Carefully monitor the cooking and temperature with a thermometer. The inside of the turbot should reach 80 °C (175F).

Leave to cool in its poaching liquid; this is even more important for turbot than for other fish.

Glazing

Remove the fish on the rack and let it drain.

Wipe the surface dry with a hand towel.

Carefully peel off the dark skin, leaving it on the head, tail and border of fins.

The fish is too delicate to turn over to remove the skin on the other side, so it remains.

Dry the surface again and chill until ready to glaze.

Make a thick chaud-froid sauce. With a spoon or a pastry brush, apply a coat of chaud-froid to the surface of the filets, leaving the head, tail and fins uncoated, as shown. Chill to set before applying a second coat.

To increase the number of servings, the extra salmon mousse may be shaped in a cylinder by wrapping it up in several layers of plastic wrap and poaching at 190 ⁰C (370F) for about 45 minutes. In this case, slice the cylinder of mousse into medallions and coat them with chaud-froid also.

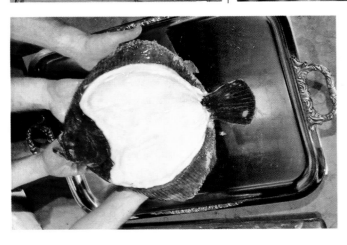

Making the Garnishes

The Mussels

Select nice mussels about the same size and wash them carefully. Cook them "à la marinière", leave to cool and drain. Remove the shells and the dark rim or "beard" around each one. Put each mussel on a half-shell and fill to the rim with a curry flavored chaud-froid sauce. Two layers of sauce will give the best results.

Decorate the top with a slice of stuffed green olive. Chill, then brush with a layer of clear aspic.

The Hard-boiled Eggs and Cherry Tomatoes

Cut the eggs in half widthwise, then cut a little off each end so the halves sit flat.

Brush with a coat of clear aspic, decorate with a bit of truffle or tomato paste piped through a paper cone.

Chill, then glaze with aspic again.

The cherry tomatoes are glazed with aspic, then decorated with truffle.

The Croutons

Cut out rounds of "pain de mie" (enriched white bread). Lightly butter them on both sides and toast in the oven until crisp and golden.

With a pastry bag and star tip, pipe a rosette of salmon or crab mousse on each crouton.

Chill until the mousse is firm, then brush on a coat of aspic. Decorate with a sprig of dill.

The Crayfish Barquettes

Remove the dark "vein" of intestine from each crayfish by twisting the center tail fin and gently pulling it out. Sauté the crayfish in a little olive oil over high heat for 1-2 minutes until they turn bright red. Drain them, then while still warm, remove the tail meat. Reserve the shells for decoration.

Use blind baked barquette shells made with pie pastry.

Place a dab of seasoned mayonnaise in the bottom of each barquette.

Place a crayfish tail and a little vegetable julienne in each barquette.

Assembly

Carefully place the turbot on a large presentation platter. This may require two people, as the turbot is large and quite fragile.

Lay the medallions of mousse down the center of the turbot, slightly overlapping. Brush the entire surface of the fish with clear aspic.

Arrange the mussels around the turbot, which highlight its large size and dramatic shape. Arrange the remaining garnishes on the platter in an attractive pattern.

Decorate the base of the platter with aspic cut into fine dice and piped from a pastry bag.

Keep chilled, covered with plastic wrap to prevent it from drying out.

Touch up the aspic before serving if necessary.

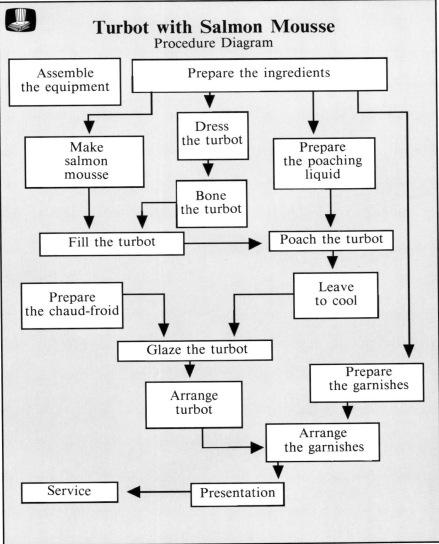

Turbot with Salmon Mousse
Procedure Diagram

Chapter 8
Lobsters

Presented split and filled on a plate, or whole in all their glory on a platter, lobsters make a spectacular display.

The Star of the Buffet

The texture and subtle flavor of lobster makes it a perennial favorite.

These are classic preparations that have graced French tables for centuries.

The lobsters can be majestically arranged on platters as the main attraction on a buffet or split and filled with colorful ingredients for an easy-to-serve, elegant dish.

The basic techniques involved are not difficult.

The cost of lobster is usually very high, so these luxurious preparations are most often served for special occasions.

General Advice for Preparing Lobsters

Choosing Lobsters

The lobsters shown here are called " langoustes " in French, and are known as spiny or rock lobsters in English. They are found worldwide in temperate coastal waters. Regular lobsters can be used, though they are not as spectacular on a platter display.

For the classic buffet showpiece pictured at the beginning of this chapter, choose large lobsters (2-3kg (4 1/2-6 1/2lbs)) with the antennae intact for the presentation.

Individual portions made by splitting a cooked lobster in half are made with lobsters weighing 700-800g (1 1/2-1 3/4lb).

Always buy the lobsters just before they are to be prepared and keep them alive until they are cooked.

Storage of Live Lobsters

The live lobsters can be kept refrigerated for up to 24 hours.

Do not be tempted to put them in a basin of water, which would lack the oxygen to keep them alive.

It is recommended to leave them in the case they are shipped in. Algae is often used to pack them to maintain a humid environment.

Once the lobster dies, it dries out very quickly and the flesh becomes tough and rubbery.

Prepare the Lobsters for Cooking

Before cooking, clean the shell of the lobster by scrubbing with a vegetable brush and rinsing under cold water to remove algae, sand and impurities.

The cooking process stiffens the flesh and therefore sets the shape of the lobster. For this reason, a lobster to be displayed on a platter must have its tail flattened and tied to a board as shown. The head is raised with a small block of wood or a ball of aluminum foil so that the cooked lobster will sit on the platter in the described upswept position.

The board should be just wide enough to fit under the tail and longer than the lobster to facilitate handling.

The smaller lobsters to be split do not need to be tied to a board. The tail naturally curls during cooking, which gives the lobster an attractive shape on the plate.

Cooking the Lobsters

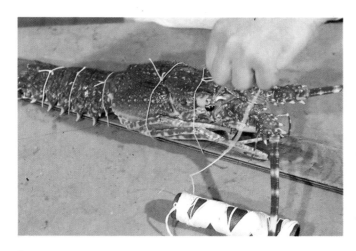

Cooking lobsters is not difficult. They are simply plunged, alive, into a boiling liquid.

The Cooking Liquid

Lobsters are usually boiled in lightly salted water. The cooking liquid can also be court-bouillon, which is flavored with vegetables. However, the taste of the court-bouillon should not be strong enough to overpower the delicate meat of the lobster. (See recipe at the end of this section.)

Cooking

Bring the water or court-bouillon to a boil in a pot large enough to hold the lobster easily. A tall stockpot is especially functional for the lobsters that have been tied to a board.

When the water has come to a boil, submerge the lobster.

Be very careful with lobsters that are not secured to a board, as they will sometimes flip their tail and splash boiling water.

Maintain the cooking liquid at a low steady boil during the cooking process.

The cooking time varies with the size of the lobster.

- 8 minutes for a 700g (1 1/2lb) lobster

- 12 minutes for a 1.5kg (3 1/4lb) lobster

Draining the Lobsters

Place the cooked lobsters on a cooling rack to drain. Cooking

liquid will also fill cavities in the lobster shell during cooking.

To drain the inside of the lobster, make an incision with a stiff-bladed knife between the eyes.

Turn the lobster upside down so the liquid trapped inside pours out.

NOTE: For all of the preparations in this chapter, the lobsters are split and filled after they are thoroughly cooled. Therefore it is necessary to cook them a day in advance.

Storage

The cooked and drained lobsters are refrigerated until ready to assemble; they will keep 4-5 days.

Splitting the Lobster in Half

Half of a lobster provides an individual portion appropriate for a refreshing first course or light main course. (The size of the lobster can vary depending on how they will be served.)

The decorative shape of the lobster and bright color makes a stunning plate presentation. The shell is a natural container to serve the delicious meat from the tail combined with an array of other ingredients.

Attention is needed at this stage to cut the shell neatly and exactly in half so each serving is identical and attractive.

Place the lobster on a cutting board with the underside next to the board as shown.

Using a well-sharpened large chef's knife, make an incision with the point of a knife in the center just above the tail.

Hold the head of the lobster with the other hand and grasp the knife and firmly draw it down through the tail, applying steady pressure on the knife.

Turn the lobster around and repeat the process. Place the tip of the knife into the incision in the middle and draw the knife down, this time cutting through the head.

Remove the dark vein (the intestine) that is visible along the outer edge of the tail. The vein may be on one half or the other or cut in two.

Lift out the tail meat in one piece and trim the thin skin that envelops the flesh. Scrub out the shell with a vegetable brush to make a clean container for the presentation.

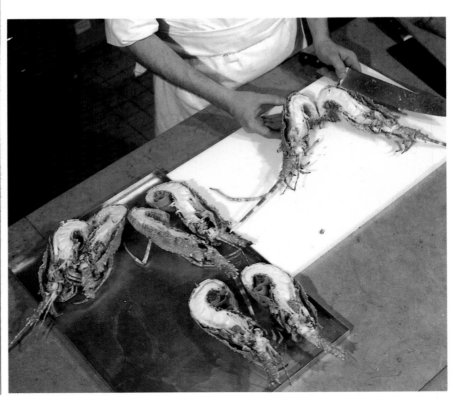

Preparing the Whole Lobster

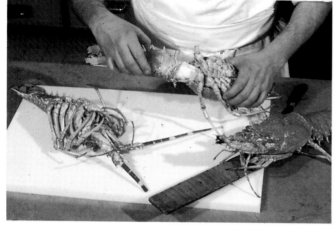

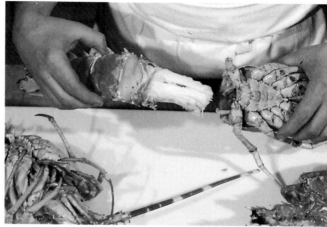

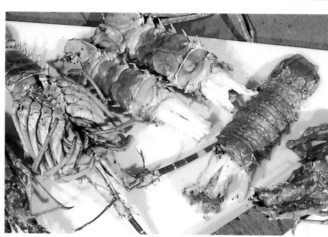

In French, a platter presentation with neatly arranged and highly decorated foods is called "bellevue" or "beautiful sight".

Lobsters are often featured "en bellevue" as the centerpiece of a fancy buffet. The most flamboyant presentation includes two lobsters with the bodies arched and the dramatic antennae reaching high in the air.

It is therefore important to remove the meat carefully so the empty shell of the whole lobster can be reassembled for the beautiful display.

The lobsters have been tied to a board with their tails flat and straight and heads raised.

To remove the tail meat in one piece, cut the scales on the underside of the tail.

Do not press too hard as you cut so the shell is not crushed.

It is highly recommended to use a hand towel to hold the lobster to protect you from the sharp scales.

Pull the tail meat out with your fingers or a fork.

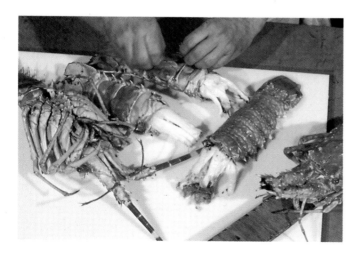

Preparing a Whole Lobster (continued)

Make a shallow incision down the center of the top of the tail to expose the dark vein (intestine) and remove it carefully using the tip of a small knife.

Trim all the dark bits of flesh that are attached to the meat that would mar the appearance of the finished dish.

Using a small knife, pull off the very thin fibrous skin that envelops the tail meat.

Storage

Once the meat is removed from the shell, it oxidizes very quickly, which darkens the meat and dries it out.

Procedure for Preparing Lobsters

Make the court-bouillon or heat the water in a large pot

Wash the lobsters

If necessary, tie them to the wooden planks

Cook the lobsters by plunging them in boiling liquid

Drain the lobsters on a rack

Pierce the shell to let trapped liquid drain out

Leave to cool completely

Keep refrigerated (4 C (40F)) until ready to use

Cut the lobsters on a cutting board with a large chef's knife

Garnish the lobsters according to the chosen recipe

Remember the cooked lobsters keep 4-5 days in their shells.

For best results, remove the meat for split and whole lobsters just before assembling.

If preparing large quantities, the lobster tails or half lobsters can be refrigerated a few hours covered with plastic wrap.

Ingredients for Court-Bouillon

For 12 liters (12 quarts) water

120g (4oz) coarse salt	200g (7oz) onions
2 bay leaves	300g (10oz) tomatoes
3 sprigs thyme	6 cloves garlic
12 parsley stems	150g (5oz) leek green
40 peppercorns	120g (4oz) celery stalks
300g (10oz) carrots	3 slices lemon

Simmer for 30 minutes.

Lobster with Mayonnaise

Introduction

This is the simplest presentation for a split lobster. The decoration can be more elaborate than shown here but should always harmonize with the taste and color of the lobster.

Ingredients

1 lobster 700-800g
  (1 1/2-1 3/4lbs)
1 hard-boiled egg
1 tomato
Truffle
Parsley

Sauce

Mayonnaise
1 egg yolk
1/2 teaspoon mustard
Salt, cayenne pepper
1/4L (1 cup) oil
Few drops vinegar or lemon

Chive vinaigrette
1cl (2 tsp) wine vinegar
Salt, pepper
4cl (8 tsp) oil
6 chive sprigs

Procedure

The Lobster

Clean and cook the lobsters as described at the beginning of this chapter. Cool and cut in half.

Remove the dark vein from each half, then pull out the tail meat. Cut the meat into neat pieces and replace it in the shell. This operation makes the dish easy to handle for the guests.

The Sauce

The mayonnaise should be made stiff enough to be piped and it should be well seasoned. Using a pastry bag fitted with a medium or small star tip, make an attractive pattern with the mayonnaise.

A sauceboat of vinaigrette, accented with fresh herbs, can be served alongside.

Glazing and Decoration

Before placing the decoration on the lobster, brush on a very thin coat of fish aspic. (For this dish the aspic does not need to be chilled and thickened over ice because the aspic is not applied to make a shiny finish, but rather to keep the lobster moist and prevent it from darkening.)

The simple decoration here consists of a slice of hard-boiled egg with a thin slice of truffle providing contrast. Tomato wedges and parsley add a dash of color.

A " macedoine " (small dice) of vegetables with a mayonnaise dressing can be spooned into the head of the lobster.

Storage

If a large quantity is being prepared in advance, the lobsters can be wrapped in plastic wrap and refrigerated for a few hours. (Whole, they will keep refrigerated 4-5 days.)

Serving

Remove the prepared lobsters from the refrigerator a little while before serving to take the chill off. Brush on a fresh coat of aspic to moisten them.

" Manhattan " Lobster

Introduction

This American style salad combines the lobster with avocado and red pepper, and the mayonnaise is accented with ketchup.

The ingredients are diced, mixed with the dressing then spooned into the shell which is lined with a lettuce leaf.

Ingredients

(For a 700-800g (1 1/2-1 3/4lb) lobster
1/2 avocado (75g (2 1/2oz))
1/4 red pepper (45g (1 1/2oz))
Sauce
150g (5oz) mayonnaise
Few drops vodka
2cl (4 tsp) ketchup
Salt, cayenne pepper
Tabasco

Decoration

Lettuce leaves
Quartered hard-boiled eggs
Quartered tomatoes
Black olives
Chervil sprigs

Procedure

The Lobster

Clean and cook the lobsters as described at the beginning of this chapter. Cool and cut in half.

Remove the dark vein and lift out the tail meat from each half.

Trim the thin skin if necessary and cut the meat into 1.5cm (1/2 in.) dice. Cover and refrigerate until ready to assemble the dish.

The Avocado

Choose a ripe avocado that is firm enough that it can be cut into neat dice and will not become mushy when mixed with the other ingredients. The dice should be a little smaller than the lobster, about 1cm (3/8in).

The Red Pepper

Choose bright unblemished peppers, rinse them and remove the peel, seeds and white ribs on the inside.

Cut the pepper into small dice, 4-5mm (1/8-1/4in).

Making the Sauce

Make a classic mayonnaise and add a dash of ketchup. Season with a few drops of tabasco, a few drops of vodka and a little salt.

Assembly

Mix all of the ingredients with the sauce. Add some freshly chopped chervil if available.

Line the hollow shells with fresh, crisp lettuce leaves that have been washed and dried thoroughly.

Spoon the lobster salad into the shell from the head to the tip of the tail as shown.

For this presentation, quail eggs, tomato wedges and olives decorate

the finished dish as well as a sprig of fresh chervil.

Storage

If preparing in advance, cover with plastic wrap and refrigerate.

Serving

Remove the prepared lobster from the refrigerator a little while before being served to "take the chill off" and serve chilled but not too cold.

Lobster with Vegetable Julienne

Introduction

Delicate shoe-string julienne are quickly made with a "mandoline"--a specialized manual slicer on which vegetables are shaped very efficiently with a "strumming" motion. The settings on the mandoline can be adjusted to make thin strips or thicker ones.

Garnish

75g (2 1/2oz) cucumber
60g (2oz) zucchini
60g (2oz) carrots
15g (1/2oz) truffle

Sauce

2cl (4 tsp) wine vinegar
8cl (1/3 cup) oil
Salt and pepper

Decoration

Dill
Chives

Ingredients

(For a 700-800g (1 1/2-1 3/4lb) lobster)

Procedure

The Lobster

Clean and cook the lobster as described at the beginning of this chapter. Cool and cut in half.

Pull off the dark vein and lift out the tail meat.

Trim the thin skin from the tail meat and cut away dark pieces of flesh.

Cut the meat into even slices, keeping the tail together so it will fit back into the shell. Clean the interior of the shell and replace the meat.

The Garnish

The julienne of vegetables that accompanies the sliced lobster consists of cucumber, carrot, zucchini and truffle.

Peel the cucumber and cut in 5cm (2in) pieces. Cut each piece in quarters lengthwise to remove the seeds in the center. Using a mandoline, slice each piece of cucumber thinly, then cut the slices into a thin julienne with a chef's knife.

Peel and rinse the carrot. Cut into 5cm (2in) pieces and slice thinly on the mandoline. Cut the slices into thin julienne with a chef's knife.

Rinse the zucchini and remove the dark green outer layer carefully with a vegetable peeler without pulling too much of the light flesh of the zucchini underneath. Cut the skin of the zucchini into 5cm (2in) lengths and cut them into fine julienne.

Slice the truffle very thinly with a sharp thin-bladed knife and cut the slices into julienne.

Assembly

Make a well-seasoned vinaigrette.

Toss the julienne of vegetables with the vinaigrette. Taste and add salt and pepper if necessary.

When ready to serve, cover the head of the lobster with an ample portion of the seasoned julienne of vegetables.

Brush the sliced meat with a little olive oil or fish aspic to protect the flesh and make it look moist.

Sprinkle some chopped chives over the tail meat. Finish the decoration with a sprig of dill at the top.

Storage and Serving

If not serving immediately, cover with plastic wrap and refrigerate.

Allow the refrigerated lobster to sit at room temperature briefly before being served to "take the chill off". Serve cool but not icy cold.

Serve with vinaigrette in a sauceboat.

Lobster " en Salpicon "

Introduction

A " salpicon " is a mixture of diced ingredients. The colorful assortment in this recipe makes the presentation lively and fresh.

Each ingredient is prepared separately, as they have very different textures.

Ingredients

(For a 700-800g (1 1/2-1 3/4lb) lobster)

Garnish
45g (1 1/2oz) mangoes
75g (2 1/2oz) tomatoes
45g (1 1/2oz) carrots
45g (1 1/2oz) green beans
15g (1/2oz) truffles

Sauce
2cl (4tsp) wine vinegar
8cl (1/3 cup) oil
Salt and pepper

Decoration
Lettuce leaves

Procedure

The Lobster

Clean and cook the lobster as described at the beginning of this chapter. Cool and cut in half.

The " Salpicon "

This colorful salpicon is made with green beans, tomatoes, carrots, mangoes and truffles.

The Green Beans

Choose extra thin green beans. Rinse them and remove the strings.

Cook them in rapidly boiling salted water until tender but still firm.

Transfer the cooked beans immediately to a basin of ice water to stop the cooking.

Drain them on a hand towel, then cut into 1cm (3/8in) pieces.

The Carrots

Rinse the carrots, peel them and cut in thin slices (3-4mm (about 1/8in)) on a mandoline.

Cut the slices into strips, then cut the strips into small dice.

Cook the carrots in rapidly boiling salted water until tender but firm.

Transfer the cooked carrots immediately to a basin of ice water to stop the cooking.

Drain on a hand towel.

The Tomatoes

Choose firm ripe tomatoes. If they are too soft, they will not hold their shape in the salad.

Plunge the tomatoes into boiling water for a few seconds to loosen the skin. Peel away the skin, cut in half and squeeze out the seeds.

Cut the tomatoes into 1cm (3/8in) dice using a very sharp knife that will slice neatly without crushing the fragile flesh of the tomato.

The Lobster Meat

Remove the dark vein (intestine) and lift out the tail meat in one piece.

Trim the thin skin off the meat and cut away any dark bits of flesh that are attached.

Cut the meat into 1.5cm (1/2in) dice and store in the refrigerator until ready to assemble the dish.

Clean the inside of the shell.

The Mango

Choose a ripe mango that is not too soft. Not ripe enough and it will be bland, too ripe and the mango will not hold its shape in the salad.

Peel the mango and cut it in 1cm (3/8in) slices. Cut the slices into strips, then into even dice.

The Truffle

Cut the truffle into very fine dice and cover with plastic wrap.

Assembly

Whisk together the vinaigrette ingredients.

Gently toss all of the diced ingredients together in a bowl.

Stir in the vinaigrette without crushing the delicate elements. The sauce will season the mixture and make it shine.

Line the clean shells with lettuce leaves, pressing them into the hollow of the shell so the salad can fill the cavity.

Spoon the salpicon above the rim of the shell so the portion is ample.

NOTE: Lettuce is always used when the lobster meat is removed and mixed with other ingredients, then replaced in the shell.

No further decoration is needed for this festive dish.

Storage and Serving

If not serving immediately, cover with plastic wrap and refrigerate.

Allow the refrigerated lobster to sit at room temperature briefly before serving to "take the chill off". Serve cool but not icy cold.

Serve with vinaigrette in a sauceboat.

Lobsters " en Bellevue "

Introduction

Whole lobsters are spectacular when arranged on platters and beautifully decorated " en bellevue ".

The flattened tail and raised head make the lobster look majestic and the simple decoration on the platter is very elegant.

One or more lobsters can be arranged on a platter. Two lobsters head to head make a particularly dramatic presentation.

The trimmed tail meat is cut into neat medallions and are the main garnish on the platter.

The meat from the two lobsters is usually not enough, so several need to be cooked to fill the platter.

Choosing the Lobster

Choose fresh lively lobsters with undamaged shells and antennae.

The lobsters for platter presentation can vary between 1-3kg (2-6 1/2lb). If presenting 2 or more on the same platter, they should all be the same size.

Cutting Medallions

When the lobster has completely cooled (overnight), remove the tail meat as described, being sure to hold the lobster securely with a hand towel to prevent the sharp scales from injuring you.

Remove the dark vein (intestine), pull off the thin skin and trim away any dark bits of flesh that are attached to the tail meat. Cut the meat in even medallions about 1cm (3/8in) thick.

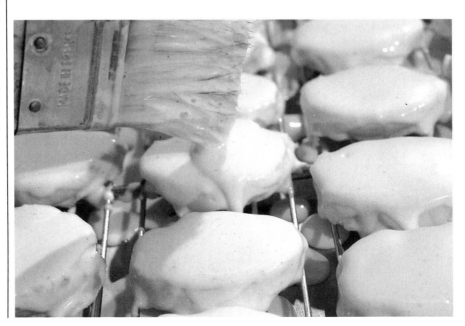

Glazing the Medallions

Arrange the medallions on a stainless steel rack set over a stainless steel baking sheet, in rows so they can be glazed in assembly-line fashion.

Shown here, some of the medallions are covered with chaud-froid sauce and others simply with a crystal clear aspic.

The chaud-froid can be a classic velouté based sauce or a better tasting mayonnaise with flavorful fish aspic blended in.

The chaud-froid is stirred over ice to thicken slightly, then brushed or spooned over the medallions. Two coats are necessary to give a smooth neat finish.

Decorating the Medallions

Truffles are the perfect decoration for the medallions of lobster. The jet-black truffle cut in neat shapes contrasts beautifully against the snowy white lobster and ivory-colored chaud-froid to make a very elegant display.

Other decorations that marry well with the luxurious lobster are

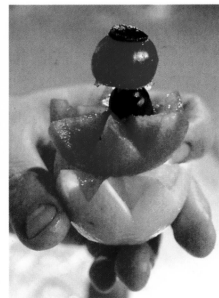

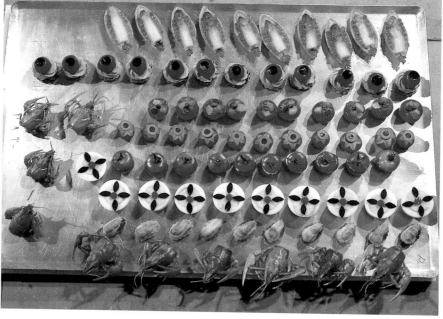

red pepper, tomatoes, hard-boiled egg white, green part of the leek, dill and parsley.

Classically, the final presentation is quite austere to put the lobster in a place of prominence.

Once the decorations are arranged, chill before applying a final coat of aspic to make them shine and hold them in place.

Preparing the Garnishes

As shown in the chapter on Fish in Aspic, the platters are decorated with assorted garnishes.

The variety is endless and the choice will depend on the tastes and budget of the customer.

Barquettes or boat-shaped pastry shells are blind baked and cooled.

The simple filling used here is an asparagus tip sitting on a little mayonnaise with salmon eggs placed on either side of the asparagus.

The barquette is chilled, then brushed with aspic and decorated with dill or parsley.

Croutons made of close-textured bread can be cut out in rounds, diamonds or squares with a pastry cutter.

The shapes are buttered on both sides and toasted in the oven until crispy and golden brown.

Here the cooled croutons are topped with a rosette of delicate salmon mousse decorated with a tomato and a round of truffle. They are chilled, then brushed with aspic.

Cherry tomatoes with the top 1/3 cut off, are scooped out with a small melon baller and filled with a tiny julienne of vegetables.

They can also be cut in half, scooped out and filled with a rosette of herbed cheese and decorated with chives.

Radishes cut in " flowers " are a lovely decoration.

Hard-boiled eggs, are cut in slices and topped with a geometric shape made from olives or truffles and red peppers.

Small toasts, round or oval, can be topped with pepper compote, vegetables in aspic. Another elegant filling is shrimp mousse with a crayfish tail placed on top.

Crayfish shells, are colorful additions to the presentation.

Peeled tomatoes cut in half and decorated with truffle and egg white are elegant when juxtaposed with eggs cut in half and decorated with truffles and red pepper.

Tomato roses and *zigzag lemon halves* complete the stunning choices for garnishes.

Platter with One Lobster

Procedure

1. Glaze the platter with aspic
2. Set the lobster on the platter
3. Arrange the medallions
4. Add the garnishes
5. Decorate with chopped aspic

Advice

Arrange the medallions and garnishes in a balanced pattern, playing with the colors and shapes, without overcrowding the platter.

Platter with Two Lobsters

On a large elegant platter, place the two lobsters so they are centered and achieve an upswept motion.

A triangular piece of bread can be used under the heads to support them, with the antennae straight in the air.

Arrange some of the medallions, overlapping on the tail of each lobster and place the others in even rows on either side.

The other garnishes are arranged around the medallions, playing with shape and color to create a balanced display.

Fill in the space between the garnishes with aspic cut in cubes or chopped and piped with a pastry bag.

The finishing touches of parsley, tomato roses and cut lemons are added at the last moment.

Cover with plastic wrap and refrigerate until ready to serve.

Just before serving, brush a thin coat of aspic over the medallions and garnishes to make them shine.

Chapter 9

Poultry in Aspic

A Principal Role in the Caterer's Repertoire

Poultry in aspic plays an important role in catering. The range of flavors and forms is wide, allowing limitless variation on recipes and presentations.

This versatility encourages the caterer's creativity because so many different sauces, finishes and garnishes complement the taste of poultry.

General Advice

Choosing Poultry

There is a great variety of poultry to choose from. The first consideration should be the flavor of the bird, and then the available sizes.

For a large buffet, a mix of poultry is possible, where the caterer may offer large centerpieces as well as individual portion sizes.

The selection presented in this chapter illustrates the diversity of poultry in aspic.

1. Cubed Turkey in Aspic

2. Chicken in Chaud-Froid with Truffles

3. Chicken in Aspic

4. Duck à l'Orange in Aspic

5. Quails with Foie Gras in Aspic

These examples can serve as a springboard from which the caterer can develop many other variations.

Cooking Poultry

There are several distinct cooking methods that can be used:

• poaching

• roasting in an oven

• spit-roasting

• pot-roasting

The choice of cooking method should be the one that best preserves and enhances the flavor and texture of the particular bird.

Assembly

The bird will be cut up and assembled to correspond to the way in which it will be presented and sold. For example, a service at a buffet requires a dish that is easy to eat without too much manipulation, so the bird should be pre-cut into slices or cubes.

A caterer may offer poultry in the following methods of sale:

- in a specialty food shop

- in " quick " restaurant service

- at sit-down meals (lunch or dinner)

- at a small buffet

- at a large spectacular buffet

Glazing

The choice of glaze is important

- for flavor

- for decoration

- for protection from dryness and to hold the dish together

The range of glazes runs from plain aspic to aspic flavored with herbs or alcohols to chaud-froid sauce, a favorite glaze because of its beautiful appearance.

The glaze is applied in several successive layers and the poultry is chilled thoroughly before each application for a perfect finish.

Garnishing

Garnishes add visual interest to a presentation as well as introduce flavors and textures that harmonize with the poultry.

All sorts of bases, such as croutons and pastry barquettes, can be topped with flavorful, colorful ingredients.

Presentation

The final presentation of the dish will integrate all the flavors, textures and shapes of the ingredients.

It is here that the caterer's skill becomes visible, and much attention should be paid to presentation, in order to have impeccable results that do justice to the ingredients.

The edible garnishes will serve as decoration as well, and other decorative elements may be used also such as frilled toothpicks or paper frills to cover the ends of the legs.

The serving platter must be the correct size for the dish. The elements should not be overcrowded on the platter and yet the dish must appear copious.

Storage

If preparing the dishes in advance, cover with pastic wrap and refrigerate for 48 hours maximum.

Serving

For the cubed presentations, provide toothpicks for easy handling.

The dishes coated with chaud-froid are usually not served with a sauce.

Cubed Turkey in Aspic

Introduction

In France, roast turkey with stuffing features in festive end-of-the-year holiday meals. Nonetheless, turkey is delicious cold, and is eaten year-round.

The best quality production and attention to cooking and preparation are crucial to client satisfaction.

The turkey's large size makes for a striking presentation on a buffet table.

The method of preparation presented in this recipe may be applied to slightly smaller birds as well, such as chicken and duck.

Suggested garnishes include slices of chicken breast, small aspic molds, pastry barquettes filled with macedoine of vegetables and croutons topped with liver mousse.

Equipment

Roasting pan, ladle, cutting board, trussing needle, kitchen twine, chef's knife, paring knife, palette knife, thin-bladed flexible knife, mixing bowls, 2-pronged fork, spatula, whisk, pastry scraper, pastry bag and star tip, pastry brush, oval pastry cutter, white frilled toothpicks, platter, cooling rack, sheet pan

Ingredients

Main Ingredients

4.5kg (10lb) turkey (for cooking)
100g (3 1/2oz) clarified butter
5cl (1/4 cup) oil
Salt, pepper

Assembly Ingredients

500g (1lb) goose liver purée

Glazing Ingredients

3/4L (3 cups) chicken aspic

Garnish Ingredients

16 croutons, made from " pain de mie " (enriched white bread)
30g (1oz) butter
100g (3 1/2oz) goose liver purée
Truffles

Decoration Ingredients

Tomato roses
1L (1qt) aspic cut in cubes

Procedure

Preparing the Turkey

Singe off any feathers by passing the bird over a flame such as a gas burner. Wipe the skin clean with a hand towel.

Cut the feet off a little bit above the joint.

Cut off the wing tips.

Cut the neck skin on the underside and loosen the neck. Cut off the head and cut the neck from the body, taking care not to pierce the skin close to the body.

Insert your fingertips into the neck opening and run them around the carcass to loosen the lungs.

Make a small incision (2.5cm (1in)) in the tail end opening of the turkey to enlarge it. Carefully loosen and pull out the entrails. Check by touch and sight that the cavity is empty and clean. Wipe it out with paper towels or a hand towel.

Discard everything but the liver, gizzard and heart.

Carefully remove and discard the green bile sack; do not puncture it or the bile will ruin the liver. Cut away any yellow or green spots on the liver.

Cut the gizzard on the wide end and remove the inner section that contains undigested grain. Rinse the gizzard and reserve for another use.

Remove the thin skin enveloping the heart, along with any bits of fat. Make a small incision to open the heart and rinse out any blood.

Trussing the Turkey

Use a trussing needle and kitchen twine. Lay the turkey on its back on a cutting board.

Position the legs at the level of the breast. Insert the trussing needle at the joint between the leg and thigh. Turn the bird over and bring the needle under the end of the wing. Pull the neck skin taut underneath and pass the needle through.

Repeat the procedure in the opposite direction, beginning with the wing and ending with the thigh.

Tie the two ends of twine together, securing with several knots. Tie up the two leg ends so the bird is closed up.

Cooking the Turkey

Season the inside of the turkey with a little salt and pepper. (If the salt were on the outside, it would dry out the skin.)

Heat the roasting pan and add some oil and butter. Lay the turkey in the pan and brown it over medium heat, turning carefully a few times so it becomes an even golden brown. Be sure not to pierce the skin.

Transfer the turkey (on its back) to a 200C (375F) oven and roast. For the 4.5kg (10lb) turkey pictured here, count on approximately 1 1/2 hours.

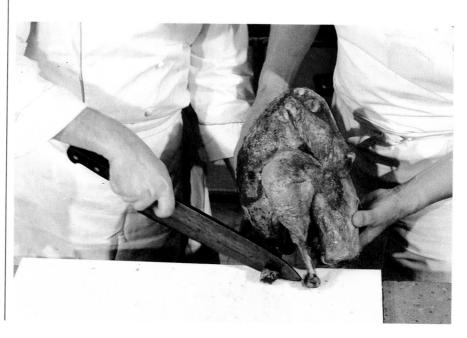

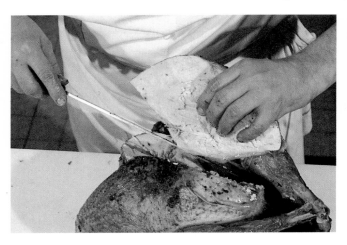

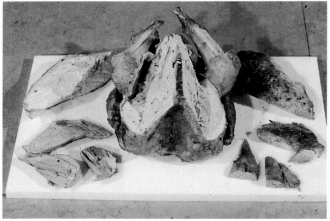

NOTE: For a moist, evenly cooked bird, be sure to baste it frequently and turn it over from time to time during cooking.

Checking the Cooking

The golden color of the turkey should be even.

Carefully lift up the turkey to let juices run from its interior; they should be clear, with no trace of blood. Transfer immediately to a cooling rack; place the turkey on its back.

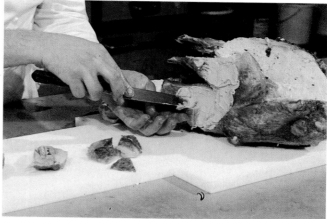

The roasting and cooling should be done a day in advance to allow for easy cutting and assembling.

Cutting the Turkey into Cubes

Set the turkey firmly on its back.

Carefully cut off the two breast filets, as shown, and set aside.

With a very sharp knife, cut off the meat from the legs. This must be done with precision so as not to separate the legs from the body-- they should remain positioned tightly against the body.

To remove the leg meat, make a neat incision down to the bone at the top and bottom of the leg, then with the knife angled slightly toward the bone, slice off the meat.

Lay the meat that has been removed in a neat order so it will be easy to put back on the bird.

Repeat the process on the other leg.

Cut the meat from the legs and breast in neat cubes and place them in their original position on the work surface.

Preparing the Aspic

Make the aspic from chicken or meat stock. Clarify it using classic techniques.

The amount of additional gelatin required will depend on the natural gelatin in the stock. Estimate 16-20g per liter (1/2 to 2/3 oz per quart). To test the consistency, pour a little in a shallow dish and refrigerate until set.

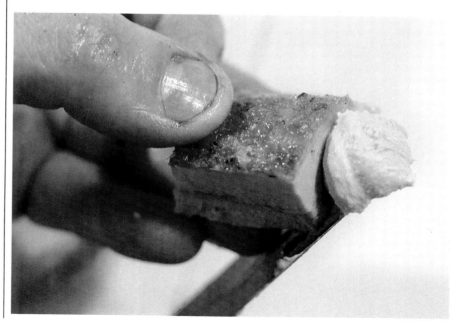

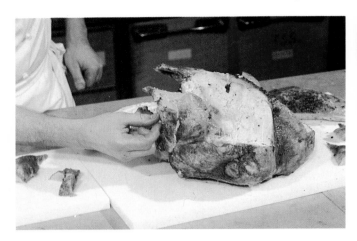

Preparing the Garnish and Decorations

Using an oval pastry cutter, stamp out croutons from pain de mie (enriched white bread) that has been cut into 8mm (about 3/8in) thick slices.

Butter the croutons lightly and toast them in the oven until crisp and golden.

Leave to cool, then using a star tip, pipe on some purée of goose liver. Decorate with a bit of truffle or black olive.

For the cubed aspic, pour some aspic in a shallow pan and chill to set.

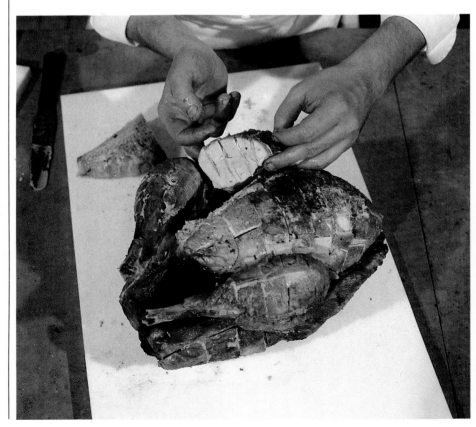

To make the tomato roses, select red, firm round tomatoes. With a small sharp knife, cut away the skin in a spiral, keeping the strip of skin thin and even. Twist the pared skin back up to form the rose.

Beat the goose liver purée until soft and creamy.

Assembly

Reshaping the Turkey

With a small palette knife, spread a layer of goose liver purée over the carcass where the meat has been cut away.

Stick the cubes of meat back on the turkey to give it its original shape. If pieces of meat start to slip, fix them in place temporarily with a toothpick.

Pipe a decorative border of purée of goose liver, using a star tip, that will serve to hide any large seams in the meat.

Chill in the freezer to stiffen the purée before beginning the glazing.

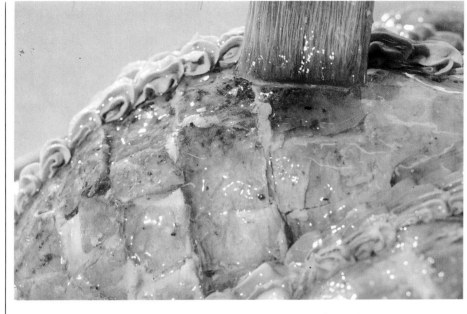

Adding an Aspic Glaze

Stir the aspic over crushed ice until it begins to thicken.

With a pastry brush, apply a coat of aspic to the meat and the decorations as well.

Chill to set, then repeat the process for a smooth finish.

Decorating

Place the tomato roses on the prepared turkey and secure them with a toothpick and brush them with aspic. Decorate with frilled toothpicks.

286

Arrange the turkey and decorations on the platter.

Once the pan of aspic has set, turn it out onto a hand towel and with a chef's knife, cut it into cubes.

Sprinkle the aspic cubes on the platter in an attractive pattern.

Storage

Store up to 48 hours at 4 °C (40F), covered with plastic wrap. To serve, touch up the aspic glaze if necessary.

Cubed Turkey in Aspic
Procedure Diagram

Assemble the equipment

Prepare the ingredients

Prepare the turkey

Cook the turkey

Cool

Prepare the assembly ingredient

Cut the turkey into cubes

Reshape the turkey

Pipe the liver purée on the turkey

Make the aspic

Chill to set

Brush on the aspic

Arrange on the platter

Prepare the garnish and decorations

Assemble the croutons

Thicken the aspic

Make the tomato roses

Cut the aspic into cubes

Arrange the garnish and decorations

Add the roses and toothpicks

Presentation and service

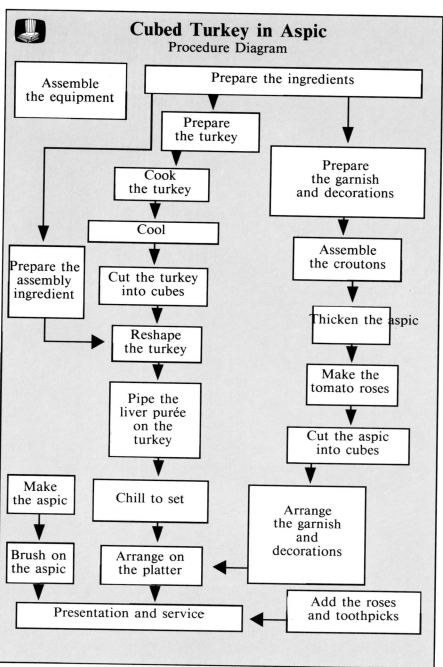

287

Chicken in Chaud-Froid with Truffles

Introduction

This is a dish to make for a large buffet. As represented here, the platter contains a whole chicken that was sliced and reconstituted, a second whole chicken cut into parts and extra breast meat cut into slices.

The platter is garnished with pastry barquettes filled with goose liver purée.

Both chicken and garnish are coated in an ivory chaud-froid, tastefully decorated with truffles and hard-boiled egg white, then sealed with a thin layer of chicken aspic.

Always choose the best quality chicken available (free-range farm-raised if possible).

The poaching liquid can be made into the aspic by clarifying it and adding gelatin.

The easy-to-make chaud-froid sauce is a combination of mayonnaise and aspic.

The classic black and white decorative motif is called " demi-deuil ", which means " half mourning ".

Equipment

Cutting board, large stockpot, thermometer, paring knife, vegetable peeler, chef's knife, trussing needle, kitchen twine, palette knife, plates, mixing bowls, spatula, fine-meshed conical sieve, serrated knife, whisk, pastry scraper, cooling rack, sheet pan, pastry brush, spoon, ladle, truffle cutter, barquette molds, oval pastry cutter, baking sheet, platter, decorative skewers, cutlet frills

Ingredients

Main Ingredients

2 1.5kg (3 1/4lb) chickens
2 chicken breasts (optional) (for poaching)
5L (5 qts) chicken stock
Aromatic vegetables: carrots, 2 onions, 2 shallots, 3 cloves garlic, 1 leek, 1 celery branch, 1 bouquet garni (thyme, parsley stems, bay leaf), salt, pepper, cloves
300g (10oz) goose liver purée (for assembly)

Garnish Ingredients

16 pre-baked barquette shells
100g (3 1/2oz) goose liver purée
Truffles

Glazing Ingredients

1.5L (6 cups) chaud-froid sauce (1/2L (2 cups) mayonnaise + 1L (4 cups) chicken aspic)
3/4L (3 cups) chicken aspic

Decoration Ingredients

Truffles
Hard-boiled egg whites
Tomatoes
Hard-boiled egg
Chopped aspic

Procedure

Preparing the Chickens

Peel, rinse and cut into medium dice the carrot, onions and shallots. Tie together the celery and leek and make a bouquet garni with parsley stems, thyme and bay leaf.

Place the chickens in a large stockpot and cover with cold chicken stock.

Add the vegetables and the bouquet garni. Season with salt, pepper and a few cloves tied up in a piece of cheesecloth.

It is best to put the chickens in the pot breast side up so the fragile breast meat is not close to the heat source.

Gradually increase the heat so the poaching liquid reaches 80-85 °C (175-185F) and poach the chickens for about 1 hour. The actual time will depend on the size of the chickens and tenderness of their meat.

Place a damp hand towel on the surface of the stock, which will help keep the chickens submerged during poaching.

NOTE: Remove the two breasts from the pot after about 30 minutes, as they will cook quicker than the whole birds.

Leave the chickens to cool in their poaching liquid and keep refrigerated. This step should be done one day in advance to allow for complete cooling.

Cutting Up the Chickens

The Whole Chicken

Remove all the skin, without pulling off any flesh.

Cut the meat off and cut into cubes, following the technique described in the preceding turkey recipe.

Spread the carcass with the purée of goose liver and reconstruct the chicken. Chill until ready to glaze.

The Chicken Pieces

Remove the skin from the second chicken and the breasts. Cut the whole chicken into pieces, starting by removing the leg and thigh in one piece from the body, by cutting through the joint.

Cut the leg from the thigh. Repeat on the other side, then set the four pieces aside.

Cut off the wings, cutting deeply into the breast in order to have a nice portion. Set aside.

Remove the breasts from the carcass with a thin-bladed flexible knife and cut them, along with the two extra breasts, into strips (approximately 4 per breast).

Spreading with Goose Liver Purée

Stir the purée so that it is a spreadable consistency.

Spread the upperside of all the pieces, including the whole chicken, with a 2mm (about 1/8in) layer of purée of goose liver. Chill to harden the layer of purée.

Preparing the Glaze

Make a classic mayonnaise.

Whisk some cold liquid aspic into the mayonnaise until it has a good pouring consistency.

Do not whisk too vigorously or air will be incorporated into the sauce, creating an unattractive bubbly texture.

Preparing the Decoration

Slice the truffles and cut out shapes with the truffle cutter. Slice the egg whites and cut out more shapes.

Cut the tomato in half in a sawtooth pattern and place a whole, peeled hard-boiled egg on top.

Decorate the egg with some truffle. Insert a small decorative skewer. Set aside.

Pour some aspic into a shallow pan and chill to set. Turn it out onto a hand towel and with a chef's knife, cut it into cubes. Keep chilled until ready to use.

Chill the baked pastry barquettes shells. Fill with purée of goose liver and shape into a shallow dome, using a palette knife. Chill until ready to use.

Glazing

Gently stir the chaud-froid sauce over ice until creamy.

Holding each piece of chicken with two fingers, pour over the chaud-froid sauce to coat, then replace on the cooling rack.

If necessary, repeat to obtain a perfect surface.

Brush all the pieces with a thin layer of aspic. Chill again to set.

Brush the chilled barquettes with aspic and chill until ready to assemble the dish.

Assembly

Arrange the pieces on the presentation platter in an attractive pattern.

There are many possibilities, with the general rule being to have the whole chicken at one end, flanked by the chicken pieces, then to arrange the slices and the barquettes around the edge.

For the whole chicken, it is best to apply the first coat with a brush, then pour on the second coat. Chill to set.

Decorate the pieces with the truffle and egg shapes. Chill to set.

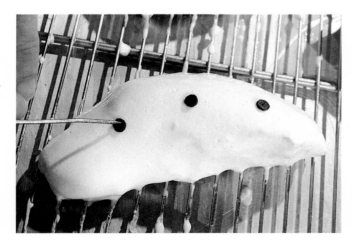

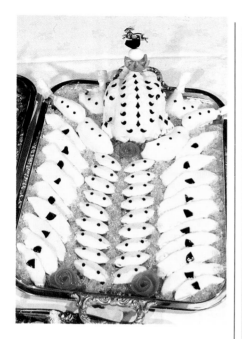

Decorate the base of the platter with the chopped aspic, either added with a spoon or piped using a pastry bag.

Top the whole chicken with the skewer of tomato, egg and truffle.

Storage

Store up to 24 hours at 4 °C (40F).

Chicken in Chaud-Froid with Truffles
Procedure Diagram

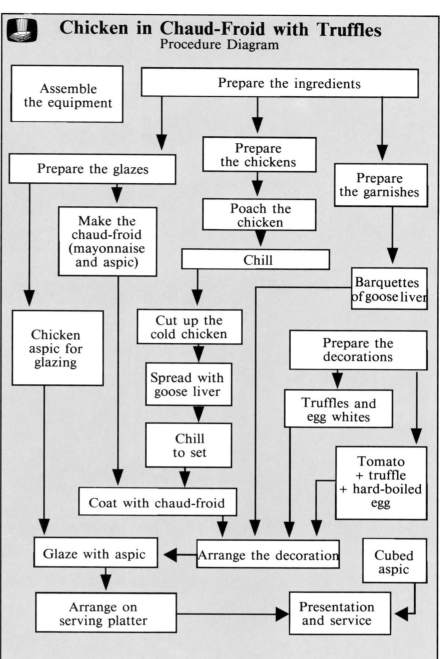

Assemble the equipment

Prepare the ingredients

Prepare the glazes

Prepare the chickens

Prepare the garnishes

Make the chaud-froid (mayonnaise and aspic)

Poach the chicken

Chill

Barquettes of goose liver

Chicken aspic for glazing

Cut up the cold chicken

Prepare the decorations

Spread with goose liver

Truffles and egg whites

Chill to set

Tomato + truffle + hard-boiled egg

Coat with chaud-froid

Glaze with aspic → Arrange the decoration

Cubed aspic

Arrange on serving platter

Presentation and service

Chicken with Truffles in Aspic

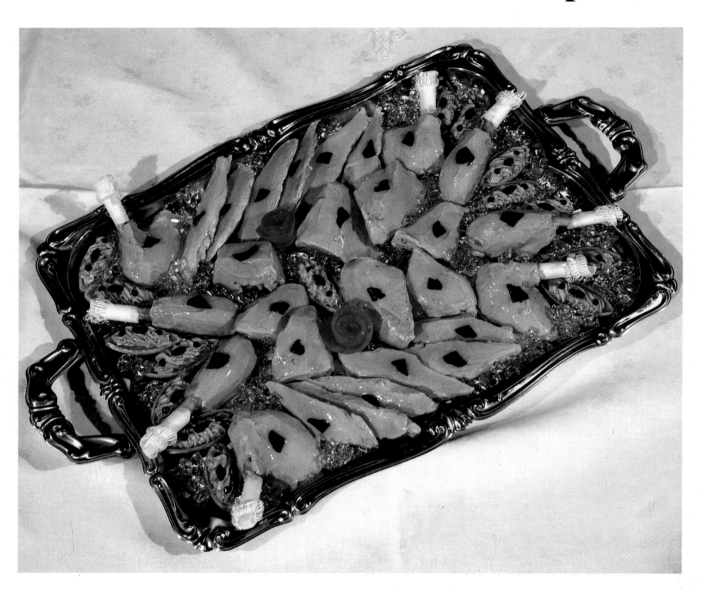

Introduction

This dish is less grand than those in the two preceding recipes, and therefore it is more versatile. It is just as appropriate for service at a sit-down dinner as it would at a buffet.

Select the best quality chicken and cook it with care. The initial steps for this dish are similar to those for the first two recipes, yet it has a different look, allowing the caterer to round out his selection.

Equipment

Cutting board, large stock pot, thermometer, paring knife, vegetable peeler, chef's knife, trussing needle, kitchen twine, palette knife, plates, mixing bowls, spatula, fine-meshed conical sieve, serrated knife, whisk, pastry scraper, cooling rack, sheet pan, pastry brush, spoon, ladle, truffle cutter, barquette mold, oval pastry cutter, baking sheet, platter, decorative skewer, cutlet frills

Ingredients

Main Ingredients

2 1.5kg (3 1/4lb) chickens
5L (5 qts) chicken stock (for the
    poaching liquid)
Aromatic vegetables: carrots, 2 on-
    ions, 2 shallots, 3 cloves garlic,
    1 leek, 1 celery branch, 1 bou-
    quet garni (thyme, parsley stems,
    bay leaf), salt, pepper, cloves
300g (10oz) goose liver purée (for
    assembly)

Garnish Ingredients

15 pre-baked barquettes
100g (3 1/2oz) goose liver purée
Truffles

Glazing Ingredient

1.5L (1 1/2 qts) chicken aspic

Decoration Ingredients

Chopped aspic
2 tomatoes

Procedure

Preparing the Chickens

Pass the chicken over an open
flame, such as a gas burner, to singe
off any feathers. Wipe the skin
clean with a hand towel.

Cut off the feet. Cut off the wing
tips and the neck and set aside for
the stock.

Empty the chicken carefully, sort
out the heart, liver and gizzard and
truss the chicken following the
techniques described in the preceding recipes.

Poaching the Chicken

Use a chicken or light veal stock.
Alternatively, make a "minute
stock".

To make this quick stock, put the
chopped vegetables (carrot, onion,
shallot) the garlic, celery and leek
tied together, bouquet garni and
spices into a stock pot.

Add the chicken wing tips, neck,
heart, and gizzard and add water.
Add about 25% more water than is
necesssary to cover the ingredients,
as it will be evaporated during
cooking.

Bring the ingredients to a boil
and simmer, partially covered, for
about one hour. Leave to cool, then
add the chickens and continue with
the poaching as described in the
preceding recipes.

Cooling the Chicken

Leave the chickens to cool completely in the poaching liquid and
chill at 4 °C (40F) until ready to use.

Preparing the Aspic

For a special touch, flavor the aspic with madeira, port or sherry or with an aromatic herb such as chervil, tarragon, basil or mint.

Depending on the consistency of the stock to be used for the aspic, add 16-20g (1/2 oz) more gelatin per liter (per quart). Pour a little in a shallow dish and chill until set to test the consistency.

Preparing the Garnish

Make barquette shells using basic pie pastry, blind bake and cool.

Fill them with purée of goose liver, using a pastry bag fitted with a star tip.

Decorate with truffles and chill.

Cutting Up the Chicken

Carefully remove the skin and cut the chicken into pieces as for the second chicken in the preceding recipe.

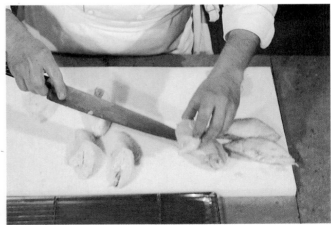

Slice the truffles and cut out shapes with the truffle cutter.

Choose red, round, firm tomatoes.

With a very sharp small knife, cut away the tomato skin in an even spiral, then twist the skin into the shape of a rose.

Pour some aspic in a shallow pan and chill to set. Turn out the aspic on a hand towel and chop into cubes with a chef's knife.

With a palette knife, spread the upper side of each piece of chicken with purée of goose liver.

Chill to harden the purée before glazing. Add the truffle decoration.

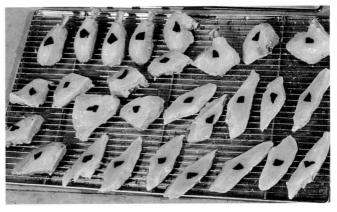

Adding an Aspic Glaze

Gently stir the aspic over crushed ice until it thickens slightly.

With a soft pastry brush, apply a first coat.

Chill to set, then add a second coat to obtain a smooth brilliant surface. Chill again before arranging on the platter.

Arranging on the Platter

Arrange the legs in a " V " shape at each end of the platter, with a wing on either side, then add the thighs.

Lay the slices of breast in a uniform pattern, overlapping the edge of the platter slightly.

Put the barquettes in the middle of the platter. Decorate the base of the platter with the cubes of aspic and place the tomato roses in the center.

The bones of the legs and wings can be encased with paper cutlet frills.

Storage

Store up to 48 hours at 4 °C (40F).

Touch up the aspic before serving, if necessary.

Chicken with Truffles in Aspic
Procedure Diagram

```
Assemble                 Prepare the ingredients
the equipment
                              Prepare
                            the chickens
                                               Prepare
                              Poach          the garnishes
                            the chickens
        Prepare
        the aspic           Chill the
                            chickens
                                              Barquettes
           Prepare the       Cut up            + purée
           decorations     the chickens

  Cut the
  aspic in    Truffles    Spread the pieces
  cubes                   with goose liver

                                  Chill

  Tomato
  roses       Decorate
            with truffles  ◄  Glaze with aspic

               Glaze
             with aspic

            Arrange on platter

                         Presentation
                         and service
```

Duck à l'Orange in Aspic

Introduction

The sweet and sour tastes in this dish may not be to everyone's liking, however with the correct balance of flavors in the sauce, this dish can be truly delicious.

The sweetness is minimized in the recipe, as it is not a dominant flavor in French cuisine.

The dish may be presented in several ways:

- in a specialty food shop as a meal for several people

- in a specialty food shop in individual servings

- as part of a buffet, with the pieces sliced and reshaped

Pastry barquettes filled with duck liver mousse can garnish the platter.

Select a good quality young duck that is plump and not too fatty.

Each duck should yield about four servings--one piece plus two slices of breast.

The citrus fruit should also be top quality--juicy and meaty with few or no seeds.

Equipment

Cutting board, chef's knife, paring knife, trussing needle, kitchen twine, roasting pan, sauté pan, vegetable peeler, mixing bowls, 2-pronged fork, measuring cup, saucepans, tablespoon, ladle, thin-bladed flexible knife, plates, drum sieve, pastry scraper, spatula, pastry bag and tip, barquette molds, baking sheets, colander, fine-meshed conical sieve, whisk, pastry bag, cooling racks, sheet pans, platter

Ingredients

Main Ingredients

1 1.5kg (3 1/4lb) young duck
For cooking:
30g (1oz) clarified butter
Salt and pepper

Garnish Ingredients

4 pre-baked barquettes
10g (1/3oz) clarified butter
1 duck liver
30g (1oz) purée of goose liver
Few drops cognac
Salt, pepper

Glazing Ingredients

5cl (1/4 cup) white wine
20g (2/3oz) sugar
Zest of 1/2 lemon
Zest of 1 orange
3cl (2 tbsp) vinegar
3cl (2 tbsp) orange juice
2cl (4 tsp) lemon juice
3/4L (3 cups) duck stock
45g (1 1/2oz) cooked roux (optional)
12-14g (1/3-1/5oz) gelatin
Chicken aspic (to finish)

Decoration Ingredients

Orange segments
Approx. 1L (1qt) chopped aspic

Procedure

Preparing the Duck

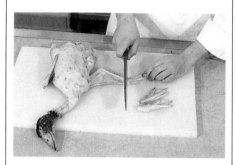

Pass the ducks over a flame, such as a gas burner, to singe off any feathers. Wipe the skin clean with a hand towel.

Cut off the feet a little above the joint. Cut off the wing tips.

Make a small incision in the neck skin, pull out the neck and cut it off.

Cut out the "Y" shaped wishbone to facilitate cutting up the duck.

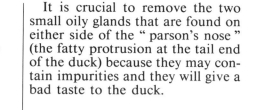

It is crucial to remove the two small oily glands that are found on either side of the " parson's nose " (the fatty protrusion at the tail end of the duck) because they may contain impurities and they will give a bad taste to the duck.

Empty the duck following the techniques described in the turkey recipe.

Remove the liver, taking care to discard the bile sack and cutting away any green or yellow spots on the liver. Set it aside for the duck liver mousse.

Trim the gizzard and reserve for another use. Truss the duck like the

other birds in this chapter, so it keeps its form during cooking.

Cooking the Duck

Season the inside with salt and pepper, then lightly season the outside as well.

Heat the roasting pan, add clarified butter, then lightly brown the duck on all sides.

Take care not to pierce the skin, which would allow the loss of juices.

When the duck is golden brown, put it in an oven at 240C (465F) and roast it for 40-45 minutes, basting and turning the duck every 10 minutes.

The duck should remain slightly pink, for the best flavor and texture.

Immediately transfer the duck to a cooling rack to drain, away from the heat. Reserve the roasting pan to make the sauce. Cool the duck until completely cold.

NOTE: It is best to roast the duck at least 6 hours ahead, if not one day, to allow for complete cooling.

Making the Garnish

Wash and wipe dry the oranges and lemon. Cut off the ends.

Remove the zest using a vegetable peeler; cut away only the colored part, not the white pith, which is bitter. Try to cut wide strips of zest.

Take half of the zest strips (use the least perfect ones) and put them in a small pan of cold water. Bring the water to a boil for two minutes. Drain and refresh in cold water.

Cut the other half of the zests into fine, even julienne. Blanch these, refresh and set aside.

With a sharp knife, trim the oranges and lemon to remove all the white pith. Cut out the segments from between the membrane. Work over a bowl to catch all the juices.

Set aside the segments, the juice and the leftover membrane.

Making the Barquettes

Lightly season the duck liver with salt and pepper. Sauté it in clarified butter until just pink. Flame with cognac.

Pass the liver through a drum sieve, then add to the pre-made purée and stir until smooth.

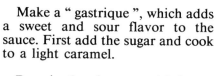

Make a "gastrique", which adds a sweet and sour flavor to the sauce. First add the sugar and cook to a light caramel.

Pour in the vinegar and bring to a boil to melt the caramel. Chop the wide strips of zest and add to the gastrique to infuse.

Making the Sauce

Heat the pan in which the duck was cooked to caramelize the meat juices left in the bottom. Pour off any fat.

Deglaze the pan with white wine and scrape up any brown bits with a wooden spoon.

With a star tip, pipe the mousse into prebaked barquettes made with pie pastry. Lay a segment of orange on each barquette.

Chill until ready to use.

Squeeze the remaining juices from the membranes of the fruit, combine with the reserved juice and add to the caramel. Boil until reduced by half, scraping the bottom of the pan.

Add the duck stock and cook to blend the flavors. Bind the sauce with the cooked roux to give it a smooth texture. Correct the seasoning, then strain through a fine-meshed conical sieve.

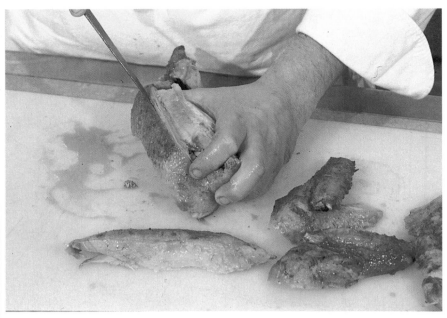

Measure the sauce and add 8-18g (1/4-1/2oz) gelatin per liter (per quart) of sauce. Test the consistency by pouring a little sauce in a shallow dish and chilling to set.

Cutting the Duck Meat

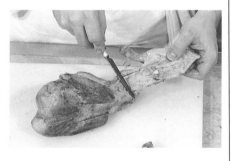

Cut off the legs and thighs in one piece, and the wings, cutting into the breast to make a nice portion. Cut off the breasts.

Remove all the skin and fat from the pieces.

Cut each breast into four slices.

Lay the pieces of duck and the prepared barquettes on a cooling rack.

Glazing

Gently stir the duck sauce over crushed ice to thicken slightly.

With a spoon, coat evenly each piece of meat with sauce. Repeat this step 2 or 3 times to obtain a perfectly smooth finish, chilling between each application.

Chill to set, then brush on a thin coat of clear aspic to enhance the shine and protect the sauce.

Brush the barquettes with aspic and chill.

Assembly

Place the pieces on the platter, with the largest ones around the outside.

Fan out the slices of breast, then arrange the barquettes down the middle.

Garnish the platter with chopped aspic.

Drain the citrus segments on a hand towel, then arrange them on the duck. Sprinkle the julienne of zest over the large pieces.

The platter could be further decorated with whole oranges cut in slices or saw-tooth.

Storage

Store the duck up to 48 hours at 4 °C (40F). Touch up the aspic before serving if necessary. If the julienne of zest dries out, replace it with fresh.

Serving

This rich dish is usually served without a sauce.

The colors are stiking on a buffet and the fresh flavor is a welcome change of pace.

Remove the platter from the refrigerator a little while before serving to take the chill off.

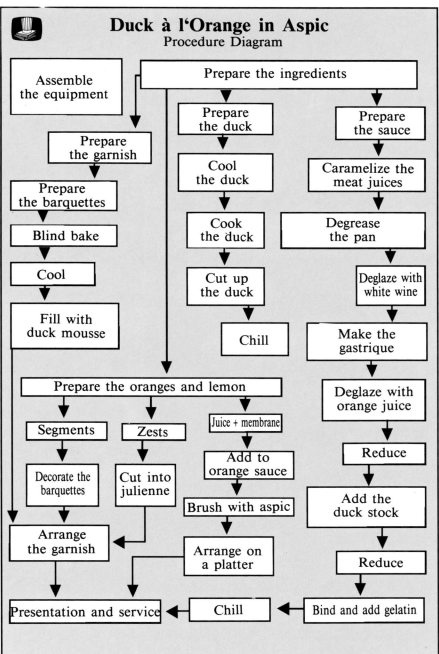

Duck à l'Orange in Aspic
Procedure Diagram

```
Assemble              Prepare the ingredients
the equipment
                  Prepare          Prepare
                  the duck         the sauce
    Prepare
    the garnish       Cool         Caramelize the
                  the duck         meat juices
    Prepare
    the barquettes    Cook         Degrease
                  the duck         the pan
    Blind bake
                  Cut up           Deglaze with
    Cool          the duck         white wine

    Fill with         Chill        Make the
    duck mousse                    gastrique

       Prepare the oranges and lemon    Deglaze with
                                        orange juice
    Segments    Zests    Juice + membrane
                                          Reduce
    Decorate the  Cut into   Add to
    barquettes    julienne   orange sauce
                                        Add the
                    Brush with aspic    duck stock
    Arrange
    the garnish     Arrange on          Reduce
                    a platter

    Presentation and service   Chill   Bind and add gelatin
```

Page 309

Quails with Foie Gras in Aspic

Introduction

This quail dish used to be very seasonal because quails were only available during hunting season. Nowadays, however, quails are raised and therefore are available year-round to make this dish and its variations.

Quail has tasty fine-textured flesh that is not too "gamey".

Their small size makes them a perfect individual portion, to be served on a plate or arranged on a large platter.

They may be served plain or filled with a delicious foie gras stuffing that is sure to please.

Equipment

Cutting board, paring knife, mixing bowls, plates, meat grinder (optional), trussing needle, kitchen twine, pastry bag and star tip, deep pot and lid, cooling rack, sheet pan, round rack, 18 tartelette molds, round plain pastry cutter, round baking sheets, spatula, chef's knife, pastry brush, pastry scraper, platter, frilled toothpicks

Ingredients

Main Ingredients

6 quails, about 120g (4oz) each
150g (5oz) forcemeat (made with 75g (2 1/2oz) pork and 75g (2 1/2oz) veal)
45g (1 1/2oz) foie gras
30g (1oz) clarified butter
10g (1/3oz) truffles
Salt, pepper

Garnish Ingredients

18 tartelette shells made with pie pastry
150g (5oz) purée of goose liver
18 green grapes

Glazing Ingredients

3/4L (3 cups) aspic
1dl (1/2 cup) Sauternes, or other sweet white wine

Decoration

3/4L (3 cups) aspic cut in cubes

Procedure

Preparing the Quails

Remove any feathers by passing the quail over an open flame, such as a gas burner. Do this carefully, as the quail's skin is delicate.

Cut off the neck.

Gently empty the entrails and wipe out the cavity.

Season the inside with salt and pepper.

Making the Forcemeat

Put the pork and veal through a meat grinder fitted with a fine disk. Add the foie gras, season with salt and pepper, add the chopped truffles, then beat to combine thoroughly.

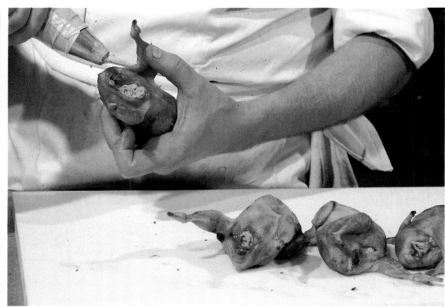

With a pastry bag fitted with a plain tip, pipe the forcemeat into the quails.

Truss the birds so they are securely closed.

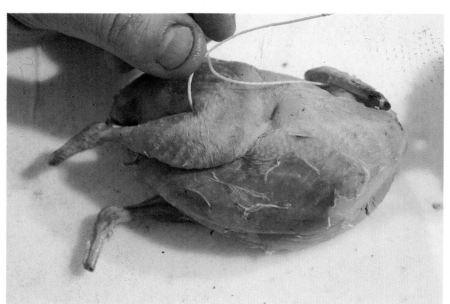

Cooking the Quails

Use a pan large enough to hold all the quails at once.

Heat the clarified butter in the pan and brown the quails over high heat, turning the quails frequently to color them evenly.

Cover the pan and continue cooking.

Estimate 30-35 minutes cooking time over moderate heat, which will allow the heat to penetrate to the interior of the stuffing.

Baste and turn the quails frequently during cooking.

To check doneness, pierce the leg to check that the juices are clear.

Verify that the forcemeat is cooked as well by inserting a skewer for a few seconds and feeling the temperature; it should feel hot along the length of the skewer.

When cooked, transfer immediately to a rack to drain.

Leave to cool completely.

It is best to cook and cool the quails the day before.

Remove the trussing strings.

Preparing the Garnish

Line the tartelette molds with pie pastry and blind bake.

Cool the tartelettes completely, then using a pastry bag and a star tip, pipe a rosette of foie gras purée in the center.

Top each rosette with a grape.

Chill until ready to glaze.

Preparing the Aspic

Melt the chicken aspic and flavor it with Sauternes.

Over crushed ice, gently stir the aspic until it thickens slightly.

Glazing the Quails

The Sauternes-flavored aspic is a perfect match for the taste of foie gras, white grapes and the delicate quail meat.

With a pastry brush, apply a first coat of aspic. Chill to set, then brush on a second coat to achieve a perfectly smooth finish.

Brush the chilled tartelettes with aspic and chill until ready to assemble the dish.

Assembly

Place the quails in a nice pattern on the platter.

Decorate with chopped aspic, added with a spoon or piped through a star tip. Place the foie gras tartelettes around the quails.

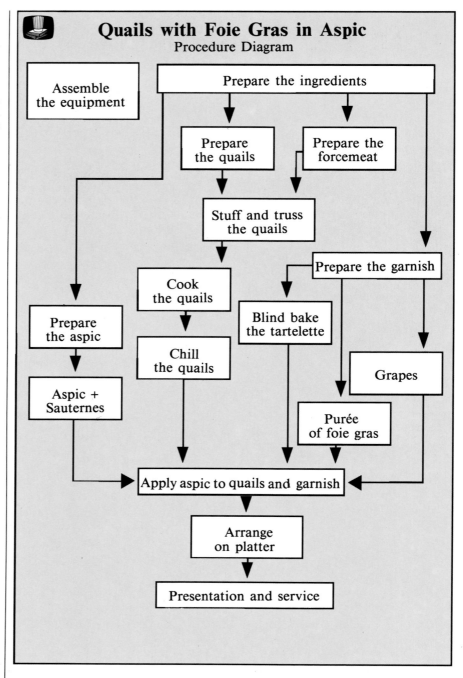

Quails with Foie Gras in Aspic
Procedure Diagram

```
Assemble          Prepare the ingredients
the equipment
                    │              │
                    ▼              │
              Prepare          Prepare the
              the quails       forcemeat
                    │              │
                    ▼              │
              Stuff and truss ◄────┘
              the quails
                    │
                    ▼                    Prepare the garnish
              Cook                         │
              the quails      Blind bake   │
                    │         the tartelette
   Prepare          ▼              │      Grapes
   the aspic   Chill                │        │
      │        the quails           │        │
      ▼             │         Purée         │
   Aspic +          │         of foie gras  │
   Sauternes        │              │        │
      │             ▼              ▼        ▼
      └──►  Apply aspic to quails and garnish  ◄──
                    │
                    ▼
              Arrange
              on platter
                    │
                    ▼
          Presentation and service
```

Storage and Serving

Store up to 48 hours at 4 °C (40F). Touch up the aspic finish before serving if necessary. Serve chilled but not too cold.

These lovely individual portions are ideal for sale in a specialty food shop. For display, they can be packaged in small disposable containers or arranged on platters.

In the Professional Caterer Series

Volume 1

Pastry Hors d'œuvres - Assorted Snacks
Canapés - Centerpieces
Hot Hors d'œuvres
Cold Brochettes - Centerpieces

Volume 2

Individual Cold Dishes - Pâtés
Terrines - Galantines and Ballotines
Aspics - Pizzas and Quiches

Translator's Notes

Because these volumes were originally written for the French audience, some of the ingredients and equipment may need explanation.

Butter is always unsalted, unless otherwise indicated.

Clarified butter is obtained by melting butter, then pouring the pure fat portion off the top, and discarding the milk solids that settle at the bottom and which tend to burn at high temperatures.

Aspic is an important ingredient in catering as it gives a shiny finish to many cold items, as well as keeps the item fresh looking and tasting by sealing out the air. Basic aspic recipes are readily found in reliable cookbooks; top quality powdered aspic is a possible substitute for fresh.

Eggs are always large size (60g/2oz).

" Américaine " sauce is called for in several recipes. The main ingredients include fish stock, tomato, cognac and tarragon. Refer to a reliable source for a recipe.

Drum sieves have many uses in a French kitchen. The large size allows flour to be sifted quickly; meat and vegetable purées are forced through the mesh to obtain smooth mixtures.

Plastic pastry scrapers are an indispensable tool for the French chef, who uses them to scrape bowls clean, transfer mixtures efficiently, keep the work surface clean, as well as to mix pastry doughs.

Hand towels are an essential part of the French chef's equipment. Tucked into the apron, they are an ever-ready pot holder. They are often used to absorb moisture from draining vegetables or other foods; when dampened, they can be used to cover food to prevent drying. When they are in direct contact with food, the hand towels must be perfectly clean.

Sheet pans in France are made from heavy gauge iron that conducts heat evenly. Choose the heaviest sheet pans available.

Measurements are provided in both metric and U.S. units. Most U.S. conversions have been rounded off to the nearest half-unit, except for smaller quantities where accuracy is crucial.

Denis Ruffel:

A Widely-Respected Young Chef

Very early in his career, Denis Ruffel made a name for himself as one of the most talented young chefs of the new generation.

Creative and skilled, meticulous and energetic, empassioned by teaching and always willing to share his knowledge, Ruffel is the ideal author for this series, The Professional Caterer.

After all, who could be more qualified than Denis Ruffel to cover such a field, which includes a wide range of dishes and varied and complex culinary techniques? From the simplest procedure to the most complicated " tricks of the trade " involved in these top-of-the-line recipes, Denis Ruffel offers food professionals a tool that will quickly prove itself indispensable.

For over fifteen years, I have had the pleasure of watching Denis Ruffel's remarkable professional development. Ever since his apprenticeship with Jean Millet, he has had a firm grasp of the fundamental techniques so essential to all top quality work.

Generous with his friends and devoted to his work, he is a paragon of dedication to our profession.

Through working with Denis Ruffel on several seminars, I came to know many of his qualities, including his wealth of knowledge, his modest nature, his friendly disposition, his constant smile and, above all, his outstanding talent for teaching.

His skills, which are equally strong in pastry, catering and cuisine, are limitless and without equal.

The Professional Caterer is the culmination of much hard work and planning, and it stands alone in the field of culinary cookbooks, offering recipes for appetizers to gala buffet fare, and covering the whole range of the catering repertoire.

In these books, Denis Ruffel unites simplicity with perfection. The professional as well as the newcomer to the field can choose from a wide variety of hors d'œuvres, canapés, appetizers, terrines and pâtés and quiches, as well as many other delicious preparations. The recipes are easy to follow, and they are made even clearer by excellent step-by-step photographs.

I would like to express my congratulations and thanks for this marvellous achievment. It is through the work of true professionals like Denis Ruffel--passionate, skilled and dedicated--that our profession will continue to grow.

M. A. Roux

Born in 1950, Denis Ruffel entered the field at the age of fourteen. He received his C.A.P. in Pastry at the Centre Ferrandi in Paris, with Jean Millet as his "maître d'apprentissage", who very quickly recognized his talents.

Passionate about cooking, Ruffel completed his training by receiving his C.A.P. in Cuisine, and worked, among other places, at La Bourgogne, under Monassier, and L'Archestrate, under Senderens.

Always striving for improvement, Ruffel received the Brevet de Maîtrise de Pâtissier-Confiseur-Glacier, and also studied at the Académie du Vin.

Since the late 1970s, he heads the kitchens of Jean Millet, maintaining the excellent reputation of Maison Millet, especially its prestigious catering department. Despite the heavy workload, Denis Ruffel finds time to participate in many other professional activities:

- Training classes at the Paris Chamber of Commerce
- Administrator for apprenticeship program at the Ecole Nationale de la Pâtisserie d'Yssingeaux
- Chef-instructor at Ecole de Cuisine La Varenne in Paris
- Winner of the Concours du Centenaire de la Saint-Michel
- Member of the Association Internationale des Maîtres Pâtissiers "Relais Dessert"
- Gold-medal winner 1985 of the Confédération Nationale de la Pâtisserie-Confiserie-Glacerie de France
- Honory member of the Confédération National de la Pâtisserie-Confiserie Japonaise
- Winner of the 1985 Culinary Trophy
- Winner of the Confédération Nationale de la Pâtisserie-Confiserie Espagnole (Salon Alimentaria en 1986)

The Professional Caterer is the product of Denis Ruffel's vast range of experience.

First published as *L'Artisan Traiteur* by Editions St-Honoré, Paris, France: copyright © 1988.

English translation copyright © 1990 by Van Nostrand Reinhold for the United States of America and Canada; by CICEM (Compagnie Internationale de Consultation *Education* et *Media*) for the rest of the world.

Van Nostrand Reinhold
115 Fifth Avenue
New York, New York 10003
Macmillan of Canada
Division of Canada Publishing Corporation
164 Commander Boulevard
Agincourt, Ontario MIS 3C7, Canada
ISBN 0-442-00142-8 (vol. 3)

CICEM, 229, rue St-Honoré
75001 PARIS (France)

© CICEM ISBN 2-86871-016-0
Dépôt légal 1er trimestre 1990
Imprimé en France par l'Imprimerie Ⴔ Alençonnaise

Library of Congress Cataloging-in-Publication Data

Ruffel, Denis :

Collective title: The professional caterer series / by Denis Ruffel (Born in 1950)

Contents:
Vol. 1. Pastry hors d'œuvres, assorted snacks, canapés, centerpieces, hot hors d'œuvres, cold brochette's.
Vol. 2. Individual cold dishes, pates, terrines, galantines, and ballotines, aspics, pizzas, and quiches.
Vol. 3. Croustades, quenelles, souffles, beignets, individual hot dishes, mixed salads, fish in aspic, lobsters, poultry in aspic.
Vol. 4. Meat and Games, Sauces and Bases, Planning, Execution, Display and Decoration for Buffets and Receptions.
1. Quantity cooking. 2. Caterers and catering. I.
Title : The professional caterer series.
TX820.R843 1990 641.5'7--dc20 89-22600
ISBN 0-442-00142-8 (vol. 3)